"I have found numerology to be particularly meaningful in interpreting human behavior. I most enthusiastically recommend Ellin Dodge's books to those who are seriously interested in delving into the scientific art of numerology."
—Joan Friedrich, M.A., Ph.D.

"In the hands of an expert such as Ellin Dodge, numerology can be an invaluable tool for everyday life."
—Rona Barrett

"An extremely useful adjunct to psychotherapy."
—Carolyn Berent Lamberg, A.C.S.W.

ELLIN DODGE

NUMEROLOGY
has your
NUMBER

A FIRESIDE BOOK
Published by Simon & Schuster Inc.
New York   London   Toronto   Sydney   Tokyo

A FIRESIDE BOOK
Published by Simon & Schuster Inc.
Simon & Schuster Building
Rockefeller Center
1230 Avenue of the Americas
New York, NY 10020

Designed by Barbara Marks Graphic Design
Illustrations by Doug Horne
Manufactured in the United States of America
10 9 8 7 6 5 4 3 2
Library of Congress Cataloging in Publication Data
Dodge, Ellin.
Numerology has your number / Ellin Dodge.
p. cm.
"A Fireside book."
Bibliography: p.
ISBN 0-671-64243-X
1. Symbolism of numbers. I. Title.
BF1623.P9D54 1988   88-11354
133.3'35—dc19   CIP
ISBN 0-671-64243-X

In memory of Wingate Holmes Paine

Dedicated to Harold "Skip" William Pearce, Jr.

◄◄◄ ACKNOWLEDGMENTS ►►►

Thanks to Beth Meyer, who has made my public relations public and my private relations warm and friendly . . .

and Alan Colmes, Michael Dixon, Toby Gold, Barry Landers, Barry Young, Earl Baldwin, Preston Westmoreland, Ellen Schenk, Tom Carroll, Patrice Brown, Richard Bey—to name a few of the many radio and TV hosts who have been kind and generous . . .

and caring Fireside editor Barbara Gess . . .

and encouraging literary agent Ellen Levine . . .

and my dad, and my Betty.

You all have my number, and I am grateful.

◄◄◄ CONTENTS ►►►

NUMEROLOGY
◄◄◄ *has your* ►►►
NUMBER

WHAT IS
NUMEROLOGY?

Looking for a new dimension? A channel to flawless timing? An appraiser of personal assets? If you can count your fingers effortlessly, you can use numerology to find your answers. Numerology is a mystical arithmetic system that reveals character, personality, and experience through the sensible progressions of numbers.

Numerology's simple arithmetic bases its startling revelations on over 11,000 years of coincidence. Prehistoric, ancient-Greek, and Elizabethan-Age societies all recognized its efficacy. Clan leaders, philosophers, and priests throughout the ages have organized its psychical information. Modernized in the sixth century B.C., today it is a down-to-earth, straightforward, speedy system for self-examination and charting opportunities.

Numerology elongates the vision of the nearsighted, blasts through tunnel vision, and just plain sheds light when we want clarity. Numbers are not just cumulative values to be totaled by a calculator or applied to odds at a crap table. This is the eighties, the age of numbers, and the duality of their importance is even more in focus. We are drawn to people, places, and things that vibe with us, and most of us find one or two numbers that feel lucky or seem to turn up in addresses or phone numbers no matter how often we change them. When you understand the gist of the number meanings, you will be able to understand the types of people and experiences that your changing home, phone, and auto repeatedly attract.

For those interested in metaphysics, numerology can sharpen mind-expansion techniques and prepare the mind to use extrasensory perceptions and mental transference easily. Numerology prods one to stretch the imagination. You may visualize how you look, feel, and act at your highest possible potential based on its number meanings. As the ancients knew and today's forecasters believe, whatever the mind can visualize, one can achieve.

Numerology provides a complete personality-lifestyle profile when we apply the meanings of individual numbers to our birth names and birth dates. The numbers of our names describe the things that we are born knowing. The numbers of our birth dates describe the things that we have to learn.

The number symbols for the letters in your name outline your natural instincts, self-image, and talents. People relate immediately to their names. Metaphysicians believe that the soul selects its name prior to birth to reflect the sound of its capacities. To the listener a name is the person's melody, and those who are soulmates respond favorably when it is spoken. Names attract or repel according to their vibrations. If you compared the name numbers of best friends and intimate lovers, you would find the same numbers in their numerology charts. Uncomfortable relationships will have name numbers that are not compatible. That's because, according to Pythagoras, the father of modern numerology, "like" numbers have an affinity for one another. Certain numbers that crop up in a person's life repeatedly—in addresses, telephone listings, auto license plates, bank accounts, social security numbers— originate in the numbers of their name or birth date.

The numbers in your birth date describe lifetime experiences and their objectives. The subdivisions of the birth date—the month, day, and year numbers—are symbols for three major cycles of life experiences, and the total number meaning explains the types of people and experiences you will meet along the way, otherwise known as your destiny.

The birth-month and birthday-number meanings describe attitudes and actions. The birth-month—number meaning describes youthful impressions and environments. The birthday number symbolizes experiences during the twenty-seven—year mid-life productivity cycle, including the period from approximately age twenty-eight to age thirty-six, when you mature and stabilize. The day-of-birth number can help during that time by putting a focus on your career and explaining options.

Then there is the challenge number. I believe this number, found through a subtraction of your birth-date numbers, is one of the most important numbers in a person's life because it describes how you will *cope* with your destiny. It tells how you will use your natural instincts and talents (symbolized by your birth-name number) and how you will deal with the people and experiences you meet (symbolized by your birth-date number). And, after all, it is not your *fate* but your *attitude* toward it that determines success or failure, happiness or misery.

According to psychologists and therapists who have listened to their clients' taped numerology counselings, the perceptions of the challenge-number meanings are accurate and usually prove to be valuable tools for growth. While the childhood training ground for what later becomes obsessive and compulsive behavior may take years to identify in therapy, with numerology it is simply a matter of subtracting the month, day, and year of birth numbers. After these patterns are identified, trained professionals can offer methods for behavior modification. Of course, knowledge of challenge-number meanings alone cannot change behavior. It takes desire and commitment, too. If the interpretation of your challenge number brings past mistakes to mind, it's up to you whether the experience sparks self-delusion or a new awakening. As always, you have a choice.

But while challenge numbers describe self-destructive attitudes, negative habits, angers, and frustrations, they can also be the key to revealing hidden talents and opportunities and can help point the way to success. Challenge patterns are deeply ingrained in us from childhood, and when we learn to balance their extremes, challenges can become major pluses. At their negative extreme these numerological "Freudian slips" describe think-stuck attitudes, inappropriate reactions, and unrealistic self-appraisals. But by identifying these unpleasant tendencies, challenges can trigger the desire to finally call a halt to black-and-white decision making, self-destructive behavior, and the mental, emotional, and physical problems they create.

When you use numerology as a companion to common sense, all things are possible. For people who will take all the help they can get, numerology can be a wonderful copemate. If you wish to explore the greater significance of character, to uncloak disturbing habits, and to gain a purposeful perspective, NUMEROLOGY HAS YOUR NUMBER.

CHAPTER TWO

NUMBER
PHILOSOPHY

Wₑ believe the unexplainable when we say "he's number one." Why is a person "dressed to the nines" when obviously well turned out? Why are we "at sixes and sevens" when in conflict? Why do people say that cats have only nine lives? Why not ten or seventeen? Is there a numerological explanation for the "seven-year itch"? There sure is. When one knows the number meanings, these superstitions make sense.

To get a basic grounding in the number meanings, let's take a look at the way the numbers evolve from 1 through 9. Pythagoras believed that the numbers 1 through 9 led to perfection, symbolized by the number 10. Here's how it works:

We begin with 1, an idea that grows in a predictable, step-by-step progression.

Number 2 symbolizes that idea reaching out, being received by others, and getting the cooperation needed to continue its growth.

The number 3 brings the idea to others for inspection and approval.

Number 4 brings the idea to practical application and corrects impracticalities.

Number 5 adds promotion and exposure to public opinion. Five, the central number, opens the door of unexpected pluses or minuses. Here the idea makes the transition from an individual concept to a community awareness.

Number 6 is the symbol for group participation and community responsibility. It broadens the concept to serve a larger purpose.

Number 7 is the symbol for debugging, questioning, and perfecting the idea technically until it can be brought to a major material result.

Number 8 stands for stamina, mental and physical organization, and practical power. It brings body, mind, and spirit together to produce tangible results. Ideas come to form through the planning, work, and structure applied during the influence of a number 8.

Number 9 polishes, develops the skills necessary to bring the idea to a broad marketplace, and concludes the process.

This process relates to everything we do. Ambitions grow through the activities or experiences indicated by the number meanings. The stages of growth during the nine months of pregnancy and the final perfection of the fetus in the ninth month are a prime example of the evolution of the numbers 1 through 9. The birth of the child begins a new life a few days after the conclusion of the ninth month. The child, a new concept, starts the cycles of life at its birth—the tenth month. In numerology, number 10 becomes a number 1 when we add 1 + 0, which results in a 1. The pregnancy ended in a number 9 month—9, the number of endings. Life begins in a number 1—the number of beginnings.

Let's see if, knowing all this, we can make sense out of one of those superstitions that we mentioned earlier. The "seven-year itch" can be explained by its meaning as the seventh year in the first cycle of nine years of marriage. Seven indicates a year that focuses on debugging and questioning. It slows down commercial ambitions and drains physical stamina. The spouse is left with time to reflect, analyze, and mature. The seventh year dims fantasies with logic, which sparks an inner search for practical perfection. Since nothing is perfect, one is always disappointed and disillusioned. Personal problems are blamed on the marriage. But impulsive actions should not be taken in the seventh year of marriage or any partnership. One needs to understand that during the introspective, serious 7 year, each spouse has a craving to be a private person. The intimacies of marriage will feel uncomfortable then. Lovers and partners should not draw conclusions or make changes until after the eighth year, with its practical, material, problem-solving process that integrates work, commerce, and common sense. People who take time out to sort individual priorities in this way and who don't impulsively consult a lawyer use the seventh year to redefine their personal identity. Patient thinkers usually do not end up regretting a "seven-year itch" divorce. But watch out for the seventh year in the next nine-year cycle! It will be equally introspective.

These physically debilitating, loner periods arise when we face the seventh, sixteenth, twenty-fifth, thirty-fourth, forty-third, fifty-second, sixty-first, seventieth, seventy-ninth, eighty-eighth, and ninety-seventh year of marriage or life. The seventh year in the nine-year cycles of experience affects the outcome of things begun seven years before, and the self-analysis undertaken during the seventh year leads to a rebirth three years later.

A LITTLE HISTORY

Since 14,000 B.C., when Cro-Magnon man walked the icy glaciers, people have been sensing, feeling, and responding to the vibrations of numbers. Cave people showed their interpretation of the duality of numbers with primitive pictures on cave walls and floors. The elders or leaders of cave clans began the mystery behind a system for counting when they declined to share their knowledge. Number magic, as important as healing techniques, was passed on only to the most trusted and intelligent clan members. Although mentally lumbering, when early man socialized with others to farm or barter, it is likely that he developed a sense of counting by comparing a four-legged animal to four animal skins. Language was primitive, however, and man had to contrive sounds for numbers. He used words that allied themselves to examples that were observed in his natural environment.

Early man evolved picture words for numbers. The name of a six-petaled flower may have been the symbol for a word that indicated a cumulative value of six. Pictures were "worth a thousand words" that were not available in their vocabulary.

Man's ability to communicate was limited, but he could calculate. To indicate that a caveman had three wives, he might draw a female form next to a three-sided leaf. Observers in the clan retained and used the pictures repeatedly. And like the childhood game of "telephone"—where one word changes from passer-on to passer-on—the meaning intended by the original caveman artist changed too. The use of symbols, and sensing the meanings of their combinations, led to the mystical aspects of cumulative symbols (numbers) indicating more than their obvious quantity.

Numerology as we use it today incorporates the investigation, imagination, and intellectual idealizations of these and other ancient societies. About 3000 B.C., the Sumerians established the sophisticated numbers system that has given us the sixty-minute hour and the sixty-second minute. Their knowledge was passed on and refined by the Babylonians. Modern numerology began with the Greek civilizations of the sixth century B.C. All the ancients (the Sumerians, Babylonians, and Chaldeans, later Pythagoras and Plato, and still later the believers of the Renaissance) believed that the basic elements of tone, idea, and thought had a mathematical basis, which in turn had vibration. Early-Christian art was informed by numerology through the Byzantine application of six as the perfect number of creation. Six animals, six-cornered objects, six flying birds, were found in mosaics and drawings of that era, symbolizing perfection. Since man's evolution from primeval caves and glacial frosts, until about 632 B.C. and the establishment of the Pythagorean numerology system, different numbers provoked additional concepts.

The tarot cards, for example, forerunners of modern playing cards, are based on a picture and number system. Card reading began when humans conceptualized an inner consciousness, built self-control, and tried to master fate. Picture interpretation began with a throw of colored stones, which in more sophisticated cultures were changed to mosaic tiles. The interpretation of colors, amounts, and images was put to a system based on coincidence—the positions that the stones took repeatedly.

How number cards originated or when they materialized in the form of a pack or deck is unknown. In excavations from Babylonian, Egyptian, Judaic, Mexican, Indian, and Chinese archaeological digs, decks of tarot cards, mosaic murals, and sculptures depicting the twenty-two picture cards comprising the major arcana of the tarot system, have been found. These were the tools for character evaluation and forecasting. Their insights were secretly passed from teacher to disciple. Leaders guarded the mystical power that instilled fear in the average citizen.

It was the Jewish people, with their dedication to the idea of preserving tradition, who kept tarot meanings pure. The keys to the Old Testament's Egyptian-Hebrew writings in the Books of Moses (far more complex than the reader of letters alone suspects) are only understood by talmudic scholars who link tarot numbers to the cabala. The cabala holds the key to unknown vowel placement necessary for interpretation. Twenty-two numbers and letters describe the primitive Hebrew alphabet. Each row of letters is also a row of numbers that sum up a word, name, or phrase revealing the complexity of the Torah, the Jewish scriptures. To this day, Jews put a high value on knowledge and continue to study numbers. It is thanks to the significance they placed on cabalistic interpretation of their scriptures that we have documentation for part of the evolution that led to modern numerology. But they are not the only ones to have developed a system of pictures and numbers.

The tarot number system was also used by the European Gypsies, who, it is believed, had Egyptian or Hindu origins, and did not receive their knowledge from the Jews. The Egyptian priests, like other ancient hierarchies, used their knowledge of metaphysical techniques to add to their control over others. They were arrogant, kept secrets, and inspired fear in uneducated people who were dependent upon birthright or survival of the fittest. Their predictions were given to leaders who used numerology to outrank and forecast the actions of opponents. The belief has been passed down (some say that Pythagoras believed it, too) that both Egyptians and Eastern Indians traced back to Atlantis and that this is where the "magic" knowledge had come from. Could Pythagoras have learned numerology's "divine knowledge" and perfections when he'd traveled as a young man? Fable or truth? Who can tell, when these early beliefs were shrouded in religious secrecy and power plays?

We do know that with tarot began the desire to understand self-image with pictures and numbers. Interpretation changed with the times and according to the society in which it was used. When writing began, the number figures may have been taken from a visual or a finger—a mental picture of the purpose of 1. For example: number 1, as a graphic, stands straight, unaided, and alone. It is not difficult to understand how the numerological interpretation, "independence," could be applied to a 1 type of personality or a destiny. Stretch your imagination and put yourself in the place of the ancients who were trying to make sense of all the things one cannot touch, taste, smell, hear, see, or spend. See how easy it would be to associate the number 1 with the character of an independent person. Life unfolds for a number 1 destiny only if independence is learned. A 1 challenge requires one to balance one's independent actions. Is it possible that this is the way numerology was born?

Systems continued to differ according to religious beliefs until Pythagoras began his Greek mystery school. His religious belief was based upon a scientific and mathematical understanding of the relationship of universal truths to numbers.

PYTHAGORAS, FATHER OF NUMEROLOGY

It was charismatic Pythagoras of Samos, born in 580 B.C., who put his serene genius to calling forms and ideas by number. During an age when humans and Gods interacted, it was only natural that after his enlightening world travels Pythagoras would attract and win over followers. His intention was to raise man from 1 (egocentricity) to 9 (selflessness). The nature of his evaluations and conclusions led Pythagoras—as later they inspired Jesus of Nazareth—to relay to others the knowledge gained from various foreign cultures. He integrated mathematics, music, mysticism, science, astronomy, and philosophy and used them as the basis for his practical applications. Eventually, he founded a school-based religion that upheld his principles.

Revered as "the master" or "that man," Pythagoras led his followers in a "way of life." He developed his belief that there existed a harmony in the spheres, which related to progressive number interpretations. He was preoccupied with the thought that words could not adequately bring understanding to concepts and objects. He believed that numbers could describe them best.

His inquiring nature caused him to travel widely in his youth. Perceived as an enlightened being, he met and studied with the spiritual leaders of India, Arabia, Persia, Palestine, Phoenicia, Chaldea, Babylon, and Egypt. Brahmans, Egyptian priests, rabbis, Zoroastrians, and the magi of Babylon shared knowledge that influenced his understanding of the soul, people, and life, with all its vicissitudes.

Pythagoras's works were passed on by respectful disciples.

As texts, they may have been lost or never existed. His convictions and theories had an impact on the teachings of Plato, St. Thomas Aquinas, St. Augustine, Aristotle, and Francis Bacon. There were many mystery schools of Greece, but none studied, disciplined, and educated each potential student as carefully as Pythagoras's. His school experimented with human relationships and inspired the lingering loyalties of disciples for centuries.

Prior to acceptance, each disciple's family background, emotional balance, and attitudes were examined by Pythagoras. The initiate was required to spend five years in silence. This discipline was intended to produce the necessary poise, purification, and mastery of self that resulted in men free of vice—men who would be certain candidates for rebirth (Pythagoras believed in karma and reincarnation). Silence was intended to heighten the individual's ability to listen to the basic truths springing from within, while meditation freed the mind to reach the pure senses. Quiet also allowed one to receive information from without. But, above all, Pythagoras taught that we reap whatever we sow.

His understanding of levels of consciousness, lifestyle, and mathematical sciences was carried into the fourth and fifth centuries B.C. It served as a foundation for art, music's diatonic scale, astronomy, and geometry. Pythagoras believed in living a practical reality and married late in life. He had seven children and died at about eighty. He was so influential right to the end that even his death was mysteriously shrouded in politically confusing circumstances.

NUMBERS OF UPHEAVAL

Should we refuse the extra jelly doughnut in a baker's dozen because it may invite disaster? Thirteen is considered—irrationally—to be malefic. Thirteen sat at Jesus Christ's table for the Last Supper, and a death followed. Is it tempting fate to chance that one will die after seating thirteen at a dinner table?

Rarely do we find a thirteenth floor in multiple dwellings or office buildings. Is there more to 13 than 1 + 12?

To the numerologist, 13 indicates transformation. It usually portends upheaval and decline leading to reconstruction on a higher level. When Judas, the thirteenth at Christ's table, began the actions that led to Jesus' crucifixion, he began the cycle of rebirth and evolution of universal Christianity. He took Christ's philosophy out of the kitchen and into the world. The thirteenth guest created a hue and cry that galvanized followers from around the universe. It's true that death occurred after the seating of thirteen. However, Christ's higher self lives on in the practical and structured religious belief organized by his converts.

Thirteen is only one of the testing numbers that take humanity to the heights or the depths. The numbers 13, 14, 16, and 19 are not malefic; they are demanding. In the Christian belief, Jesus lived his life according to the basic, common values of honesty, truth, and love. It is said that he worked for the constructive good and did not fall prey to superficial or egocentric values (the meanings of 1 and 3, which make up 13). Thirteen, in a numerology chart, indicates a testing of faith during life. It is a test of its sum number 4 (13 = 1 + 3 = 4). So numerology believes the number 13 attracts successes and failures that lead to a test of economy, self-discipline, positiveness—with a focus on working. Number 13 demands practicality, common sense, and a dedication to work for constructive values. The number 13 person is repeatedly offered reconstructive options.

Thirteen was divine and powerful to the ancients. It is a number that is misunderstood today. It is simply explained as a number having exceptional influence and requiring a down-to-earth desire to ignore superficial values and frivolity. Numerology always provides reasonable explanations for numbers that have historically attracted attention.

CHAPTER THREE

HOW TO USE THIS BOOK

1. To learn the basics of numerology, prepare to do numerology charts with the following tools at hand:
  • Pencils with erasers
  • Scratch paper for additions
  • An adding machine or calculator if you prefer not to add with your fingers or in your head:

2. Begin by following the instructions starting on page 45 for finding the single-digit number for each of the five categories in your life (challenge, self-motivation, self-image, self-expression, and destiny).

3. Write in the single-digit category numbers on the numerology category list sheet (page 38).

4. Read the appropriate category number meanings listed in the number-meanings section of this book.

5. Make note of the correspondents for each of your category numbers and read about how to use them in the correspondents sections.

6. To analyze a personal chart: compare challenge-number meanings to other category-number meanings. Use the challenge-number meanings to identify pitfalls. Use personality categories to confirm self-knowledge. Use destiny descriptions to forecast options.

7. To analyze and compare two charts: compare the category numbers to establish compatibility. Refer to the general compatibility or incompatibility numbers listed under correspondents.

8. If you wish to commit the numerology system to memory:
First, learn the number values for the alphabet. Do at least ten complete chartings for friends and family. Read the category-number meanings for each chart, from *Numerology Has Your Number*, into a tape recorder. Forget the sound of your own voice, if you do not like it. Your listeners are only concerned with the words that you are saying about them. Be friendly. Interject the person's name. If you think something is cute or funny, react. If you feel sympathetic, sound like you are. Expect to use a one-hour tape.

Read personality categories, destiny, personal year (the current year), and personal month (the current month), in that order. Save the challenge meanings for last.

Give numerology tapes as birthday, engagement, divorce, or holiday gifts. The positive feedback you receive will build self-confidence. The more tapes you do, the more you will want to do. Note the applause you'll get for originality. Look at the money you'll save!

Repeated readings of the number meanings will help you remember them. Memorizing should not be a problem.

Get into the habit of adding mentally. The trick is to visualize the column of numbers before you attempt to add.

Remember that 9 added to any number leaves the reduced number unchanged, so do not bother adding 9. Think of the name "Virlis." $(V)4 + (L)3 + (S)1 = 8$. If we bothered with the I, R, and I (all 9s), we'd come up with $4 + 9 + 9 + 3 + 9 + 1 = 35$ and $3 + 5 = 8$ anyway.

9. COCKTAIL PARTY NUMEROLOGY

You can be the life of the party after committing the system to memory. Use the first name (only the self-expression category) and personal year numbers. They are "quick and dirty" attention-getters.

You lose your audience while trying to find a pencil and paper at a party, so don't. While you are tantalizing acquaintances with your "psychic" ability, take time to think—and add.

Interpret the first letter of the first name as a "point of view," the last letter as a challenge, and each of the other letters as a positive-number meaning. Calculate the vowels (self-motivation), to explain the single reduced number as the person's "natural instinct."

Strike an introspective pose. Speak with conviction. Do not rush. Let the audience use their recall and imagination. If you do not resort to terrestrial writing tools, astounded listeners will imagine that you are "channeling" or "trancing." Don't spoil their fun by explaining too much.

USING THE CORRESPONDENTS

At the beginning of each number-meanings section you will find places and things that have vibrations corresponding to that particular number. There are letters, colors, foods, crystals, vegetation, musical instruments and notes, as well as locations that will feel familiar or be receptive to the people who have the same number vibrations in their self-motivation, self-image, self-expression, or destiny. Correspondents will become assets during the personal years, months, and days sharing the same numbers. When challenge numbers match up with the correspondents, these objects and locations trigger emotional responses.

Generally people are automatically attracted to their own number correspondents. It is not necessary to surround yourself with jewels, foods, colors, or music that correspond to the numbers in your chart or for you to avoid the things that are challenges. However, your daily life may be energized by having unchallenged correspondents in your surroundings. Challenged objects or locations may be abrasive.

Your correspondents seem to demand actions or reactions when they match up with your charted numbers. By using, eating, listening to, or residing with the objects or locations that are akin to your numbers, you are creating your personal environment and putting the spotlight on the people or experiences that make your life more profitable and relaxed.

COLORS, GEMS, CRYSTALS, AND VEGETATION

Colors, gems, crystals, and vegetation may be used to set moods and attract help. The ones that correspond to your personal numbers complement you and should be worn or used when decorating your home to add serenity, invite kindred spirits, or enhance enjoyable activities. For example, a turquoise ring on the hand of a person with a number 5 destiny sends out a subliminal invitation to people who have the number 5 in their personality numbers, their destiny, or their changing personal year, month, or day numbers.

The color, gem, crystal, or vegetation that corresponds to your *challenge* number should NOT be used unless you are modifying behavior and have achieved some balance in your personality and your life. When wearing a challenge correspondent, expect to attract people and experiences that trigger emotional overreactions to practical situations. Decorating with challenge correspondents sets challenging moods.

The color, gem, crystal, or vegetation corresponding to your *self-motivation* number should be worn at home or when relaxing. It will attract people and experiences that make you comfortable. Your *self-image* correspondent should be worn for effect, to enhance the first impression. Your *self-expression* correspondent should be worn to support self-expression and career ambitions. Your *destiny* correspondent should be worn to attract new people and experiences that teach the meaning of the destiny number. Wearing the color, gem, crystal, or vegetation that corresponds to your *personal year, month, or day* will attract people and experiences that enhance that number meaning. Wear red on a number 1 day to send out a self-assertive vibe. It is amusing to note that, without planning, on a 1 personal day, most people wear the color red instinctively.

FOODS

"We are what we eat" numerologically. Foods that are correspondents of *challenge* numbers may give you indigestion. You may overeat to get as much of their taste as you can or you may avoid them—there is no balance in your attitude toward challenge correspondents. In some cases, avoiding challenge-number foods may improve your health. For example, if people who have the number 1 challenge avoid eating number 1 correspondent foods like baked beans, lobster, or chocolate, they may find that their diarrhea, cellulite, or hernia problems abate or go away.

If you eat the foods that correspond to personality numbers, they have a bolstering effect on health. *Destiny* numbers put correspondent foods in your path—they are offered to you; you are intended to learn about them. Changing tastes can be identified by *personal year, month, and day* numbers. Foods that correspond to your *self-motivation* number may be combined with other personality-number correspondent foods. Try to use your correspondents to support their categories: *self-motivation* number foods for relaxation, *self-image* foods to support first impressions, *self-expression* foods in combination with talents, *destiny* foods for new experiences.

MUSICAL NOTES, APPEALS, AND INSTRUMENTS

Music has been said to soothe the savage breast. You will find pleasure in the musical correspondents listed for your *self-motivation, self-image,* and *self-expression* numbers.

Challenge-number correspondents may be offensive and bring up emotional responses that can speed or delay behavior modification. If you listen to the melody of a favorite love song, it may bring you to tears of depression or tears of joy. You will love or hate the challenge music correspondents, and may wish to use them to create a mood that will cause you to get in touch with your feelings. For people who do not sit still long enough to follow their emotions and dig into the reasons why moods overcome them, musical challenge correspondents can become a tool for the therapist working to help them.

Destiny-number musical correspondents crop up during one lifetime and seem to become symbols or focuses for that lifetime. As for *personal year, month, and day* correspondents, you will be drawn to or encounter the types of music indicated by these numbers during that particular time period.

LOCATIONS

Before making a move to a different location, consider the reason for the move. Locations attract the people who want to exemplify their number meanings. Investigate the states that correspond to your *self-expression* number in order to feel at home immediately. People there will be participating in the activities indicated by that number. Investigate the states that correspond to the *self-motivation* number when changing jobs. The people there will be attracted to the talents and methods of self-expression indicated by the number meaning. Investigate the states that correspond to the *destiny* number to make a fresh start.

Note: Only a few cities are listed for each number. To find the numbers for additional cities, use the same method you used to find your self-motivation, self-image, and self-expression numbers. Substitute the name of the city for your name. You will discover what people living there desire, how they want to appear, and what types of careers or businesses they are focused upon.

Use correspondents with common sense. However, use them.

◄◄◄ NUMEROLOGY CATEGORY LIST ►►►

Categories		Name	Name	Name
		Susie		
Challenge Numbers	1st	3		
	2nd	5		
	3rd	2		
	4th	2		
Self-motivation Number		8		
Self-image Number		2		
Self-expression Number		1		
Destiny Number		2		
Personal-Year Number		3		
Personal-Month Number		*James* 9		
Personal-Day Number				

◄◄◄ NUMEROLOGY CATEGORY LIST ►►►

Categories		Name	Name	Name
Challenge Numbers	1st	____	____	____
	2nd	____	____	____
	3rd	____	____	____
	4th	____	____	____
Self-motivation Number		____	____	____
Self-image Number		____	____	____
Self-expression Number		____	____	____
Destiny Number		____	____	____
Personal-Year Number		____	____	____
Personal-Month Number		____	____	____
Personal-Day Number		____	____	____

CHAPTER FOUR

HOW TO FIND
YOUR NUMBERS

CHALLENGE NUMBER

This is the first numerology book to place emphasis on the challenge numbers. Their impact, importance, and value have not been tapped or explained in depth before. *Numerology Has Your Number* makes challenge-number descriptions more important than personality- and destiny-number descriptions. So, before finding your personality and destiny numbers, find your challenge numbers.

Their meanings should be read first, in the hope that it will be easier to view them dispassionately. In this context there is no accuser—no need to get adrenaline flowing to "defend." Personality and destiny descriptions will make more sense when challenges are outlined beforehand. Then, too, when you go on to read the positives of your number descriptions, you can focus on them without thinking "Numerology cannot be valid. It only gives me good points." Go ahead and focus on the good points! We all have more than enough neurotic shticks to work on. Take all the help you can get!

Challenge holders should read the other categories (self-motivation, self-image, etc.) for their challenge numbers, too. They may be helpful when trying to "gray down" the black-and-white opinions of the challenged aspect of the number. When a challenge number is the same as a personality-category number, derived from the name or birth date, the challenge number points to exact personality areas that need destined balance. When challenge numbers do not appear in other personality categories, they touch all aspects of the personality.

• CHALLENGES are best understood by the person whose name and birth date are being charted. They are tools for self-analysis—keys to honest self-assessments.

• CHALLENGE-number meanings supply the very personal reasons for stress. Challenges stem from childhood experiences. After maturity they manifest in symptoms that cloud logic and create emotional overreactions.

• CHALLENGES are the reasons behind the repeated mistakes one makes and the emotional extremes to which one goes. They describe personality assets that are used in positive or negative extremes. The challenge holder does not have childhood points of reference to indicate the balanced attitude.

• CHALLENGES EXPLAIN THE REASON ONE HAS MANY OPTIONS. One may see a glass of water half-full—another sees it half-empty.

• CHALLENGES show how one copes with destiny. It is a person's attitudes, not *fate*, that breeds success or disappointment. "Fate is the sum of the reactions to our actions. Therefore we must change ourselves in order that fate may also change."

—Elisabeth Haich
Wisdom of the Tarot
(translated by D. Q. Stephenson)

ABOUT THE CHALLENGES . . .

You have control over your fate and your challenges. It is your attitude that determines whether you are a winner or a loser, an adult or a baby. Numerology accurately predicts the people and experiences that you can expect to encounter. You behave toward them according to how you perceive yourself. Challenges reveal your childhood perceptions that linger to maturity.

Challenge-number meanings describe the personality extremes that lead to emotional, physical, and intellectual stresses. Challenge symptoms waste potential, time, and energy. The challenge-number sections include suggestions for identifying and changing unproductive habits or asinine behavior patterns. Numerology's suggestions lead to new options for the challenge holder. Recognizing and balancing challenge extremes can lead to additional means of self-expression . . . plus, a calmer, healthier, more multifaceted person is freed from fruitless self-induced pressures.

Challenges describe irrational fears and imply a stressful use of abilities. These stressful extremes lead to changes in body chemistry that alter mental, physical, and intuitional energy levels. Here's how it works.

Emotions filter through the mind. The mind signals the brain. The brain relays messages to the body. When a one-hundred-twenty-pound untrained woman sees her child pinned under the wheels of a car, what happens to her emotions? She might faint, or she might lift the car to free her child. In either case, body chemistry changes. Another example: when too happy or too sad, some people react with a case of hives or psoriasis. Feelings are censored as they travel through the mind. The process causes physical reactions. The schools of psychosomatic and holistic medicine, to name a few, agree on that.

Mary Baker Eddy's Christian Science philosophy adds to the concept: "Disease is an image of thought externalized. . . . We classify disease as error, which nothing but truth and mind can heal.

"An experience of mortal mind . . . it is fear made manifest on the body."

Challenge-number descriptions include the areas of the body that are susceptible to dis-ease. A variety of healing philosophies indicate that our thoughts can make us sick, depressed, and inactive. Challenge-number meanings point out those attitudes and actions that tend to have unpleasant effects on our physical and mental health.

Challenge numbers describe uncomfortable personality traits and habits that are born in childhood and expand in youth. These habits may appear to spur one on to achievement, but in the end they drain energy, open the door to physical problems, delay progress, and prevent one from doing what comes naturally.

Challenge numbers describe defensive attitudes and habits. Inappropriate, childlike perceptions and expectations of instant approval (or disapproval) cause personal and business problems. In our challenged areas we may back away from confrontations or force issues. Communications with loved ones become snarled. We may aggressively build walls with manipulative threats or submit to another's control.

Using one's work to avoid investigating uncomfortable feelings is a challenge habit, too. Challenge holders may be compulsively busy. They appear to be achievers. In reality, they may be drowning in a well of details, unable to see the ocean for the waves—anything to avoid sitting still! It is their habit to live rigidly, governed by youthful disciplines. As a result, challenge holders do the impersonal "right thing" for all the wrong personal reasons.

Usually challenge holders do not learn from past experience, repeating mistakes that undermine self-esteem. In order to feel valuable, some challenge holders make money, status, or power too important. Attempts to "show the world" often begin with panic and set one up for rejection. No matter how old we get, no matter how intelligent or talented we are, challenge numbers describe our feelings of inadequacy.

Challenges reveal the cause and effect of too much parental attention or neglect. As infants, we cannot change the overly concerned mother who lovingly smothers us into self-absorption. We cannot insist upon affection and approval from our forever-working, preoccupied father. As adults, we repeat our mother's pattern or become politely concerned parents in order to avoid her mistakes. As adult breadwinners, we may become workaholics or refuse to let practical financial concerns take us away from home. The feelings we could not express as tots have a profound effect on our adult personalities and expectations.

Childhood suppressions result in challenges. As adults, we cannot suck our thumbs or carry little blue blankets to the job. Challenges reveal the bases for a lifetime of hidden feelings that surface as overreactions.

IN A NUTSHELL . . .

There are nine types of challenges, symbolized by each of the numbers 1 through 9. Personal-challenge numbers are found by a birth date subtraction routine. The challenge-number meanings describe cause, effect, and cure for inappropriate adult habits based on a child's-eye emotional view. These habits cause stress, and affect the way we cope with asinine, destructive demonstrations of black-or-white opinions and actions. The gray shades of constructive compromise are elusive because they are the unknowns of childhood. Challenge-number meanings fill in many childhood blanks and open our eyes to a happier maturity.

FIND THE CHALLENGE NUMBERS

Numerology has a basic rule: All double numbers are added together and reduced to a single number by adding from left to right.

Example: $45 = 4 + 5 = 9$
$34 = 3 + 4 = 7$
28 is tricky; it calls for double action.
$28 = 2 + 8 = 10;$
$1 + 0 = 1,$
so a 28 becomes a 1 in numerology.

Zero has a challenge meaning, equivalent to 9, which is described in the meanings of the 9 number section.

FOR CHALLENGE SUBTRACTION AND PURPOSES OF ADDITION, 11 (1+1) IS REDUCED TO 2, 22 (2+2) IS REDUCED TO 4, 33 (3+3) IS REDUCED TO 6, AND 44 (4+4) IS REDUCED TO 8.

CHALLENGE NUMBER CHART INSTRUCTIONS

Refer to the month, day, and year of birth to find the challenge numbers.

Step 1. Convert the month of birth to a number by finding its place in the calendar.

> January = 1, February = 2, March = 3, April = 4, May = 5, June = 6, July = 7, August = 8, September = 9, October = 1, November = 2, December = 3

Step 2. Reduce birth-date number to a single number, if necessary.

Step 3. Reduce birth-year number to a single number.

Example: 1937 = 2

> Add 1 + 9 + 3 + 7 = 20; reduce to a single number.
> 2 + 0 = 2; THE YEAR 1937 = 2
> 1954 = 1
> Add 1 + 9 + 5 + 4 = 19; reduce to a single number.
> 1 + 9 = 10; reduce 10 to a single number
> 1 + 0 = 1; THE YEAR 1954 = 1

CHALLENGE NUMBER SYSTEM

Step 1. Fill in the single-digit numbers of your birth date:

A _7_   B _4_   C _9_
Month   Day   Year

Note: Always subtract the smaller number from the higher number.

Step 2. A − B = _____*3*_____ (Birth to age 28)

Step 3. B − C = _____*5*_____ (After age 28)

Step 4. Subtract the remainders of A − B and B − C from each other:

_____*2*_____ (Lifetime)

Step 5. A − C = _____*2*_____ (Lifetime)

Example: July 12, 1937 is Bill Cosby's birth date.

July is the 7th calendar month = 7

12 (1 + 2) is added to become a 3 = 3

1937 = 1 + 9 + 3 + 7 = 20, and 2 + 0 = 2

Step 1. Bill Cosby's birth date by number: 7 (month), 3 (day), 2 (year)

Step 2. 7 − 3 = 4; has its strongest focus in youth and touches mid-life.

Step 3. 3 − 2 = 1; has its strongest focus mid-life and after.

Step 4. 4 − 1 = 3; focus is for the lifetime.

Step 5. 7 − 2 = 5; focus is for the lifetime.

Birth-date challenges for Bill Cosby are 4, 1, 3, and 5.

Example: June 1, 1926—Marilyn Monroe's birth date.

Step 1. Birth date by number: 6 (month) 1 (day) 9 (year)
(1 + 9 + 2 + 6 = 18; 1 + 8 = 9)

Step 2. 6 − 1 = 5 (switch numbers of month and day)

Step 3. 9 − 1 = 8

Step 4. 8 − 5 = 3

Step 5. 9 − 6 = 3

Birth-date challenges for Marilyn Monroe are 5, 8, and 3.

Example: February 22, 1932—Edward (Ted) Kennedy's birth date.

Step 1. Birth date by number: 2 (month) 4 (day) 6 (year)

Step 2. 4 − 2 = 2

Step 3. 6 − 4 = 2

Step 4. 2 − 2 = 0

Step 5. 6 − 2 = 4

Birth-date challenges for Ted Kennedy are 2, 2, 0, and 4.

CHALLENGE NUMBER TIMING

Notice that Ted Kennedy and Marilyn Monroe both have double challenge numbers. Ted Kennedy has the double-detail and mother-conscious 2, and Marilyn Monroe has the socially insecure, facade-conscious 3. When a challenge number appears more than once, it is a difficult challenge to overcome. Double challenge numbers warn that childhood influences or environments do not change after maturity. These challenges are reinforced consistently. It is more desirable for the challenge holder to digest them slowly, over a long period of time. Situations will arise to bring their meaning into focus.

Refer to the Challenge Chart. . . .

Step 2. FIRST CHALLENGE: The subtraction of the month and day provides the number that describes the challenge felt strongly until approximately the twenty-eighth birthday.

Step 3. SECOND CHALLENGE: The subtraction of the day and year provides the number that describes the challenge felt strongly in mid-life, which may hang in to touch the late years.

Steps 4 and 5. THIRD AND FOURTH CHALLENGES: The subtractions of the remainders and of the day and year require attention throughout life.

PERSONALITY CATEGORIES

Personality is divided into three categories—self-motivation, self-image, and self-expression. You will be finding your personality category numbers by using your entire birth name.

BASIC RULES FOR NAME INTERPRETATION

To construct a chart, use only the exact letters of the names printed on the certificate of birth or its equivalent.

Nicknames, baptismal names, early-name changes, mar-

◄◄◄ CHALLENGE NUMBER SYSTEM ►►►

BLANK CHARTS

Step 1: Birth date

A _____ B _____ C _____
   month   day   year

Step 2: A − B = _____ (Birth to age 28)

Step 3: B − C = _____ (After age 28)

Step 4: Subtract the remainders of A − B and B − C from

each other: _____ (Lifetime)

Step 5: A − C = _____ (Lifetime)

Step 1: Birth date

A _____ B _____ C _____
   month   day   year

Step 2: A − B = _____ (Birth to age 28)

Step 3: B − C = _____ (After age 28)

Step 4: Subtract the remainders of A − B and B − C from

each other: _____ (Lifetime)

Step 5: A − C = _____ (Lifetime)

Step 1: Birth date

A _____ B _____ C _____
      month   day   year

Step 2: A − B = _____ (Birth to age 28)

Step 3: B − C = _____ (After age 28)

Step 4: Subtract the remainders of A − B and B − C from

each other: _____ (Lifetime)

Step 5: A − C = _____ (Lifetime)

Step 1: Birth date

A _____ B _____ C _____
      month   day   year

Step 2: A − B = _____ (Birth to age 28)

Step 3: B − C = _____ (After age 28)

Step 4: Subtract the remainders of A − B and B − C from

each other: _____ (Lifetime)

Step 5: A − C = _____ (Lifetime)

riage names, and professional names should not be used to construct a numerology chart.

Junior, the II, III, IV, etc., are not included as part of a name chart. It is accepted that the child will have the characteristics of the name, which were the same for the original name holder. Uniqueness is explained by opportunities offered by different birth dates.

If baby, boy, girl, infant, male, female, an initial (A., B., C., etc.) or a name that has never been used but has been registered on a birth certificate or in the recordkeeper (family Bible, etc.) of any culture, that is the name used to prepare a numerology chart. The first record is understood to have been chosen by the new soul that has come to Earth for its purposes.

Note: There are all sorts of logical reasons for calling this numerology rule impossible, ridiculous, or crazy, and many clients have told me "But I never used that name—it was a mistake." However, parascientists, metaphysicians, and numerologists believe that there is a purpose and a plan for everyone—there are no mistakes.

Ancients believed that the parents, siblings, or esteemed friend that names the baby is the tool the soul uses on this material plane. This belief in karma, reincarnation, and the self-determination of the soul existed for the ancients and is accepted as truth by many cultures today.

Keep in mind that numerology's documentation has been lost. It may not seem logical, but it works!

PERSONALITY CATEGORIES— PURPOSE AND INSTRUCTIONS

SELF-MOTIVATION

Your *self-motivation* number is derived from the number values of the vowels in your entire birth name. Refer to the name as it appears on a birth certificate or the first name recorded, as is the custom in different countries and cultures. The number equivalents for the vowels in the entire birth name, added together and reduced to a single number, reveal what we desire, feel inclined to do, and want to have to feel contented.

We instinctively set our heart and soul on the values described by the self-motivation number. It describes what it is we desire to be and what we want out of life.

To add depth and scope to your understanding of the self-motivation number, you should also read the number meaning for each individual name in the entire birth name. The single reduced number for the vowels in a first name indicate practical instincts. The single reduced number for the vowels in the middle name(s) describe emotional instincts. The reduced number for the vowels in the last name reveals spiritual instincts for the bearer and the paternal side of the family.

Metaphysically self-motivation is called the "soul urge."

To find the self-motivation number meaning

The single reduced number meanings for the vowels in the name self-motivation are explained in the number meanings section. Please continue reading the explanation. The self-motivation, self-image, and self-expression numbers will be calculated on one chart.

Instructions and blank chart follow after "Self-expression."

SELF-IMAGE

Your *self-image* number is derived from the number values of the consonants in your birth name.

The single number calculated for your *entire* name is the most important. However, the numbers for individual names within a birth name add to understanding what it is we wish to show the world.

The self-image number reveals the impression that onlookers receive of us when we walk out of an elevator thinking ourselves unnoticed or enter a room unannounced—the first impression we make. It is the visualization of success that we cherished as youngsters, when we daydreamed and planned the way we would walk, talk, dress, and progress as adults.

When we live up to our self-image number meanings, we disregard the demands made by others and instead send out number vibrations that attract our dreams. Our self-image is born in the imagination. It is the key to understanding the way we see ourselves at our best.

To find meanings for the self-image category

Meanings for the single reduced numbers of the consonants in the name self-image are to be found in the number meanings section. Please keep reading the explanation. The instructions and chart for self-motivation, self-image, and self-expression follow after "Self-expression."

SELF-EXPRESSION

Your *self-expression* number is derived by adding *all* the number values of the letters in the full given name. The numbers for each name are totaled separately and reduced to one number. These numbers are then added together and reduced to one number. To find the overall picture, read the meaning of the single number value for *all* the letters. Individual names in the full birth name, when reduced to their single number meaning, describe talents, potentials, and methods of self-expression. The meanings of the single reduced numbers for first, middle, and last names in the entire birth name may be read for additional information.

The self-expression number indicates your career talents and sums up your capabilities. Its ingredients suggest career choices that make use of material abilities. As a homemaker, a hobbyist, or a dedicated professional, you are most comfortable focusing on the meanings of the self-expression numbers to attract recognition.

Note: Please do not shortcut numerology by taking the single, reduced number of the sum of vowels and consonants to find the self-expression number.

Number meanings for self-expression, as well as for self-motivation and self-image, can be found in the number meanings section. When you have completed the instructions for all three categories and noted the numbers by category, read the number meanings. In order to gain a broad perspective, heighten perceptions, and compare with challenge numbers, it is desirable to read and analyze in one sitting.

NUMBERS HAVE A NEGATIVE AND A POSITIVE SIDE

It is necessary to complete a numerology charting before reading the individual meanings of the numbers because all the complex parts of our natures must be viewed as a whole.

To fully comprehend a numerology personality profile and its destiny, we must recognize that each number description has a negative and positive side. Most people are not consistently positive or negative . . . or balanced.

The complexities within our natures become clear when our number meanings are read one after another. People are not simple. We often confuse ourselves and our intimates by revealing conflicting desires. A complete personality chart sheds light on these dichotomies.

After reading all the personal number values new options arise for us. The previously undreamed-of possibilities indicated by a personality-category number may light a fire under the Scarlett O'Haras among us who will "think about it tomorrow." Seeing time spans defined may spark a sense of immediacy. Scanning lifetime opportunities may relieve the concerns of people who think that life is passing them by.

Too often we are caught up in the happenings of the moment. Our past efforts and future aspirations may be shelved when we think that an emergency has arisen. It is only human to zero in on numerology's number meanings to find solutions for immediate problems, but it is best to come back to the long-term possibilities, indicated by our destiny-number description, as soon as an emergency is over.

Numerology helps us to understand when and how time can heal emotional wounds or solve problems. By waiting to read the number meanings for the entire personality category list, we can discover additional assets. Extraordinary timing may be available for the future. A more promising solution may be found, which often reduces anxiety and places less importance on what appears to be an immediate need for action.

In order to benefit from the lateral vision that numerology offers, it is better to chart first and read later.

INSTRUCTIONS AND WORKSHEET FOR CHARTING SELF-MOTIVATION, SELF-IMAGE, AND SELF-EXPRESSION NUMBERS

NOTE: When charting self-motivation, y becomes a vowel if a, e, i, o, or u are not in a syllable. A, e, i, o, and u are vowels. All remaining letters are consonants. Example: Marilyn = Mar-i-lyn; y is a vowel. Kennedy = Ken-ne-dy; y is a vowel. Lynne; y is not a vowel. Nancy = Nan-cy; y is a vowel. Mary = Mar-y; y is a vowel. Harley = Har-ley; y is not a vowel. Raymond = Ray-mond; y is not a vowel. Yolanda = Yo-lan-da; y is not a vowel. Cynthia = Cyn-thi-a; y is a vowel.

Okay, here we go. Let's learn how to calculate the self-motivation, self-image, and self-expression numbers by doing a few examples.

Example # 1: WILLIAM HENRY COSBY, JUNIOR

Note: William's nickname, Bill, is not used to prepare a chart.

"Junior" is also not used in preparation of a chart.

Step 1. Have a pencil with an eraser.

Step 2. Using the grid below, print the name as it appears on the birth certificate; William Henry Cosby.

Step 3. Using the letter-values chart as your guide, print the number value below each letter in the name on the grid.

Step 4. Print the number values for each of the consonants in the name in the appropriate boxes.

Step 5. Print the number values for each of the vowels in the name in the appropriate boxes.

Step 6. Total the numbers listed for each individual name on all three lines. All totals that equal 10 or more should be reduced to a single digit number by adding the two numbers together (11 = 1 + 1 = 2).

Step 7: Add the individual name numbers to make a grand total for each line. Reduce the grand totals to single digit numbers.

Step 8. Transfer the single reduced numbers for each category onto the Category List (page 38).

Full name—self-expression

Consonants—self-image

Vowels—self-motivation

Step 9. To determine Cosby's personality ingredients, read the number meanings for the grand totals of all categories.

Step 10. Read the number meanings of each individual name to add depth to your understanding.

Bill Cosby's personality numbers are:

Self-motivation: 8

Self-image: 7

Self-expression: 6

LETTER VALUES

1	2	3	4	5	6	7	8	9
A	B	C	D	E	F	G	H	I
J	K	L	M	N	O	P	Q	R
S	T	U	V	W	X	Y	Z	

LETTER VALUE WORKSHEET

Step 2.
Full Name

W	I	L	L	I	A	M		H	E	N	R	Y		C	O	S	B	Y		

T T

Step 3.
Letter Values
of Full Names T

5	9	3	3	9	1	4	34	8	5	5	9	7	34	3	6	1	2	7	19
			7								7							1	

15   6

T T

Step 4.
Consonant Letter
Values T

5		3	3			4	15	8	5		9		22	3		1	2		6
			6								4							6	

16   7

T T

Step 5.
Vowel Letter
Values T

9				9	1		19			5		7	12		6			7	13
9							1			3								4	

8   8

T T

Example #2: Edward Moore (Ted) Kennedy

Step 1. Have a pencil with an eraser.

Step 2. Using the grid below, print the name as it appears on the birth certificate; Edward Moore Kennedy.

Step 3. Using the letter-values chart as your guide, print the number value below each letter in the name on the grid.

Step 4. Print the number values for each of the consonants in the name in the appropriate boxes.

Step 5. Print the number values for each of the vowels in the name in the appropriate boxes.

Step 6. Total the numbers listed for each individual name on all three lines. All totals that equal 10 or more should be reduced to a single-digit number by adding the two numbers together (11 = 1 + 1 = 2).

Step 7. Add the individual name numbers to make a grand total for each line. Reduce the grand totals to single-digit numbers.

Step 8. Transfer the single reduced numbers for each category onto the Category List (page 38).

Full name—self-expression

Consonants—self-image

Vowels—self-motivation

Step 9. To determine Kennedy's personality ingredients, read the number meanings for the grand totals of all categories.

Step 10. Read the number meanings of each individual name to add depth to your understanding.

Ted Kennedy's personality numbers are:

Self-motivation: 4

Self-image: 6

Self-expression: 1

LETTER VALUES

1	2	3	4	5	6	7	8	9
A	B	C	D	E	F	G	H	I
J	K	L	M	N	O	P	Q	R
S	T	U	V	W	X	Y	Z	

LETTER VALUE WORKSHEET

Step 2.
Full Name: E D W A R D | M O O R E | K E N N E D Y | T T

Step 3.
Letter Values of Full Names T:
5 4 5 1 9 4 | 2 8 4 6 6 9 5 | 30 2 5 5 5 5 4 7 | 33
3   6   10 1   T T

Step 4.
Consonant Letter Values T:
4 5 | 9 4 22 4 | 9 | 13 2 | 5 5 | 4 | 16   15 6
4   4   7   T T

Step 5.
Vowel Letter Values T:
5 | 1 | 6 6 | 5 17 5 | 5 7 17   22 4
6   8   8   T T

Example #3: Norma Jean Mortenson (Marilyn Monroe)

Step 1. Have a pencil with an eraser.

Step 2. Using the grid below, print the name as it appears on the birth certificate; Norma Jean Mortenson.

Step 3. Using the letter values chart as your guide, print the number value below each letter in the name on the grid.

Step 4. Print the number values for each of the consonants in the name in the appropriate boxes.

Step 5. Print the number values for the vowels in the name in the appropriate boxes.

Step 6. Total the numbers listed for each individual name on all three lines. All totals that equal 10 or more should be reduced to a single digit number by adding the two numbers together (11 = 1 + 1 = 2)

Step 7. Add the individual name numbers to make a grand total for each line. Reduce the grand totals to single digit numbers.

Step 8. Transfer the single reduced numbers for each category onto the Category List (page 38).

Full name—self-expression

Consonants—self-image

Vowels—self-motivation

Step 9. To determine Marilyn's personality ingredients, read the number meanings for the grand totals of all categories.

Step 10. Read the number meanings of each individual name to add depth to your understanding.

Marilyn Monroe's personality numbers are:

Self-motivation: 3

Self-image: 5

Self-expression: 8

LETTER VALUES

	1	2	3	4	5	6	7	8	9
	A	B	C	D	E	F	G	H	I
	J	K	L	M	N	O	P	Q	R
	S	T	U	V	W	X	Y	Z	

LETTER VALUE WORKSHEET

Step 2.
Full Name: N O R M A   J E A N   M O R T E N S O N   T   T

Step 3.
Letter Values of Full Names:
5 6 9 4 1   [25] 1 5 1 5   [12] 4 6 9 2 5 5 1 6 5 [43]
T: 7   3   7   17   8   T   T

Step 4.
Consonant Letter Values:
5 9 4 [18] 1   5 6 4   9 2 5 1 5 [26]
T: 9   6   8   23   5   T   T

Step 5.
Vowel Letter Values:
6 1 [7]   5 1 [6]   6 5 [17]
T: 9   6   8   21   3   T   T

YOUR PERSONALITY CATEGORY WORKSHEET

Here is a worksheet for you to use with your own name. After calculating your personality category numbers and noting them on the Category List (page 38), please go on to the destiny and personal year, month, and day number instructions. Then you will be prepared to read the number meanings for a complete analysis.

Step 1. Have a pencil with an eraser.

Step 2. Using the grid below, print the name as it appears on the birth certificate.

Step 3. Using the letter-values chart as your guide, print the number value below each letter in the name on the grid.

Step 4. Print the number values for each of the consonants in the name in the appropriate boxes.

Step 5. Print the number values for each of the vowels in the name in the appropriate boxes.

Step 6. Total the numbers listed for each individual name on all three lines. All totals that equal 10 or more should be reduced to a single-digit number by adding the two numbers together (11 = 1 + 1 = 2).

Step 7. Add the individual name numbers to make a grand total for each line. Reduce the grand totals to single-digit numbers.

Step 8. Transfer the single reduced numbers for each category onto the Category List (page 38).

Full name—self-expression

Consonants—self-image

Vowels—self-motivation

Step 9. To determine your personality ingredients, read the number meanings for the grand totals of all categories.

Step 10. Read the number meanings of each individual name to add depth to your understanding of yourself.

LETTER VALUES

1	2	3	4	5	6	7	8	9
A	B	C	D	E	F	G	H	I
J	K	L	M	N	O	P	Q	R
S	T	U	V	W	X	Y	Z	

LETTER VALUE WORKSHEET

Step 2.
Full Name: SUSAN ELIZABETH ROGERS

T   T

Step 3.
Letter Values of Full Names: 1 3 1 1 5 | 5 3 9 8 1 3 5 2 8 | 4 9 6 7 5 9 1 5   10 1

T   7   T   T

Step 4.
Consonant Letter Values: 1 1 5 | 3 8 3 2 9 | 9 1 | 9 1 24   20 2

T   7   5   8   T   T

Step 5.
Vowel Letter Values: 3 1 | 4 5 9 1 5 | 20 6 5 | 11   8 8

T   4   2   2   T   T

DESTINY NUMBER—
PURPOSE AND INSTRUCTIONS

The destiny number describes what we are intended to learn. Metaphysically speaking, the destiny number describes our purpose in the plan of life. The types of people and experiences indicated by this number will be surprising unless the personality traits of self-motivation, self-image, self-expression, or birthday number are the same.

If the self-expression number is the same as the destiny number, you settle upon a career early in life, and the experiences you encounter speed your progress. If your self-motivation number is the same as the destiny number, you quickly meet the people and experiences that make you feel at ease. If your self-image number is the same as your destiny number, you have the opportunities to live up to your childhood lifestyle fantasies.

Few people have the same numbers in their personality categories and destiny. Most people live by the hunt-and-peck method and learn from experience.

By understanding numerology's destiny-number meaning, you are able to identify *who* you are meant to become, *what* you are intended to do to get there, *why* you came here to begin with, *where* you should look for help, and *when* timing is right.

How you do all these things depends upon how you cope with the challenge-number meanings.

INSTRUCTIONS FOR FINDING
THE DESTINY NUMBER

Step 1. Add the month, day, and year of birth numbers. *Or* reduce month, day, and year birth numbers to a single number and add those numbers together.

Step 2. Reduce the sum to a number between 1 and 9. The single reduced number of the sum of the month, day, and year of birth is the destiny number.

Example for Bill Cosby: July 12, 1937
July = 7
12 = 1 + 2 = 3
1937 = 1 + 9 + 3 + 7 = 20 and 2 + 0 = 2
   7 + 3 + 2 = 12 and 1 + 2 = 3
OR
   7 + 12 + 1937 = 1956 and 1 + 9 + 5 + 6 = 21 and
   2 + 1 = 3
Bill Cosby's destiny number is 3.

Example for Marilyn Monroe: June 1, 1926
June = 6
1 = 1
1926 = 1 + 9 + 2 + 6 = 18 and 1 + 8 = 9
   6 + 1 + 9 = 16 and 1 + 6 = 7
(It is interesting that Marilyn Monroe's destiny number is the
   testing number 16 under the 7.)

Example for Ted Kennedy: February 22, 1932
February = 2
22 = 2 + 2 = 4
1932 = 1 + 9 + 3 + 2 = 15 and 1 + 5 = 6
   2 + 4 + 6 = 12 and 1 + 2 = 3

YOUR DESTINY NUMBER WORKSHEET

Birth date numbers:
   ___*7*___ + ___*31*___ + ___*1944*___ = _____
   month   day   year   total
Reduce total to single number:
   ___*2*___ + ___*9*___ = ___*2*___
                              total
DESTINY NUMBER = ___*2*___

   Note the destiny number on the Numerology Category
List.
   Instructions for forecasting personal year, personal month,

and personal day (the current cycles and trends) follow. Personal year, month, and day are part of the destiny. *All* number descriptions should be read after the completion of a chart.

THE PERSONAL YEAR NUMBER— PURPOSE AND INSTRUCTIONS

Lifetimes are divided into nine-year cycles of experience. We begin new concepts in the number 1 personal year of the cycle and conclude the first cycle's goal, eight years later, in a number 9 personal year.

The seven years between the number 1 and number 9 years bring our initial concept (1) to a polish and skill of performance (9). In the number 9 personal year we let go of the past and prepare for a new direction the following year—the number 1 personal year that begins another cycle of experiences.

It is said that we live in seven-year cycles; however, few people remember to factor in the first year, when ideas take shape, or the last year, when we let go of the idea.

During the number 9 personal year we reflect on the past eight years and realize that number 1 personal-year goals have been reached. New concepts based on accomplishments or conclusions are born. The seed for change is planted. It is not possible to begin and end major projects in the same year, so after the number 9 year concludes, new things are instigated in a 1 year. They are nurtured in a 2, come to light in a 3, come down to earth in a 4, make transitions in a 5, add responsibilities in a 6, specialize in a 7, make material strides in an 8, and gain recognition in a 9.

Each year in the nine-year cycle has a purpose.

NUMBER 1 PERSONAL YEAR offers opportunities to make progressive changes. It is an outgoing year during which we can expect to start projects.

NUMBER 2 PERSONAL YEAR offers opportunities to learn the details of the projects that began in the number 1 cycle. It is a receptive detail year during which we build for future results.

NUMBER 3 PERSONAL YEAR offers opportunities to bring the goals of the number 1 cycle to light. It is an outgoing year during which we can expect to see results from social contacts.

NUMBER 4 PERSONAL YEAR offers opportunities to correct impracticalities and build security for the future. It is a receptive work year during which we build for the future.

NUMBER 5 PERSONAL YEAR offers opportunities to experiment with additional ideas, to use various means of self-promotion, and to experience physical pleasures. It is a transforming, outgoing year during which we can expect to see results.

The first four personal year cycles are rooted in independent actions. The fifth year is a pivotal cycle that opens the door to unknowns and a lifestyle transition.

NUMBER 6 PERSONAL YEAR offers opportunities to make long-term business and intimate commitments, assume obligations, and be of service. It is a receptive year during which we build for the future.

NUMBER 7 PERSONAL YEAR offers opportunities to be introspective and to reevaluate intimate, business, and spiritual goals. It is a loner year to observe, be receptive, and expect little or no commercial results.

NUMBER 8 PERSONAL YEAR offers opportunities to take control of material and commercial affairs. It is a problem-solving year to be very aggressive, courageous, and to expect high-level, tangible results.

NUMBER 9 PERSONAL YEAR offers opportunities to be philosophical, cultured, and charitable. It is a year to be receptive to the needs of many, to set an example, and to expect results of the original concepts that took shape in the number 1 personal year. It is a year to clean out dead wood. Nothing new begins.

INSTRUCTIONS FOR FINDING OUT
YOUR PERSONAL YEAR

METHOD 1: USING THE PERSONAL YEAR GRIDS

Step 1. Find the grid for the current calendar year (pages 69–77).

Step 2. Look up your birthday in the grid to find your personal year number.

METHOD 2. USING NUMEROLOGY'S
PERSONAL YEAR SYSTEM

Step 1. First you must find the single number for any calendar year. Add the calendar year numbers together and reduce them to a number between 1 and 9.

CALENDAR YEAR EXAMPLE:

$$1991 = 1 + 9 + 9 + 1 = 20$$
$$2 + 0 = 2$$
$$1991 = \text{Number 2 calendar year}$$

Step 2. Add the single number for the calendar year to your month and day-of-birth numbers.

Step 3. Totals that equal 10 or more should be reduced to a single-digit number by adding the two numbers together.

Example: BILL COSBY'S PERSONAL YEAR FOR 1989

Birthday: July 12

Step 1. $1989 = 1 + 9 + 8 + 9 = 27 = 9$

Step 2. Add 7 (for July, the seventh calendar month)

$$+ 3 (1 + 2 = 3)$$
$$+ 9 \text{ (calendar year number)}$$

TOTAL $= 19 = 10 = 1$

Bill Cosby is in a number 1 personal year in 1989.

Example: TED KENNEDY'S PERSONAL-YEAR NUMBER IN 1991 FOR HIS BIRTHDAY, FEBRUARY 22.

Add 2 (for February)

4 (for 22—2 + 2 = 4)

PERSONAL YEAR GRID FOR 1988, 1997, 2006, 2015, 2024, 2033, 2042

FIND YOUR BIRTHDAY

BIRTHDAY→	1	2	3	4	5	6	7	8	9	10	11	12	13	14	15	16	17	18	19	20	21	22	23	24	25	26	27	28	29	30	31
JANUARY	1	2	3	4	5	6	7	8	9	1	2	3	4	5	6	7	8	9	1	2	3	4	5	6	7	8	9	1	2	3	4
FEBRUARY	2	3	4	5	6	7	8	9	1	2	3	4	5	6	7	8	9	1	2	3	4	5	6	7	8	9	1	2	3		
MARCH	3	4	5	6	7	8	9	1	2	3	4	5	6	7	8	9	1	2	3	4	5	6	7	8	9	1	2	3	4	5	6
APRIL	4	5	6	7	8	9	1	2	3	4	5	6	7	8	9	1	2	3	4	5	6	7	8	9	1	2	3	4	5	6	
MAY	5	6	7	8	9	1	2	3	4	5	6	7	8	9	1	2	3	4	5	6	7	8	9	1	2	3	4	5	6	7	8
JUNE	6	7	8	9	1	2	3	4	5	6	7	8	9	1	2	3	4	5	6	7	8	9	1	2	3	4	5	6	7	8	
JULY	7	8	9	1	2	3	4	5	6	7	8	9	1	2	3	4	5	6	7	8	9	1	2	3	4	5	6	7	8	9	1
AUGUST	8	9	1	2	3	4	5	6	7	8	9	1	2	3	4	5	6	7	8	9	1	2	3	4	5	6	7	8	9	1	2
SEPTEMBER	9	1	2	3	4	5	6	7	8	9	1	2	3	4	5	6	7	8	9	1	2	3	4	5	6	7	8	9	1	2	
OCTOBER	1	2	3	4	5	6	7	8	9	1	2	3	4	5	6	7	8	9	1	2	3	4	5	6	7	8	9	1	2	3	4
NOVEMBER	2	3	4	5	6	7	8	9	1	2	3	4	5	6	7	8	9	1	2	3	4	5	6	7	8	9	1	2	3	4	
DECEMBER	3	4	5	6	7	8	9	1	2	3	4	5	6	7	8	9	1	2	3	4	5	6	7	8	9	1	2	3	4	5	6

PERSONAL YEAR GRID FOR 1989, 1998, 2007, 2016, 2025, 2034, 2043

FIND YOUR BIRTHDAY

BIRTHDAY→	1	2	3	4	5	6	7	8	9	10	11	12	13	14	15	16	17	18	19	20	21	22	23	24	25	26	27	28	29	30	31
JANUARY	2	3	4	5	6	7	8	9	1	2	3	4	5	6	7	8	9	1	2	3	4	5	6	7	8	9	1	2	3	4	5
FEBRUARY	3	4	5	6	7	8	9	1	2	3	4	5	6	7	8	9	1	2	3	4	5	6	7	8	9	1	2	3	4		
MARCH	4	5	6	7	8	9	1	2	3	4	5	6	7	8	9	1	2	3	4	5	6	7	8	9	1	2	3	4	5	6	7
APRIL	5	6	7	8	9	1	2	3	4	5	6	7	8	9	1	2	3	4	5	6	7	8	9	1	2	3	4	5	6	7	
MAY	6	7	8	9	1	2	3	4	5	6	7	8	9	1	2	3	4	5	6	7	8	9	1	2	3	4	5	6	7	8	9
JUNE	7	8	9	1	2	3	4	5	6	7	8	9	1	2	3	4	5	6	7	8	9	1	2	3	4	5	6	7	8	9	
JULY	8	9	1	2	3	4	5	6	7	8	9	1	2	3	4	5	6	7	8	9	1	2	3	4	5	6	7	8	9	1	2
AUGUST	9	1	2	3	4	5	6	7	8	9	1	2	3	4	5	6	7	8	9	1	2	3	4	5	6	7	8	9	1	2	3
SEPTEMBER	1	2	3	4	5	6	7	8	9	1	2	3	4	5	6	7	8	9	1	2	3	4	5	6	7	8	9	1	2	3	
OCTOBER	2	3	4	5	6	7	8	9	1	2	3	4	5	6	7	8	9	1	2	3	4	5	6	7	8	9	1	2	3	4	5
NOVEMBER	3	4	5	6	7	8	9	1	2	3	4	5	6	7	8	9	1	2	3	4	5	6	7	8	9	1	2	3	4	5	
DECEMBER	4	5	6	7	8	9	1	2	3	4	5	6	7	8	9	1	2	3	4	5	6	7	8	9	1	2	3	4	5	6	7

PERSONAL YEAR GRID FOR 1990, 1999, 2008, 2017, 2026, 2035, 2044

FIND YOUR BIRTHDAY

BIRTHDAY→	1	2	3	4	5	6	7	8	9	10	11	12	13	14	15	16	17	18	19	20	21	22	23	24	25	26	27	28	29	30	31
JANUARY	3	4	5	6	7	8	9	1	2	3	4	5	6	7	8	9	1	2	3	4	5	6	7	8	9	1	2	3	4	5	6
FEBRUARY	4	5	6	7	8	9	1	2	3	4	5	6	7	8	9	1	2	3	4	5	6	7	8	9	1	2	3	4	5		
MARCH	5	6	7	8	9	1	2	3	4	5	6	7	8	9	1	2	3	4	5	6	7	8	9	1	2	3	4	5	6	7	8
APRIL	6	7	8	9	1	2	3	4	5	6	7	8	9	1	2	3	4	5	6	7	8	9	1	2	3	4	5	6	7	8	
MAY	7	8	9	1	2	3	4	5	6	7	8	9	1	2	3	4	5	6	7	8	9	1	2	3	4	5	6	7	8	9	1
JUNE	8	9	1	2	3	4	5	6	7	8	9	1	2	3	4	5	6	7	8	9	1	2	3	4	5	6	7	8	9	1	
JULY	9	1	2	3	4	5	6	7	8	9	1	2	3	4	5	6	7	8	9	1	2	3	4	5	6	7	8	9	1	2	3
AUGUST	1	2	3	4	5	6	7	8	9	1	2	3	4	5	6	7	8	9	1	2	3	4	5	6	7	8	9	1	2	3	4
SEPTEMBER	2	3	4	5	6	7	8	9	1	2	3	4	5	6	7	8	9	1	2	3	4	5	6	7	8	9	1	2	3	4	
OCTOBER	3	4	5	6	7	8	9	1	2	3	4	5	6	7	8	9	1	2	3	4	5	6	7	8	9	1	2	3	4	5	6
NOVEMBER	4	5	6	7	8	9	1	2	3	4	5	6	7	8	9	1	2	3	4	5	6	7	8	9	1	2	3	4	5	6	
DECEMBER	5	6	7	8	9	1	2	3	4	5	6	7	8	9	1	2	3	4	5	6	7	8	9	1	2	3	4	5	6	7	8

PERSONAL YEAR GRID FOR 1991, 2000, 2009, 2018, 2027, 2036, 2045

FIND YOUR BIRTHDAY

BIRTHDAY→	1	2	3	4	5	6	7	8	9	10	11	12	13	14	15	16	17	18	19	20	21	22	23	24	25	26	27	28	29	30	31
JANUARY	4	5	6	7	8	9	1	2	3	4	5	6	7	8	9	1	2	3	4	5	6	7	8	9	1	2	3	4	5	6	7
FEBRUARY	5	6	7	8	9	1	2	3	4	5	6	7	8	9	1	2	3	4	5	6	7	8	9	1	2	3	4	5	6		
MARCH	6	7	8	9	1	2	3	4	5	6	7	8	9	1	2	3	4	5	6	7	8	9	1	2	3	4	5	6	7	8	9
APRIL	7	8	9	1	2	3	4	5	6	7	8	9	1	2	3	4	5	6	7	8	9	1	2	3	4	5	6	7	8	9	
MAY	8	9	1	2	3	4	5	6	7	8	9	1	2	3	4	5	6	7	8	9	1	2	3	4	5	6	7	8	9	1	2
JUNE	9	1	2	3	4	5	6	7	8	9	1	2	3	4	5	6	7	8	9	1	2	3	4	5	6	7	8	9	1	2	
JULY	1	2	3	4	5	6	7	8	9	1	2	3	4	5	6	7	8	9	1	2	3	4	5	6	7	8	9	1	2	3	4
AUGUST	2	3	4	5	6	7	8	9	1	2	3	4	5	6	7	8	9	1	2	3	4	5	6	7	8	9	1	2	3	4	5
SEPTEMBER	3	4	5	6	7	8	9	1	2	3	4	5	6	7	8	9	1	2	3	4	5	6	7	8	9	1	2	3	4	5	
OCTOBER	4	5	6	7	8	9	1	2	3	4	5	6	7	8	9	1	2	3	4	5	6	7	8	9	1	2	3	4	5	6	7
NOVEMBER	5	6	7	8	9	1	2	3	4	5	6	7	8	9	1	2	3	4	5	6	7	8	9	1	2	3	4	5	6	7	
DECEMBER	6	7	8	9	1	2	3	4	5	6	7	8	9	1	2	3	4	5	6	7	8	9	1	2	3	4	5	6	7	8	9

PERSONAL YEAR GRID FOR 1992, 2001, 2010, 2019, 2028, 2037, 2046

FIND YOUR BIRTHDAY

BIRTHDAY→	1	2	3	4	5	6	7	8	9	10	11	12	13	14	15	16	17	18	19	20	21	22	23	24	25	26	27	28	29	30	31
JANUARY	5	6	7	8	9	1	2	3	4	5	6	7	8	9	1	2	3	4	5	6	7	8	9	1	2	3	4	5	6	7	8
FEBRUARY	6	7	8	9	1	2	3	4	5	6	7	8	9	1	2	3	4	5	6	7	8	9	1	2	3	4	5	6	7		
MARCH	7	8	9	1	2	3	4	5	6	7	8	9	1	2	3	4	5	6	7	8	9	1	2	3	4	5	6	7	8	9	1
APRIL	8	9	1	2	3	4	5	6	7	8	9	1	2	3	4	5	6	7	8	9	1	2	3	4	5	6	7	8	9	1	
MAY	9	1	2	3	4	5	6	7	8	9	1	2	3	4	5	6	7	8	9	1	2	3	4	5	6	7	8	9	1	2	3
JUNE	1	2	3	4	5	6	7	8	9	1	2	3	4	5	6	7	8	9	1	2	3	4	5	6	7	8	9	1	2	3	
JULY	2	3	4	5	6	7	8	9	1	2	3	4	5	6	7	8	9	1	2	3	4	5	6	7	8	9	1	2	3	4	5
AUGUST	3	4	5	6	7	8	9	1	2	3	4	5	6	7	8	9	1	2	3	4	5	6	7	8	9	1	2	3	4	5	6
SEPTEMBER	4	5	6	7	8	9	1	2	3	4	5	6	7	8	9	1	2	3	4	5	6	7	8	9	1	2	3	4	5	6	
OCTOBER	5	6	7	8	9	1	2	3	4	5	6	7	8	9	1	2	3	4	5	6	7	8	9	1	2	3	4	5	6	7	8
NOVEMBER	6	7	8	9	1	2	3	4	5	6	7	8	9	1	2	3	4	5	6	7	8	9	1	2	3	4	5	6	7	8	
DECEMBER	7	8	9	1	2	3	4	5	6	7	8	9	1	2	3	4	5	6	7	8	9	1	2	3	4	5	6	7	8	9	1

PERSONAL YEAR GRID FOR 1993, 2002, 2011, 2020, 2029, 2038, 2047

FIND YOUR BIRTHDAY

BIRTHDAY→	1	2	3	4	5	6	7	8	9	10	11	12	13	14	15	16	17	18	19	20	21	22	23	24	25	26	27	28	29	30	31
JANUARY	6	7	8	9	1	2	3	4	5	6	7	8	9	1	2	3	4	5	6	7	8	9	1	2	3	4	5	6	7	8	9
FEBRUARY	7	8	9	1	2	3	4	5	6	7	8	9	1	2	3	4	5	6	7	8	9	1	2	3	4	5	6	7	8		
MARCH	8	9	1	2	3	4	5	6	7	8	9	1	2	3	4	5	6	7	8	9	1	2	3	4	5	6	7	8	9	1	2
APRIL	9	1	2	3	4	5	6	7	8	9	1	2	3	4	5	6	7	8	9	1	2	3	4	5	6	7	8	9	1	2	
MAY	1	2	3	4	5	6	7	8	9	1	2	3	4	5	6	7	8	9	1	2	3	4	5	6	7	8	9	1	2	3	4
JUNE	2	3	4	5	6	7	8	9	1	2	3	4	5	6	7	8	9	1	2	3	4	5	6	7	8	9	1	2	3	4	
JULY	3	4	5	6	7	8	9	1	2	3	4	5	6	7	8	9	1	2	3	4	5	6	7	8	9	1	2	3	4	5	6
AUGUST	4	5	6	7	8	9	1	2	3	4	5	6	7	8	9	1	2	3	4	5	6	7	8	9	1	2	3	4	5	6	7
SEPTEMBER	5	6	7	8	9	1	2	3	4	5	6	7	8	9	1	2	3	4	5	6	7	8	9	1	2	3	4	5	6	7	
OCTOBER	6	7	8	9	1	2	3	4	5	6	7	8	9	1	2	3	4	5	6	7	8	9	1	2	3	4	5	6	7	8	9
NOVEMBER	7	8	9	1	2	3	4	5	6	7	8	9	1	2	3	4	5	6	7	8	9	1	2	3	4	5	6	7	8	9	
DECEMBER	8	9	1	2	3	4	5	6	7	8	9	1	2	3	4	5	6	7	8	9	1	2	3	4	5	6	7	8	9	1	2

PERSONAL YEAR GRID FOR 1994, 2003, 2012, 2021, 2030, 2039, 2048

FIND YOUR BIRTHDAY

BIRTHDAY→	1	2	3	4	5	6	7	8	9	10	11	12	13	14	15	16	17	18	19	20	21	22	23	24	25	26	27	28	29	30	31
JANUARY	7	8	9	1	2	3	4	5	6	7	8	9	1	2	3	4	5	6	7	8	9	1	2	3	4	5	6	7	8	9	1
FEBRUARY	8	9	1	2	3	4	5	6	7	8	9	1	2	3	4	5	6	7	8	9	1	2	3	4	5	6	7	8	9		
MARCH	9	1	2	3	4	5	6	7	8	9	1	2	3	4	5	6	7	8	9	1	2	3	4	5	6	7	8	9	1	2	3
APRIL	1	2	3	4	5	6	7	8	9	1	2	3	4	5	6	7	8	9	1	2	3	4	5	6	7	8	9	1	2	3	
MAY	2	3	4	5	6	7	8	9	1	2	3	4	5	6	7	8	9	1	2	3	4	5	6	7	8	9	1	2	3	4	5
JUNE	3	4	5	6	7	8	9	1	2	3	4	5	6	7	8	9	1	2	3	4	5	6	7	8	9	1	2	3	4	5	
JULY	4	5	6	7	8	9	1	2	3	4	5	6	7	8	9	1	2	3	4	5	6	7	8	9	1	2	3	4	5	6	7
AUGUST	5	6	7	8	9	1	2	3	4	5	6	7	8	9	1	2	3	4	5	6	7	8	9	1	2	3	4	5	6	7	8
SEPTEMBER	6	7	8	9	1	2	3	4	5	6	7	8	9	1	2	3	4	5	6	7	8	9	1	2	3	4	5	6	7	8	
OCTOBER	7	8	9	1	2	3	4	5	6	7	8	9	1	2	3	4	5	6	7	8	9	1	2	3	4	5	6	7	8	9	1
NOVEMBER	8	9	1	2	3	4	5	6	7	8	9	1	2	3	4	5	6	7	8	9	1	2	3	4	5	6	7	8	9	1	
DECEMBER	9	1	2	3	4	5	6	7	8	9	1	2	3	4	5	6	7	8	9	1	2	3	4	5	6	7	8	9	1	2	3

PERSONAL YEAR GRID FOR 1995, 2004, 2013, 2022, 2031, 2040, 2049

FIND YOUR BIRTHDAY

BIRTHDAY→	1	2	3	4	5	6	7	8	9	10	11	12	13	14	15	16	17	18	19	20	21	22	23	24	25	26	27	28	29	30	31
JANUARY	8	9	1	2	3	4	5	6	7	8	9	1	2	3	4	5	6	7	8	9	1	2	3	4	5	6	7	8	9	1	2
FEBRUARY	9	1	2	3	4	5	6	7	8	9	1	2	3	4	5	6	7	8	9	1	2	3	4	5	6	7	8	9	1		
MARCH	1	2	3	4	5	6	7	8	9	1	2	3	4	5	6	7	8	9	1	2	3	4	5	6	7	8	9	1	2	3	4
APRIL	2	3	4	5	6	7	8	9	1	2	3	4	5	6	7	8	9	1	2	3	4	5	6	7	8	9	1	2	3	4	
MAY	3	4	5	6	7	8	9	1	2	3	4	5	6	7	8	9	1	2	3	4	5	6	7	8	9	1	2	3	4	5	6
JUNE	4	5	6	7	8	9	1	2	3	4	5	6	7	8	9	1	2	3	4	5	6	7	8	9	1	2	3	4	5	6	
JULY	5	6	7	8	9	1	2	3	4	5	6	7	8	9	1	2	3	4	5	6	7	8	9	1	2	3	4	5	6	7	8
AUGUST	6	7	8	9	1	2	3	4	5	6	7	8	9	1	2	3	4	5	6	7	8	9	1	2	3	4	5	6	7	8	9
SEPTEMBER	7	8	9	1	2	3	4	5	6	7	8	9	1	2	3	4	5	6	7	8	9	1	2	3	4	5	6	7	8	9	
OCTOBER	8	9	1	2	3	4	5	6	7	8	9	1	2	3	4	5	6	7	8	9	1	2	3	4	5	6	7	8	9	1	2
NOVEMBER	9	1	2	3	4	5	6	7	8	9	1	2	3	4	5	6	7	8	9	1	2	3	4	5	6	7	8	9	1	2	
DECEMBER	1	2	3	4	5	6	7	8	9	1	2	3	4	5	6	7	8	9	1	2	3	4	5	6	7	8	9	1	2	3	4

PERSONAL YEAR GRID FOR 1996, 2005, 2014, 2023, 2032, 2041, 2050

FIND YOUR BIRTHDAY

BIRTHDAY→	1	2	3	4	5	6	7	8	9	10	11	12	13	14	15	16	17	18	19	20	21	22	23	24	25	26	27	28	29	30	31
JANUARY	9	1	2	3	4	5	6	7	8	9	1	2	3	4	5	6	7	8	9	1	2	3	4	5	6	7	8	9	1	2	3
FEBRUARY	1	2	3	4	5	6	7	8	9	1	2	3	4	5	6	7	8	9	1	2	3	4	5	6	7	8	9	1	2		
MARCH	2	3	4	5	6	7	8	9	1	2	3	4	5	6	7	8	9	1	2	3	4	5	6	7	8	9	1	2	3	4	5
APRIL	3	4	5	6	7	8	9	1	2	3	4	5	6	7	8	9	1	2	3	4	5	6	7	8	9	1	2	3	4	5	
MAY	4	5	6	7	8	9	1	2	3	4	5	6	7	8	9	1	2	3	4	5	6	7	8	9	1	2	3	4	5	6	7
JUNE	5	6	7	8	9	1	2	3	4	5	6	7	8	9	1	2	3	4	5	6	7	8	9	1	2	3	4	5	6	7	
JULY	6	7	8	9	1	2	3	4	5	6	7	8	9	1	2	3	4	5	6	7	8	9	1	2	3	4	5	6	7	8	9
AUGUST	7	8	9	1	2	3	4	5	6	7	8	9	1	2	3	4	5	6	7	8	9	1	2	3	4	5	6	7	8	9	1
SEPTEMBER	8	9	1	2	3	4	5	6	7	8	9	1	2	3	4	5	6	7	8	9	1	2	3	4	5	6	7	8	9	1	
OCTOBER	9	1	2	3	4	5	6	7	8	9	1	2	3	4	5	6	7	8	9	1	2	3	4	5	6	7	8	9	1	2	3
NOVEMBER	1	2	3	4	5	6	7	8	9	1	2	3	4	5	6	7	8	9	1	2	3	4	5	6	7	8	9	1	2	3	
DECEMBER	2	3	4	5	6	7	8	9	1	2	3	4	5	6	7	8	9	1	2	3	4	5	6	7	8	9	1	2	3	4	5

$$\underline{2} \text{ (for 1991—1 + 9 + 9 + 1 = 20 =}$$
$$2 + 0 = 2)$$

TOTAL = 8

Ted Kennedy is in a number 8 personal year for 1991.

THE PERSONAL MONTH NUMBER— PURPOSE AND INSTRUCTIONS

Personal month number meanings describe the types of people and experiences you can expect to encounter during the calendar month in question. This number gives you additional insights to understand your personal year's step-by-step progress.

TO FIND YOUR PERSONAL MONTH NUMBER: Add your personal-year number to the calendar month number. Then add the sum to reduce it to a single-digit number.

Example: Bill Cosby's personal month number for November 1989

Bill Cosby's personal year number for 1989 = 1
Calendar month number for November = 11 = 2

November 1989 for Bill Cosby is a 3 month.

THE PERSONAL DAY NUMBER— PURPOSE AND INSTRUCTIONS

Every day our moods change, and we focus on different types of people and experiences. We alternate between being receptive and aggressive.

The old adage "Sleep on it" gains new meaning when we consider day-to-day forecasts. If a personal day number meaning indicates that you should not make changes, have patience and faith. Let the number vibrations of the new day bring a change that will work for you.

When the personal day numbers are identical to any of your challenge numbers, people and experiences you encounter that day may trigger overreactions. If large amounts of money or legal documents are involved, it may be best to put major changes or decisions on the shelf for that day. Challenge numbers warn you to expect people or experiences that trigger emotional responses to practical matters.

TO FIND YOUR PERSONAL DAY NUMBER:

Method 1: Find your personal year number grid (pages 69–77). Then look up the calendar day in the grid to find your personal day number.

Method 2: Add the current month and day numbers to your personal year number. Reduce totals of 10 or more to a single-digit number.

Example: Bill Cosby's personal day number for March 5, 1988
Add 3 (for March)
5 (for the calendar day)
9 (for Bill Cosby's personal year number)
$17 = 1 + 7 = 8$

Bill Cosby's personal day number for March 5, 1988 is 8.

HAVE YOU NOTED ALL YOUR NUMBERS ON THE CATEGORY LIST?

If you have completed the personal day instructions and entered all category numbers on the Category List, you are ready to read the number meanings. Read the meanings of personality category and destiny numbers, keeping the personality swings of the challenge-number meanings in mind.

The following section is devoted to an analysis of the numbers in a single chart or for two charts. Complete your reading of a total chart before making comparisons. Insights will be sharper on the second go-around.

NUMBER COMPARISONS

There are various ways to use number comparison within your own chart and between two charts. For instance, if you want to know whether your talents are on a destiny path that will

PERSONAL DAY GRID FOR #1 PERSONAL YEAR

TO FIND YOUR PERSONAL DAY
STEP 1. ON YOUR PERSONAL YEAR GRID . . . STEP 2. FIND THE CALENDAR DAY

DAY→	1	2	3	4	5	6	7	8	9	10	11	12	13	14	15	16	17	18	19	20	21	22	23	24	25	26	27	28	29	30	31
JANUARY	3	4	5	6	7	8	9	1	2	3	4	5	6	7	8	9	1	2	3	4	5	6	7	8	9	1	2	3	4	5	6
FEBRUARY	4	5	6	7	8	9	1	2	3	4	5	6	7	8	9	1	2	3	4	5	6	7	8	9	1	2	3	4	5		
MARCH	5	6	7	8	9	1	2	3	4	5	6	7	8	9	1	2	3	4	5	6	7	8	9	1	2	3	4	5	6	7	8
APRIL	6	7	8	9	1	2	3	4	5	6	7	8	9	1	2	3	4	5	6	7	8	9	1	2	3	4	5	6	7	8	
MAY	7	8	9	1	2	3	4	5	6	7	8	9	1	2	3	4	5	6	7	8	9	1	2	3	4	5	6	7	8	9	1
JUNE	8	9	1	2	3	4	5	6	7	8	9	1	2	3	4	5	6	7	8	9	1	2	3	4	5	6	7	8	9	1	
JULY	9	1	2	3	4	5	6	7	8	9	1	2	3	4	5	6	7	8	9	1	2	3	4	5	6	7	8	9	1	2	3
AUGUST	1	2	3	4	5	6	7	8	9	1	2	3	4	5	6	7	8	9	1	2	3	4	5	6	7	8	9	1	2	3	4
SEPTEMBER	2	3	4	5	6	7	8	9	1	2	3	4	5	6	7	8	9	1	2	3	4	5	6	7	8	9	1	2	3	4	
OCTOBER	3	4	5	6	7	8	9	1	2	3	4	5	6	7	8	9	1	2	3	4	5	6	7	8	9	1	2	3	4	5	6
NOVEMBER	4	5	6	7	8	9	1	2	3	4	5	6	7	8	9	1	2	3	4	5	6	7	8	9	1	2	3	4	5	6	
DECEMBER	5	6	7	8	9	1	2	3	4	5	6	7	8	9	1	2	3	4	5	6	7	8	9	1	2	3	4	5	6	7	8

PERSONAL DAY GRID FOR #2 PERSONAL YEAR

TO FIND YOUR PERSONAL DAY
STEP 1. ON YOUR PERSONAL YEAR GRID . . . STEP 2. FIND THE CALENDAR DAY

DAY→	1	2	3	4	5	6	7	8	9	10	11	12	13	14	15	16	17	18	19	20	21	22	23	24	25	26	27	28	29	30	31
JANUARY	4	5	6	7	8	9	1	2	3	4	5	6	7	8	9	1	2	3	4	5	6	7	8	9	1	2	3	4	5	6	7
FEBRUARY	5	6	7	8	9	1	2	3	4	5	6	7	8	9	1	2	3	4	5	6	7	8	9	1	2	3	4	5	6		
MARCH	6	7	8	9	1	2	3	4	5	6	7	8	9	1	2	3	4	5	6	7	8	9	1	2	3	4	5	6	7	8	9
APRIL	7	8	9	1	2	3	4	5	6	7	8	9	1	2	3	4	5	6	7	8	9	1	2	3	4	5	6	7	8	9	
MAY	8	9	1	2	3	4	5	6	7	8	9	1	2	3	4	5	6	7	8	9	1	2	3	4	5	6	7	8	9	1	2
JUNE	9	1	2	3	4	5	6	7	8	9	1	2	3	4	5	6	7	8	9	1	2	3	4	5	6	7	8	9	1	2	
JULY	1	2	3	4	5	6	7	8	9	1	2	3	4	5	6	7	8	9	1	2	3	4	5	6	7	8	9	1	2	3	4
AUGUST	2	3	4	5	6	7	8	9	1	2	3	4	5	6	7	8	9	1	2	3	4	5	6	7	8	9	1	2	3	4	5
SEPTEMBER	3	4	5	6	7	8	9	1	2	3	4	5	6	7	8	9	1	2	3	4	5	6	7	8	9	1	2	3	4	5	
OCTOBER	4	5	6	7	8	9	1	2	3	4	5	6	7	8	9	1	2	3	4	5	6	7	8	9	1	2	3	4	5	6	7
NOVEMBER	5	6	7	8	9	1	2	3	4	5	6	7	8	9	1	2	3	4	5	6	7	8	9	1	2	3	4	5	6	7	
DECEMBER	6	7	8	9	1	2	3	4	5	6	7	8	9	1	2	3	4	5	6	7	8	9	1	2	3	4	5	6	7	8	9

TO FIND YOUR PERSONAL DAY
STEP 1. ON YOUR PERSONAL YEAR GRID . . . STEP 2. FIND THE CALENDAR DAY

DAY→	1	2	3	4	5	6	7	8	9	10	11	12	13	14	15	16	17	18	19	20	21	22	23	24	25	26	27	28	29	30	31
JANUARY	5	6	7	8	9	1	2	3	4	5	6	7	8	9	1	2	3	4	5	6	7	8	9	1	2	3	4	5	6	7	8
FEBRUARY	6	7	8	9	1	2	3	4	5	6	7	8	9	1	2	3	4	5	6	7	8	9	1	2	3	4	5	6	7		
MARCH	7	8	9	1	2	3	4	5	6	7	8	9	1	2	3	4	5	6	7	8	9	1	2	3	4	5	6	7	8	9	1
APRIL	8	9	1	2	3	4	5	6	7	8	9	1	2	3	4	5	6	7	8	9	1	2	3	4	5	6	7	8	9	1	
MAY	9	1	2	3	4	5	6	7	8	9	1	2	3	4	5	6	7	8	9	1	2	3	4	5	6	7	8	9	1	2	3
JUNE	1	2	3	4	5	6	7	8	9	1	2	3	4	5	6	7	8	9	1	2	3	4	5	6	7	8	9	1	2	3	
JULY	2	3	4	5	6	7	8	9	1	2	3	4	5	6	7	8	9	1	2	3	4	5	6	7	8	9	1	2	3	4	5
AUGUST	3	4	5	6	7	8	9	1	2	3	4	5	6	7	8	9	1	2	3	4	5	6	7	8	9	1	2	3	4	5	6
SEPTEMBER	4	5	6	7	8	9	1	2	3	4	5	6	7	8	9	1	2	3	4	5	6	7	8	9	1	2	3	4	5	6	
OCTOBER	5	6	7	8	9	1	2	3	4	5	6	7	8	9	1	2	3	4	5	6	7	8	9	1	2	3	4	5	6	7	8
NOVEMBER	6	7	8	9	1	2	3	4	5	6	7	8	9	1	2	3	4	5	6	7	8	9	1	2	3	4	5	6	7	8	
DECEMBER	7	8	9	1	2	3	4	5	6	7	8	9	1	2	3	4	5	6	7	8	9	1	2	3	4	5	6	7	8	9	1

PERSONAL DAY GRID FOR #4 PERSONAL YEAR

TO FIND YOUR PERSONAL DAY
STEP 1. ON YOUR PERSONAL YEAR GRID . . . STEP 2. FIND THE CALENDAR DAY

DAY→	1	2	3	4	5	6	7	8	9	10	11	12	13	14	15	16	17	18	19	20	21	22	23	24	25	26	27	28	29	30	31
JANUARY	6	7	8	9	1	2	3	4	5	6	7	8	9	1	2	3	4	5	6	7	8	9	1	2	3	4	5	6	7	8	9
FEBRUARY	7	8	9	1	2	3	4	5	6	7	8	9	1	2	3	4	5	6	7	8	9	1	2	3	4	5	6	7	8		
MARCH	8	9	1	2	3	4	5	6	7	8	9	1	2	3	4	5	6	7	8	9	1	2	3	4	5	6	7	8	9	1	2
APRIL	9	1	2	3	4	5	6	7	8	9	1	2	3	4	5	6	7	8	9	1	2	3	4	5	6	7	8	9	1	2	
MAY	1	2	3	4	5	6	7	8	9	1	2	3	4	5	6	7	8	9	1	2	3	4	5	6	7	8	9	1	2	3	4
JUNE	2	3	4	5	6	7	8	9	1	2	3	4	5	6	7	8	9	1	2	3	4	5	6	7	8	9	1	2	3	4	
JULY	3	4	5	6	7	8	9	1	2	3	4	5	6	7	8	9	1	2	3	4	5	6	7	8	9	1	2	3	4	5	6
AUGUST	4	5	6	7	8	9	1	2	3	4	5	6	7	8	9	1	2	3	4	5	6	7	8	9	1	2	3	4	5	6	7
SEPTEMBER	5	6	7	8	9	1	2	3	4	5	6	7	8	9	1	2	3	4	5	6	7	8	9	1	2	3	4	5	6	7	
OCTOBER	6	7	8	9	1	2	3	4	5	6	7	8	9	1	2	3	4	5	6	7	8	9	1	2	3	4	5	6	7	8	9
NOVEMBER	7	8	9	1	2	3	4	5	6	7	8	9	1	2	3	4	5	6	7	8	9	1	2	3	4	5	6	7	8	9	
DECEMBER	8	9	1	2	3	4	5	6	7	8	9	1	2	3	4	5	6	7	8	9	1	2	3	4	5	6	7	8	9	1	2

PERSONAL DAY GRID FOR #5 PERSONAL YEAR

TO FIND YOUR PERSONAL DAY
STEP 1. ON YOUR PERSONAL YEAR GRID . . . STEP 2. FIND THE CALENDAR DAY

DAY→	1	2	3	4	5	6	7	8	9	10	11	12	13	14	15	16	17	18	19	20	21	22	23	24	25	26	27	28	29	30	31
JANUARY	7	8	9	1	2	3	4	5	6	7	8	9	1	2	3	4	5	6	7	8	9	1	2	3	4	5	6	7	8	9	1
FEBRUARY	8	9	1	2	3	4	5	6	7	8	9	1	2	3	4	5	6	7	8	9	1	2	3	4	5	6	7	8	9		
MARCH	9	1	2	3	4	5	6	7	8	9	1	2	3	4	5	6	7	8	9	1	2	3	4	5	6	7	8	9	1	2	3
APRIL	1	2	3	4	5	6	7	8	9	1	2	3	4	5	6	7	8	9	1	2	3	4	5	6	7	8	9	1	2	3	
MAY	2	3	4	5	6	7	8	9	1	2	3	4	5	6	7	8	9	1	2	3	4	5	6	7	8	9	1	2	3	4	5
JUNE	3	4	5	6	7	8	9	1	2	3	4	5	6	7	8	9	1	2	3	4	5	6	7	8	9	1	2	3	4	5	
JULY	4	5	6	7	8	9	1	2	3	4	5	6	7	8	9	1	2	3	4	5	6	7	8	9	1	2	3	4	5	6	7
AUGUST	5	6	7	8	9	1	2	3	4	5	6	7	8	9	1	2	3	4	5	6	7	8	9	1	2	3	4	5	6	7	8
SEPTEMBER	6	7	8	9	1	2	3	4	5	6	7	8	9	1	2	3	4	5	6	7	8	9	1	2	3	4	5	6	7	8	
OCTOBER	7	8	9	1	2	3	4	5	6	7	8	9	1	2	3	4	5	6	7	8	9	1	2	3	4	5	6	7	8	9	1
NOVEMBER	8	9	1	2	3	4	5	6	7	8	9	1	2	3	4	5	6	7	8	9	1	2	3	4	5	6	7	8	9	1	
DECEMBER	9	1	2	3	4	5	6	7	8	9	1	2	3	4	5	6	7	8	9	1	2	3	4	5	6	7	8	9	1	2	3

PERSONAL DAY GRID FOR #6 PERSONAL YEAR

TO FIND YOUR PERSONAL DAY
STEP 1. ON YOUR PERSONAL YEAR GRID . . . STEP 2. FIND THE CALENDAR DAY

DAY→	1	2	3	4	5	6	7	8	9	10	11	12	13	14	15	16	17	18	19	20	21	22	23	24	25	26	27	28	29	30	31
JANUARY	8	9	1	2	3	4	5	6	7	8	9	1	2	3	4	5	6	7	8	9	1	2	3	4	5	6	7	8	9	1	2
FEBRUARY	9	1	2	3	4	5	6	7	8	9	1	2	3	4	5	6	7	8	9	1	2	3	4	5	6	7	8	9	1		
MARCH	1	2	3	4	5	6	7	8	9	1	2	3	4	5	6	7	8	9	1	2	3	4	5	6	7	8	9	1	2	3	4
APRIL	2	3	4	5	6	7	8	9	1	2	3	4	5	6	7	8	9	1	2	3	4	5	6	7	8	9	1	2	3	4	
MAY	3	4	5	6	7	8	9	1	2	3	4	5	6	7	8	9	1	2	3	4	5	6	7	8	9	1	2	3	4	5	6
JUNE	4	5	6	7	8	9	1	2	3	4	5	6	7	8	9	1	2	3	4	5	6	7	8	9	1	2	3	4	5	6	
JULY	5	6	7	8	9	1	2	3	4	5	6	7	8	9	1	2	3	4	5	6	7	8	9	1	2	3	4	5	6	7	8
AUGUST	6	7	8	9	1	2	3	4	5	6	7	8	9	1	2	3	4	5	6	7	8	9	1	2	3	4	5	6	7	8	9
SEPTEMBER	7	8	9	1	2	3	4	5	6	7	8	9	1	2	3	4	5	6	7	8	9	1	2	3	4	5	6	7	8	9	
OCTOBER	8	9	1	2	3	4	5	6	7	8	9	1	2	3	4	5	6	7	8	9	1	2	3	4	5	6	7	8	9	1	2
NOVEMBER	9	1	2	3	4	5	6	7	8	9	1	2	3	4	5	6	7	8	9	1	2	3	4	5	6	7	8	9	1	2	
DECEMBER	1	2	3	4	5	6	7	8	9	1	2	3	4	5	6	7	8	9	1	2	3	4	5	6	7	8	9	1	2	3	4

PERSONAL DAY GRID FOR #7 PERSONAL YEAR

TO FIND YOUR PERSONAL DAY
STEP 1. ON YOUR PERSONAL YEAR GRID . . . STEP 2. FIND THE CALENDAR DAY

DAY→	1	2	3	4	5	6	7	8	9	10	11	12	13	14	15	16	17	18	19	20	21	22	23	24	25	26	27	28	29	30	31
JANUARY	9	1	2	3	4	5	6	7	8	9	1	2	3	4	5	6	7	8	9	1	2	3	4	5	6	7	8	9	1	2	3
FEBRUARY	1	2	3	4	5	6	7	8	9	1	2	3	4	5	6	7	8	9	1	2	3	4	5	6	7	8	9	1	2		
MARCH	2	3	4	5	6	7	8	9	1	2	3	4	5	6	7	8	9	1	2	3	4	5	6	7	8	9	1	2	3	4	5
APRIL	3	4	5	6	7	8	9	1	2	3	4	5	6	7	8	9	1	2	3	4	5	6	7	8	9	1	2	3	4	5	
MAY	4	5	6	7	8	9	1	2	3	4	5	6	7	8	9	1	2	3	4	5	6	7	8	9	1	2	3	4	5	6	7
JUNE	5	6	7	8	9	1	2	3	4	5	6	7	8	9	1	2	3	4	5	6	7	8	9	1	2	3	4	5	6	7	
JULY	6	7	8	9	1	2	3	4	5	6	7	8	9	1	2	3	4	5	6	7	8	9	1	2	3	4	5	6	7	8	9
AUGUST	7	8	9	1	2	3	4	5	6	7	8	9	1	2	3	4	5	6	7	8	9	1	2	3	4	5	6	7	8	9	1
SEPTEMBER	8	9	1	2	3	4	5	6	7	8	9	1	2	3	4	5	6	7	8	9	1	2	3	4	5	6	7	8	9	1	
OCTOBER	9	1	2	3	4	5	6	7	8	9	1	2	3	4	5	6	7	8	9	1	2	3	4	5	6	7	8	9	1	2	3
NOVEMBER	1	2	3	4	5	6	7	8	9	1	2	3	4	5	6	7	8	9	1	2	3	4	5	6	7	8	9	1	2	3	
DECEMBER	2	3	4	5	6	7	8	9	1	2	3	4	5	6	7	8	9	1	2	3	4	5	6	7	8	9	1	2	3	4	5

PERSONAL DAY GRID FOR #8 PERSONAL YEAR

TO FIND YOUR PERSONAL DAY
STEP 1. ON YOUR PERSONAL YEAR GRID . . . STEP 2. FIND THE CALENDAR DAY

DAY→	1	2	3	4	5	6	7	8	9	10	11	12	13	14	15	16	17	18	19	20	21	22	23	24	25	26	27	28	29	30	31
JANUARY	1	2	3	4	5	6	7	8	9	1	2	3	4	5	6	7	8	9	1	2	3	4	5	6	7	8	9	1	2	3	4
FEBRUARY	2	3	4	5	6	7	8	9	1	2	3	4	5	6	7	8	9	1	2	3	4	5	6	7	8	9	1	2	3		
MARCH	3	4	5	6	7	8	9	1	2	3	4	5	6	7	8	9	1	2	3	4	5	6	7	8	9	1	2	3	4	5	6
APRIL	4	5	6	7	8	9	1	2	3	4	5	6	7	8	9	1	2	3	4	5	6	7	8	9	1	2	3	4	5	6	
MAY	5	6	7	8	9	1	2	3	4	5	6	7	8	9	1	2	3	4	5	6	7	8	9	1	2	3	4	5	6	7	8
JUNE	6	7	8	9	1	2	3	4	5	6	7	8	9	1	2	3	4	5	6	7	8	9	1	2	3	4	5	6	7	8	
JULY	7	8	9	1	2	3	4	5	6	7	8	9	1	2	3	4	5	6	7	8	9	1	2	3	4	5	6	7	8	9	1
AUGUST	8	9	1	2	3	4	5	6	7	8	9	1	2	3	4	5	6	7	8	9	1	2	3	4	5	6	7	8	9	1	2
SEPTEMBER	9	1	2	3	4	5	6	7	8	9	1	2	3	4	5	6	7	8	9	1	2	3	4	5	6	7	8	9	1	2	
OCTOBER	1	2	3	4	5	6	7	8	9	1	2	3	4	5	6	7	8	9	1	2	3	4	5	6	7	8	9	1	2	3	4
NOVEMBER	2	3	4	5	6	7	8	9	1	2	3	4	5	6	7	8	9	1	2	3	4	5	6	7	8	9	1	2	3	4	
DECEMBER	3	4	5	6	7	8	9	1	2	3	4	5	6	7	8	9	1	2	3	4	5	6	7	8	9	1	2	3	4	5	6

PERSONAL DAY GRID FOR #9 PERSONAL YEAR

TO FIND YOUR PERSONAL DAY
STEP 1. ON YOUR PERSONAL YEAR GRID . . . STEP 2. FIND THE CALENDAR DAY

DAY→	1	2	3	4	5	6	7	8	9	10	11	12	13	14	15	16	17	18	19	20	21	22	23	24	25	26	27	28	29	30	31
JANUARY	2	3	4	5	6	7	8	9	1	2	3	4	5	6	7	8	9	1	2	3	4	5	6	7	8	9	1	2	3	4	5
FEBRUARY	3	4	5	6	7	8	9	1	2	3	4	5	6	7	8	9	1	2	3	4	5	6	7	8	9	1	2	3	4		
MARCH	4	5	6	7	8	9	1	2	3	4	5	6	7	8	9	1	2	3	4	5	6	7	8	9	1	2	3	4	5	6	7
APRIL	5	6	7	8	9	1	2	3	4	5	6	7	8	9	1	2	3	4	5	6	7	8	9	1	2	3	4	5	6	7	
MAY	6	7	8	9	1	2	3	4	5	6	7	8	9	1	2	3	4	5	6	7	8	9	1	2	3	4	5	6	7	8	9
JUNE	7	8	9	1	2	3	4	5	6	7	8	9	1	2	3	4	5	6	7	8	9	1	2	3	4	5	6	7	8	9	
JULY	8	9	1	2	3	4	5	6	7	8	9	1	2	3	4	5	6	7	8	9	1	2	3	4	5	6	7	8	9	1	2
AUGUST	9	1	2	3	4	5	6	7	8	9	1	2	3	4	5	6	7	8	9	1	2	3	4	5	6	7	8	9	1	2	3
SEPTEMBER	1	2	3	4	5	6	7	8	9	1	2	3	4	5	6	7	8	9	1	2	3	4	5	6	7	8	9	1	2	3	
OCTOBER	2	3	4	5	6	7	8	9	1	2	3	4	5	6	7	8	9	1	2	3	4	5	6	7	8	9	1	2	3	4	5
NOVEMBER	3	4	5	6	7	8	9	1	2	3	4	5	6	7	8	9	1	2	3	4	5	6	7	8	9	1	2	3	4	5	
DECEMBER	4	5	6	7	8	9	1	2	3	4	5	6	7	8	9	1	2	3	4	5	6	7	8	9	1	2	3	4	5	6	7

offer immediate recognition, compare your self-expression number to your destiny number. If you want to know whether you are compatible in business with an associate or a superior, compare your self-expression number to theirs. If you want to know whether your first impression is compatible with the people and experiences that you will meet in life, read the meaning of your self-image number and compare its meaning with the focus of your destiny number. Common sense is always helpful when trying to make comparisons and determine compatibility.

A quick number comparison chart follows that identifies numbers that are generally compatible and numbers that are not. But remember, you always have a choice with numerology—incompatible numbers do not have to cause strained relationships if partners or mates understand themselves and want to make a commitment to each other. There are degrees of incompatibility that may be eased by compromise when both people are willing to work with each other. But the first step is always up to the person with the smaller number. He or she will have to stretch to learn from the person with the larger number. And the one with the larger number should make a commitment to give the person with the smaller number time to learn from him or her. Communication is the key. Sharing the meanings of numbers in your chart and another's can pave the way to bettering a relationship. However, if you are thinking of starting a long-term commitment to a person whose self-motivation and destiny numbers are incompatible with yours, it may be best to agree to disagree before problems arise.

It's nice to feel like kindred spirits in any relationship, but when there are opposites and unknowns in an intimate relationship, those surprising attitudes and actions can deplete the energy of the unit. The self-motivation number describes the things that make you comfortable and the things that make you tick. The destiny number forecasts the types of people and experiences that you can expect to encounter throughout life. If both important life factors are uncomfortable for you, daily living will be filled with irritating reactions and situations. By using numerology to understand yourself and your associates, the surprises you get will be pleasant ones.

Here are a few rules of thumb for comparing numbers:
- When making comparisons between charts or within your own chart, always use the *final reduced number* for the challenge, self-motivation, self-image, self-expression, destiny, personal year, month, and day categories.
- In your own chart, compare your desires (self-motivation) to your talents (self-expression) to find out if you have the talents to get what you want.
- In your own chart, compare your self-expression number (talents) to your destiny number to see if you will meet the people and experiences that will make it easy for you to connect with a business or profession. If these numbers are incompatible, you should concentrate on the meaning of your destiny number to learn what types of environments will open doors for you.
- In your own chart, compare your challenge numbers to your self-motivation, self-image, and self-expression numbers. If they are the same, you can pinpoint the part of your personality that goes to extremes and needs behavior modification. If one of your challenge numbers is the same as your destiny number, or personal year, month or day numbers, you find it difficult to react to the people and experiences that you meet without emotionalizing practical situations. You can make your life smoother by understanding that your intense emotional reactions are triggered by the people that your destiny offers (you do not want to pick the wrong people to date, mate, or work with). You will make your life smoother by concentrating on getting along with the types of people and experiences that help you during your lifetime or the time span in question.
- In your own chart, if the single reduced number of your self-motivation is higher than your destiny number, you want

more comforts than life will offer. If your self-image number is higher than your destiny number, you appear to be more accomplished than most of the people you encounter. If your self-expression number is higher than your destiny number, you have more talent than you need to fulfill your destiny. If your name numbers are lower than your destiny number, you will have to stretch to learn what life has to offer. Always remember that the name numbers self-motivation, self-image, and self-expression relate to character, and the birthday numbers challenge, destiny, personal year, month, and day relate to the types of people and experiences you can expect to meet.

• When making comparisons between charts or within your own chart, compare personal year numbers to the month and day numbers to find out when the months and days support the year's purpose and will not be frustrating. When the smaller time spans are not conducive to speedy accomplishments, it is best to be prepared for delays for yourself and to understand that the person you are concerned about is not having an easy time either.

• To determine when to go into any partnership, marriage, or business, compare the personal year numbers. The number 9 is a year of endings and never starts anything that is lasting. The number 6 is ideal. When possible, aim to begin long-term commitments with a number 6 year. If that seems to be impossible, choose to marry in a number 6 month or day. In business the numbers 4 and 8 are fortunate, too. Just don't start anything in a number 9 year, month, or day. Also be sure to read the meaning of the personal year for both partners to understand where opportunities are focused.

• Always compare your personal day numbers with those of your intimates and coworkers. By knowing when to be a good listener and when to be assertive, you will accomplish the goals of your personal day effortlessly.

• The single reduced number of the birthday may be compared between two charts to determine compatibility from approximately 28 to 55 years of age.

• Birth month numbers may be compared between two charts to determine whether early environments offer knowns or unknowns, comfortable or uncomfortable points of reference.

The quick number comparisons charts are handy but, if you have time, it's better to read the full number meanings and thereby gain deeper insights. When in doubt or when you need to make a fast decision, use your common sense. Numerology is a tool and a copemate. Its yearly, monthly, or daily forecasts may show you how to buy time until you are sure you are doing the "right" thing.

◄◄◄ QUICK NUMBER COMPARISONS ►►►

Numbers That Are Not Compatible:

Number 1 with 6   Number 6 with 1, 5, and 7
Number 2 with 5   Number 7 with 6 and 8
Number 3 with 4   Number 8 with 7
Number 4 with 3, 5, and 9   Number 9 with 4
Number 5 with 2, 4, and 6

Compatible Numbers for Love, Friendship, and Companionship:

Number 1 with 3, 5, and 9   Number 6 with 2, 3, 4, 8,
Number 2 with 2, 4, and 6   and 9
Number 3 with 1, 3, 5,   Number 7 with 7
  and 6   Number 8 with 4 and 6
Number 4 with 2, 4, 6,   Number 9 with 1, 3, 5, 6,
  and 8   and 9
Number 5 with 1, 3, and 9

Compatible Numbers for Career, Hobbies, and Business

Number 1 with 3 and 5   Number 5 with 1, 3, 7,
Number 2 with 4, 6, 7,   and 9
  and 8   Number 6 with 2, 3, 4, 8,
Number 3 with 1, 5, 6,   and 9
  and 9   Number 7 with 2 and 5
Number 4 with 2, 4, 6,   Number 8 with 4 and 6
  and 8   Number 9 with 3, 5, 6, and 8

CHAPTER FIVE

NUMBER 1

Independence

Independence

ATTRIBUTES:
POSITIVE—Individuality, Leadership, Creativity, Positive-ness, Active Energy, Ambition, Persistence, Self-Reliance, Boldness

NEGATIVE—Egocentricity, Bossiness, Imitation, Repression, Dependence, Laziness, Passivity, Fearfulness, Weakness

CORRESPONDENTS:
LETTERS: A, J and S
ODD NUMBER: Aggressive
DISPOSITION: Mental and personally attaining
NUMBERS: 10, 19, 28, 37, 46, 55, 64, 73, 82, 91, 100
COLOR: Red
GEM: Ruby
CRYSTALS: Garnet & Pyrite
VEGETATION: Azalea, Iris, Lilac
FOODS: Salad, Baked Beans, Halibut, Lobster, Chocolate
MUSICAL INSTRUMENT AND/OR APPEAL: Piano; Opera
MUSICAL NOTE: Middle C

LOCATIONS: State: Connecticut, Idaho, Michigan, North Dakota, Rhode Island

City: Chicago, Detroit, Los Angeles, Louisville, Milwaukee, Minneapolis, Portland, Seattle, Tulsa, Washington, D.C.

PLANET: The Sun

MONTHS: January and October

BIRTHDAYS: 1, 10, 19, and 28

DAY OF THE WEEK: Sunday

GENERAL COMPATIBILITY NUMBER(S): 3, 5, 9, 11, 22, 33

INCOMPATIBILITY NUMBERS: 6, 24

Note: If an individual has the challenge to the number 1, these descriptions will swing from positive to negative until the challenge is balanced. Please be sure to read the challenge meaning.

CHALLENGE OF THE NUMBER 1

This is a challenge to the individual's uniqueness and self-respect. It stems from too much control or too little sensitive discipline from authority figures during childhood. In particular, the male parent was often too unaggressive, too overbearing, or not present during the child's nurturing. The mother may have been too assertive, acting the "male" role and confusing the child. As a result, the child becomes an adult not understanding how to be comfortable alone or communicating in order to get what he wants and needs.

As the child grows older, if independent ideas and decisions are met with criticism or overzealous adoration, the child becomes frustrated and will do inappropriate things to attract attention. He tries to please or annoy the uncomprehending parent or controlling authority. The child gets into the habit of going from one extreme to the other. Because he is not capable of autonomy, wants love but does not know how to meet personal expectations or fulfill desires, the child will be too easily controlled or will angrily attempt to take control.

Youthful defensive habits eventually grow to become an unproductive behavior pattern. The person submissively avoids leadership and confrontations or belligerently takes over and starts them. In an effort to be himself and avoid disappointments, the 1 goes to emotionally painful, stressful extremes.

Before 1s can begin to let go of anxiety induced habits and practice the type of assertive behavior that does not result in hostility, stubbornness, and egocentricity, they must focus on the end result. Children or adults with the challenge of the 1 want acceptance and praise for originality, dependability, and progressive actions. To change childlike behavior—be "grown-up"—it is essential for 1s to have self-discipline and the courage of their convictions and to accept accountability for their actions.

Unfortunately the challenged person usually allows his anger and frustration to build and explode repeatedly. He may vacillate in making decisions; in an effort to avoid making mistakes or losing love, he fails to speak up when little slights crop up. These little slights have a way of accumulating into "the straw that broke the camel's back"—the usual reason for an overreaction that, upon reflection, is considered to be self-destructive or nonproductive.

In youth, whether the authority figure was overly concerned, too unapproachable, or unavailable because of divorce or death, the child perceived acceptance or rejection as "he loves me, he loves me not." Childlike emotional judgments based upon black-or-white perceptions persist into maturity when challenges are in effect. When experimenting with creative ideas as a youngster or pioneering business concepts as an adult, the challenge holder expects to be met with disapproval or sycophantic exultation for usefulness and individualism.

If a preschooler's primitive finger painting remains glorified on the refrigerator door when that child is in high school, the child has no way of knowing whether he deserves the accolade or has overly doting parents. As an adult, that child lacks points of reference for fair self-evaluation. Self-depreciation or an extraordinary ego may be the result.

The seeds that blossom into anticipated rejection are planted by seemingly small everyday episodes. A child who fetches and carries for others may defensively hide the need for leadership while becoming self-centered. He may also appear to be accommodating while manipulating others, and/or he may arrogantly nurture a superiority complex. When challenged by the 1, a person must resist controlling others in his desire not to be controlled.

It is essential to recognize the folly of getting recognition by using subtle domination. This habit can only lead to nobody understanding the challenge bearer's personal desires—least of all himself. Until self-criticism reveals problems and a commitment to change is made, the personality will pendulate from being accommodating to acting selfishly.

During the teenage years, this challenge can force good little children to break out and seize independence too soon before they can really be self-sustaining—bringing about the rejection they fear the most. Others may get into the habit of thinking rather than listening while others talk, and overriding conversation in a hurry to gain acceptance or leadership. Number 1 challenge bearers "jump the gun" or "stay too long at the fair." The knack of knowing when to be patient and when to make changes is not learned early. It is difficult for these individuals to understand that other people assume that the 1s will do what is best for themselves. One challenge holders do not understand that relationships will prosper when their personal needs are clearly defined and requested.

Impatience also leads a number 1 challenge bearer to believe that everything must have an immediate solution. His sense of immediacy is inappropriate and speeds everyday decisions and actions to crisis proportions. The impatient challenge holder never considers the balanced approach, patiently discussing or outlining details of a clever thought or a trend-setting action.

To let down defenses and break comfortable habits can be difficult. However, the challenge holder may choose to recognize past mistakes. He may change his approach and shed distorted childhood impressions that have an aftermath of stress, contrariness, and weakness. Until 1 realizes that everyone has a right to be himself and that others need time to injest and adjust to their preferences, the bullyish or the babyish personality will rise up, throw a tantrum, retreat, and rise again.

The number 1 challenge may swing from one of the following extremes to another until each is recognized and new habits are initiated that stabilize the ego.

Too impatient or too passive.
Too independent or too devoted.
Too attaining or too unambitious.
Too creative or too imitative.
Too ambitious or too lethargic.
Too egocentric or too patronizing.
Too aggressive or too undecided.
Too assertive or too submissive.
Too controllable or too controlling.
Too obedient or too defiant.
Too selfish or too giving.
Too domineering or too compliant.
Too changeable or too lazy.
Too alone or too involved.

PHYSICAL CHALLENGES OF THE NUMBER 1

Challenges can affect physical as well as mental health. Body chemistry changes when individuals are stressed, and when we do not know what is good for us, our minds trigger anxious, angry, or frustrated habits. When we are mean to ourselves, we get sick. One's attitude sends the brain a message, and the brain tells the body to scream for help.

To get attention for their dis-ease, often people get sick or form negative habits. Numerologists believe that illness and wellness depend upon attitude, and challenges indicate the attitudes that result from needy feelings. When we do not feel needy, we feel well and balanced and do not crave attention from others. Essentially, if the personality challenges are balanced, the body chemistry is in balance, too, and therefore there is little chance of mental or physical dis-ease.

Challenge numbers indicate the ways people subconsciously punish themselves for not being consciously good to themselves.

The following list of dis-eases and negative habits relate to the challenge of the number 1.

Anorexia Nervosa	Glaucoma
Bed-Wetting	Headache
Bladder Problem	Hernia
Bone Problems	Hollering
Cellulite Problem	Impotence
Circulatory Problem	Knee Problem
Coughs	Lung Problems
Deafness	Menopause Problem
Diarrhea	Rheumatism
Edema	Sinus Problem
Fever	Shaky Hands
Foot Problems	Stress

TO BALANCE THE CHALLENGE OF THE 1 AND BRING IT OUT AS A TALENT . . .

The first step to balancing the challenge is to feel comfortable when saying "I need . . . " When you feel that you are intimidated by authoritative, dogmatic, or fast-moving people, speak out. You have a right to make your own decisions because your desires are just as worthwhile as anyone else's. Remember to focus on your ambitions. You may risk losing supporters because some of your ideas may be unconventional, but assume responsibility for yourself and move forward. It may be necessary to make unpopular moves or to act when others want to wait. You must have the courage to try your original ideas.

If you are instigating untried concepts, you have to be a nonconformist. But you should also think about practical applications before you set the wheels in motion. When you are fully conscious of all repercussions, have listened to opposing arguments, and have considered the needs or desires of others, do what is best for yourself.

If you never try anything, obviously you will not fail. If you do many things, the odds are you won't get it right the first time all the time. You will learn to make up your own mind, however, and that's what you need to do. You will be happier when you know you are in control of your life.

Forget the expectations of others, dare to be yourself, and recognize that as pioneering, ingenious, independent individuals, "we win some and we lose some."

SELF-MOTIVATION

Youth:

As a tot, the child feels an intense urge to be left to his own devices. This is a difficult time in life for a child who desires to explore. Children may not make their own decisions; therefore, the number 1 motivation makes the tot feel frustrated when unable to follow his own instincts.

Parents may be swept along initially by the independence and creativity exhibited by the youngster. This child enjoys doing things alone and tends to ask for help only if he gets into trouble. If given too much independence, however, the youngster develops negative habits before he is taught to relate to others. As a result, he may act impatient, bossy, and stubborn when given direction.

In an attempt to encourage or discourage the tot's obvious

needs, parents and authorities may allow him too much dominance or cramp his style completely. Such a child is changeable and resolute. If controls are clamped on the youngster, he may selfishly rebel or lose initiative.

The strong-willed 1 loner may find it hard to adjust to the regimens adopted by concerned parents and will become disobedient; too many constraints may make the tot feel defeated, insecure, and powerless. In addition, a child's stronger dependence may result in tantrums or inertia if it is not tempered by a balance that safely encourages individuality. Finally, for parents, other authorities, and child, the period prior to emotional and financial independence is particularly hard to handle.
Maturity:

The 1 adult wants to control his own activities and rarely listens to the advice of others. The 1 wants—but does not need—supportive partners. He is a comfortable loner, planning accomplishments he hopes will attract praise and followers. Generally a comfortable leader and director, the number 1 prefers to leave details to subordinates or to a significant other. When involved personally or professionally with associates, the individual takes pride in executive ability and is easily embarrassed by the incompetence of subordinates. If caught in a personal mistake, the number 1 is humiliated and takes immediate steps to upgrade appearances.

A desire for progress inclines number 1s to feel changeable, to be continually on the move. Number 1s have the willpower, vigor, and determination to successfully get what they want. Their outlook is correspondingly original and creative. As far as 1s are concerned, systems and traditions are just rules to be changed for the better.

Number 1 individuals think that anything can be improved: they will reinvent the wheel repeatedly. Because of uninterest in the methods of predecessors, and often lacking the patience to read instructions, these individuals repeatedly aim to build better mousetraps, or waste time trying.

For these self-sufficient, mentally governed individuals, love and marriage may not be a prime motivation. Number 1s oscillate between introversion and companionability . . . depending upon their immediate objective. They may feel bold after achieving ambitions and decide that it is time to start a family. When feeling the need for self-glorification, they may make up their minds to be the center of someone's world, without giving up their independence.

Balanced number 1s will not allow others to possess them. They need relationships with cooperative, tactful admirers who obviously recognize (and applaud) their originality and accomplishments. The marriage of two number 1 motivations will have its attraction based upon activity and experimentation. Little time is left for individual recognition. Since the self-motivation number describes what we need in order to be comfortable, the partnership of two number 1 motivations will result in both self-important aspirants straining for accommodations from the other.

SELF-IMAGE

Youth:

When lying on the bed, listening to music, and imagining "What am I going to be like when I grow up? How will I walk, dress, and talk?" Number 1 preteens visualize themselves becoming unique individuals. They dream of pioneering Alpine explorations and see themselves receiving adulation for being the first to reach the mountaintop. Children with the number 1 self-image picture themselves as bosses, organizers, and inventors. They may load dishwashers creatively or redesign the vacuum cleaner. They are always in a hurry—planning ambitious ventures, impatient to reach the independence offered by maturity.

Ones appear ready to take the lead. Instigations are more attractive to them than detail work or cleaning up loose ends. They automatically make an effort to get others to do things for them; therefore, number 1 teens must be encouraged to envision themselves completing tasks—not just spurring others on or promoting the end result.

As youths, number 1s dress with originality. They may ignore fads and joining groups. It is their choice to set the pace or go it alone. Ones envisage themselves as unlike anyone else and will mix and match to create their own style. If asked what professional ambitions they may have, designing, architecture, and any free-lance business may come to their minds. Any career that incorporates speed, independence, and experimentation as job specifications will appeal to those with the number 1 self-image.

Maturity:

When walking out of an elevator or into a room—before personality or intellect come into play—number 1 adults send out a vibration of being different and on the move. Their attitude indicates strength, and they appear to be brimming with vitality. Clothing styles tend to be distinctive, with primary colors a preference. These individuals intend to be noticed for their original touches and forward-looking style sense. It is not unusual for number 1s to unconsciously select red clothing: when wearing the color red, they reveal their self-image, feel more self-sufficient, and show the world that they want leadership and action.

Number 1 adults perceive themselves as commanding people. When living up to their self-image, their first impression implies force, dominance, and self-assertiveness. The self-expression number may govern the first impression if uniforms, stylized business dress codes, or fads are indicated by the career descriptions included in the meaning of the number. The self-motivation number may influence the apparel of the bearers if they are relaxing and doing what they desire to do. However, when these individuals are living up to their self-image, they will not feature correspondent colors indicated by numbers in another part of their numerology chart unless they, too, are number 1s.

SELF-EXPRESSION

Youth:

It is obvious to adults when children have a number 1 self-expression number. In youth their talents are based in leadership. Number 1 youngsters assume that a few trusted followers will stand behind their inventive game playing. As they get older others tag along when authorities single them out for positions of leadership. At times they may even appear to be bullies, alienating peers and very proper adults alike. Ones are assertive, instigative, and energetic little egoists. It is difficult for them to sit still for long without getting bored and making innovative suggestions. These active tots keep adults on their toes. The 1 youths will be difficult to train and raise conventionally.

Number 1 talents put these children in the director's chair. They will be more capable adults if left to develop at their own pace and in their own way. Their creative ideas will immediately strike authorities. Once given praise, the number 1 inquiring mind will think up fresh projects.

As teenagers and young adults, they are wheeler-dealers, able to buy or sell anything they have explored alone. The materially ambitious will be first to want a paper route, or turn a hobby into a private income. Computer buffs will be rewriting program manuals before reading them. These trendsetters have definite ideas. Number 1 youths will feel capable of running the show for themselves and everyone else.

Maturity:

Suggested Occupations: Inventor, designer, salesperson, business owner, pilot, explorer, advertising idea person, architect, buyer, seller, actor/actress, director, promoter, writer, editor, musical conductor or musician, contractor, illustrator, cartoonist, politician, inspector, farmer, computer program originator, financial analyst, foreman, store manager, literary or theatrical agent, commercial artist, franchise owner, massage therapist, holistic metaphysician, trial lawyer, psychiatrist, and any career that requires independent action, leadership, and originality

Options:

Careers that are indicated by the meaning of the self-motivation number may not make use of readily available talents but will allow the individual to feel comfortable.

Careers indicated by the self-image number meanings will encourage the individual to live up to youthful dreams.

Careers indicated by the meaning of the destiny number, if it is not the same as the self-expression number, will require that the individual learn from incoming personalities and experiences.

If self-expression and destiny numbers are the same, the individual's talents will be recognized and utilized early in life.

Maturity: Self-expression Analysis

The number 1 individual has a potential for financial rewards for originality and assertiveness. Because of a venturesome spirit and unique ideas, public recognition and fame are possible. The basic ingredient of the number 1 is the ability to walk boldly and proudly. Ones are winners whenever their innovative, independent, progressive energy is channeled.

Ones must focus on forging ahead. If they are uncomfortable leaving associates with less active ambitions behind, they defeat their purpose. Emotionalism will not stand in the way of the unchallenged 1. A balanced number 1 talent prefers to go it alone and is comfortable ignoring the aspirations and opinions of others.

These aggressive individuals must select a career with obvious possibilities for advancement and individualization. Ones may expect immediate recognition for their self-starter qualities and ability to make quick decisions. Trivialities and cleanups should not be a job requirement. These individuals must find a niche where they are given the opportunity to work alone or create systems and start projects. They are best suited to blaze the trail and allow detail-minded associates time to fine-line 1s' objectives. The end result should be executive conditions in which self-reliance is praised and respected, and in which promotions are attracted. Since 1s are autonomous, self-employment is a desirable goal.

In selecting a career, number 1s must have the courage to act upon their convictions; they may, for example, have to buck a parent who expects them to join in the family business. If the arts are these individuals' objective, money may be considered a problem until a reputation is established. These gifted inventors are often encouraged to work at one job to maintain financial security and sideline their major interest. For number 1s to progress comfortably, it is best to minimize responsibilities. Youths should patiently build independence. Ones must have the willpower to avoid being influenced by intimates or traditional thinkers.

Individuals with the number 1 as a self-expression number must be unwavering in their determination to independently carry out their personal ideas.

DESTINY

WE ARE NOT BORN KNOWING WHAT LIFE HAS TO OFFER. INDIVIDUALS WITH THE NUMBER 1 DESTINY LEARN ABOUT INDEPENDENCE AND INDIVIDUALIZATION AS THEY ENCOUNTER THE PEOPLE AND EXPERIENCES THAT TEACH THEM TO VALUE CREATIVITY, SELF-RELIANCE, AND LEADERSHIP.

This destiny indicates a lifetime of self-development. To make the most of numerology's ability to forecast, the number 1 must never expect to be dependent upon others. The individual may choose to follow leaders in youth; if so, he is often placed in subordinate positions until he becomes indispensable. It follows that his superiors eventually form a dependency on his initiative, originality, and efficiency, and his natural leadership ability finally emerges in the eyes of all.

There are no limits to the capabilities of this destiny, nor are there boundaries. Children with the number 1 destiny rush out alone to greet new experiences or create their own opportunities. As time passes, 1s become more enterprising. Opportunities will arise for them to devise unique methods of fulfilling their adventurous destiny.

It is essential that number 1s develop physically, mentally, and spiritually in order to single-handedly govern their destiny. To progress, they need to develop courage, daring, and initiative. Ones should tactfully come right to the point or else expect to risk criticism and supporters. They often make unpopular decisions.

Individuals with the destiny of the number 1 may form partnerships with either number 1 challenge holders or people with the number 1 as a self-motivation or self-expression number: number 1 destiny holders observe the traits of their 1 counterparts and intuitively know that they must learn the meaning of independence from them. Relationships with people who have the number 1 self-motivation or self-expression should benefit number 1 destiny holders, since they have the natural instinct or impression that they must emulate.

Family or environmental expectations for the number 1 may not match the opportunities that life will offer. It may therefore be necessary for the number 1 to be willing to go his own way. Even further, he may break ground and risk becoming an outcast to learn that independence has its own rewards. The number 1 in the family, often the most unassuming member, may quickly rise to leadership and find that everything is different when he is successful. Since the 1 is proud, he may puckishly devote himself to creating a new lifestyle and to leaving the old ways behind. In destiny and all numerology explanations, the individual has choice. The number 1, after learning what life has in store, does not have to be reminded to expect to depend upon himself.

BIRTHDAY INFLUENCES WITHIN
THE DESTINY

January and October

Individuals born in January and October learn, in youth, that they must develop their own resources and be decisive and self-reliant. Situations arise that cause them to make their own decisions, and they learn that they cannot expect to lean on others if they want individuality.

Childhood's independent actions provide a training ground, and its lessons are not forgotten. Childhood itself may be remembered as a lonely time, when the youngster's independence was repressed by authorities because of his inability to provide for himself.

Birthday: 1, 10, 19, 28

THE BIRTHDAY NUMBER HAS AN INFLUENCE ON PERSONALITY AND DESTINY. IT ATTRACTS PEOPLE AND EXPERIENCES DURING MID-LIFE THAT EXEMPLIFY THE NUMBER MEANING.

The mid-life productivity cycle begins with maturity. It lasts from approximately twenty-eight to fifty-five years of age and coordinates with the destiny during that time span. The birthday-number meaning adds character traits and experiences to an individual's numerology analysis.

People born on the first, tenth, nineteenth, or twenty-eighth of the month, in addition to the character traits outlined by the number meanings for the name, are planners and diagnosticians. They may not be builders or be easily swayed by emotional needs. Individuals born on these dates blossom at maturity to become energetic, tenacious thinkers and idealists.

Between approximately twenty-eight and fifty-five years of age—the twenty-seven-year productivity cycle within the destiny—life will offer additional opportunities for independence, creative leadership, and progressive ambitions. These birthdate number insights are helpful when choosing a vocation. If you were born on the first, tenth, nineteenth, or twenty-eighth, you may anticipate opportunities to stand alone, to be accountable, and to be considered an original.

PERSONAL YEAR

The number 1 year is the first year in the cycle of nine years of experience and results in the polish of skill and performance based upon its goals. This is the time to hatch ideas conceptualized three years before. For most the people and experiences encountered during this year foster a rebirth; for others, the year focuses upon promoting new schemes and adds broader dimensions to present interests. The number 1 personal year allows the individual to tie up between January and August the loose ends that may have been left over from the preceding year. The intensification of activity and the clarity of this year's purpose is heightened in September—the number 1 month within the number 1 year.

Change and independent thinking are key issues in this powerful year. This is not the time to accommodate or vacillate. The year starts out slowly and adds surprising turns of events that alter ideas in April. July offers the individual a chance to take control—to plan, build, and act. This action then sets the stage for letting go of previous commitments in August. September's activities intensify new prospects and the need to make changes. Between September 21 and 30, the individual should check practicalities and break ground for new long-term ambitions.

If one does not forge ahead with new paths, areas, and methods—which doesn't mean limiting oneself or listening to other's cautions—one will not develop plans to be carried out during the following eight years. Projects begun now will not blossom until the number 3 personal year. Patience is paramount. In contrast, unions and partnerships begun now will grow. To maintain present relationships, individuals may have to make compromises; however, this is not the year to sacrifice for others. It is the number 1 time to make a new start. Relationships will be important and more comfortable when the number 2 cycle—which is beneficial for partnerships—comes in next year.

During the number 1 personal year, do the self-promoting groundwork. Ones must take an independent stand, launch explorations, and expect to be working toward new goals as the year closes. This is a very active year, not a time to repress actions or ideas. It is a time to keep busy doing the things one feels comfortable doing. The people intended to remain with the 1 for the next eight years will be swept along with this year's changes.

PERSONAL MONTH

The number 1 personal month within any personal year is active, and one should take the initiative. It is a month in which things get accomplished that were on the brink of completion three months before but did not materialize. Situations arise during this month that put the individual in the driver's seat. New people, situations, and ideas abound. One should be aggressive and use this time span to make changes. Decisions should be based on independent, intellectual evaluations because help and encouragement may not be forthcoming. Overall, the focus should be on beginnings.

PERSONAL DAY

Wake up with a determined attitude. Whether you are heading for a new job, a potential client, or any situation that you want to promote, a clever new focus will open previously closed doors. ESP is working; use intuition, stay firm in beliefs, and do not lose control. Prospects will be fresh, so seize this day's opportunities to be original.

You will be surprised to note that ambition, self-confidence, and creative thoughts are in the air and you will get satisfaction today. Activate today's energetic, independent mood by choosing to wear a red tie or dress. Above all, do not be lazy.

Plan all personal commitments carefully and be sure to have a definite goal. Remain sharp and employ practical assessments in order to see your ideas through to completion. As this active day has a purpose, it should definitely be used to begin something new.

CHAPTER SIX

NUMBER 2

Cooperation

Cooperation

ATTRIBUTES:
POSITIVE—Cooperative, Considerate, Diplomatic, Emotional, Modest, Patient, Supportive, Softhearted, Responsive, Adaptable

NEGATIVE—Insensitive, Weak-willed, Discourteous, Careless, Faultfinding, Shy, Fearful, Disinterested, Unresponsive, Cunning

CORRESPONDENTS:
LETTERS: B, K, T
EVEN NUMBER: Receptive
DISPOSITION: Emotional and Personally Concerned
NUMBERS: 11, 20, 29, 38, 47, 56, 65, 74, 83, 92, 101
COLOR: Orange
GEM: Moonstone
CRYSTAL: Rutile
VEGETATION: Ivy
FOODS: Eggs, Fowl, Breast of Lamb, Walnuts
MUSICAL INSTRUMENTS/APPEAL: Cello, Pipe Organ; Aria

MUSICAL NOTE: D (When Challenged: C#)
LOCATIONS: State: Colorado, Florida, Kansas, Kentucky, Louisiana, Minnesota, Nevada, Ohio, Oregon
City: Bakersfield, Fargo, Great Falls, Lynchburg, Memphis, Mobile, Muncie, New Haven, Omaha, Philadelphia, Saginaw, San Jose, Steubenville, Tucson, Wheeling, Youngstown
PLANET: The Moon
MONTHS: February, November (Shared with number 11)
BIRTHDAYS: 2, 11, 20, 29 (11 and 29 are shared with number 11)
DAY OF THE WEEK: Monday
GENERAL COMPATIBILITY NUMBERS: 2, 4, 6, 7 (8 commercially)
INCOMPATIBILITY NUMBERS: 5 (9 commercially)

Note: If an individual has the challenge to the number 2, these descriptions will swing from positive to negative until the challenge is balanced. Please be sure to read the challenge meaning.

CHALLENGE OF THE NUMBER 2

This is a challenge to the individual's personal sensitivity, perceptions, and susceptivity. It stems from too much or too little attention to the challenge holder's feelings and emotional reactions early in life. The female, usually the mother, is too responsive, too self-involved, or is absent because of illness, divorce, or death. The father may have been the gentle, receptive parent and played the "female" role, which might have thrown the child off balance. As a result, the tot becomes an adult without understanding how much or how little to expect or to give in intimate relationships.

As infants, these thin-skinned children internalize their feelings. To hold the receptive authority figure's concentration, they may have allergies or colic or refuse to eat. Chronic or trivial physical problems plague them. They are nervously energetic or too serene. As tots, they hide, constantly nag, or play underfoot. They are "Mommy's little helper," or they require consistent assistance.

As preschoolers, they may have easygoing dispositions and seem happy to have quiet conversations with a secret friend— or they are little hellions, busily collecting little things, sharing secrets, and being generally inconsiderate. They are too peaceful or create household tensions. As the child grows older, if his cooperation is reciprocated by manipulations, conspiracy, or hard-heartedness—or he is given unreasonable praise for keeping out of everyone's way—he feels hurt.

It is difficult for children with the challenge of the 2 to grow to maturity trusting themselves. They do not recognize their uniqueness or imagine how to live or work alone. Such children are often indecisive due to their talent for seeing every detail on both sides of the coin. Twos miss seeing the forest while dissecting each tree leaf. In their desire to do the right thing, they do not miss a trick but often lose the bridge game.

Twos must feel used or abused before taking a stand to get what they want. Carefully primed in youth to be aware of every raised eyebrow, as prudent adults they may think that standing out in a crowd is ungentlemanly or unladylike. Because of a lack of openness and misunderstood subtleties in childhood, they assume that an unobtrusive attitude, meticulousness, and championing leadership will give them "the power behind the throne." When pushed to extremes, 2s manipulate others. After doing things that they are not proud of they are never given as much credit as they think they deserve. It's a no-win situation.

For the most part, challenge 2 holders take themselves too seriously. They turn everyday personal problems (or projects) into overwhelming tasks. Twos spend too much time and energy contemplating or picking lint out of their navels. They have black-or-white perceptions of friendship, love, and confidentiality. They give all and expect that everyone will be sensitive to their desires.

Correspondingly, challenge 2 holders wait and watch to find a need and aim to fill it at any cost. Yet often they lack the confidence to depend upon honest relationships, and they question their desirability. As companions, they make dishmops out of themselves to maintain intimacy. Further, their self-depreciating behavior may lead to the emotional and physical drains that result in debilitating depression. Twos often lack the energy to get out of bed. After endless nights of petty thoughts they lose sight of major issues.

Number 2 challenge holders expect too much self-sacrifice from themselves and loved ones. If a parent played the martyr, the example has been set for these children to overdo. As adults, 2s often place themselves at another's disposal. Once having done this and experiencing discomfort, they will go to any extreme to avoid the same experience. They then retreat and refuse to give up anything for another. It is difficult for 2 challenge holders to realize that they are not the only ones ever touched by sorrow, loneliness, or discomfort. They are very self-absorbed.

In their gentle, subservient, quiet way, 2s will create problems for others. Their need for attention will cause them to talk about petty issues, which often instigates family or community disharmony. They are very considerate—often taking action before being asked or after being told to leave things alone. Twos provoke people—ironically, usually the people from whom they fear rejection. Number 2s will try unnecessarily to do or say the "right" thing—to avoid confrontations or to gain approval from the people who intimidate them. They aim to provide little niceties that they imagine will be praised and appreciated; too often, however, these acts go unnoticed or create problems.

How do the 2 challenge holders let down defenses, break habits, and shed distorted childhood impressions? First they must remember that the universe does not revolve around them, their sensitivities, or their emotional relationships. Their defensiveness, surprisingly, establishes habits that place their personal feelings above the rights of others. Until sensitive 2s realize that suspicion, mistrust, and nervousness give everyone around them the heebie-jeebies, too, they will be confronted with real or fancied personal slights, chronic problems that slow their ambitions, and a touch of masochism.

The number 2 challenge may swing from one of the following extremes to another until it is recognized and new habits are initiated that stabilize the sensitivity of the challenge holder.

Too sweet or too bitter.

Too personal or too impersonal.

Too open or too closed.

Too grudging or too grateful.

Too apologetic or too unregretting.

Too helpless or too helpful.

Too considerate or too rude.

Too honest or two-faced.

Too forgiving or too mean.

Too hurt or too untouched.

Too dependent or too alone.

Too soft or too hard.

Too friendly or too cool.

Too discontent or too loving.

PHYSICAL CHALLENGES OF THE NUMBER 2

Challenges can affect physical as well as mental health. Body chemistry changes when individuals are stressed, and when we do not know what is good for us, our minds trigger anxious, angry, or frustrated habits. When we are mean to ourselves, we get sick. One's attitude sends the brain a message, and the brain tells the body to scream for help.

To get attention for their dis-ease, often people get sick or form negative habits. Numerologists believe that illness and wellness depend upon attitude, and challenges indicate the attitudes that result from needy feelings. When we do not feel needy, we feel well and balanced and do not crave attention from others. Essentially, if the personality challenges are balanced, the body chemistry is in balance, too, and therefore there is little chance of mental or physical dis-ease.

Challenge numbers indicate the ways people subconsciously punish themselves for not being consciously good to themselves.

The following list of dis-eases and negative habits relate to the challenge of the number 2.

Athlete's Foot	Multiple Sclerosis
Birth Defects	Nerves
Bladder Problems	Premature Aging
Burns	Restless Leg Syndrome
Circulatory Problems	Sciatica
Constipation	Shaky Hands
Diabetes	Throat Problems
Fevers	Tonsillitis
Foot Problems	Tuberculosis
Hair Loss	Urinary Tract Infections
Liver Spots	Vaginitis
Menopause Problems	

TO BALANCE THE CHALLENGE OF THE 2 AND BRING IT OUT AS A TALENT . . .

The first step to balancing the challenge is to feel comfortable about saying "I need kindness." Ignore past insults or pessimism; forgive and forget. Always expect the best. Use a gentle manner to assert yourself without going to the extreme of prefacing a request with numerous exaggerated compliments.

If you feel self-conscious, remember that others are wondering what you think of *them*. We all look for approval, so stop criticizing. The spotlight is not on you all the time.

When you do not have time for yourself because you are slaving for another, remember that supporting, sharing, and cooperating does not mean losing your identity. It is admirable to be part of an effort, but you do not have to do all the detail work or handle everyone with kid gloves. Keep the peace, but not at the cost of your sanity.

We all depend upon others to guide us when we are inexperienced, but if you know what to do, do it. Do not wait to be told the obvious or expect minute guidelines for everything. People are not waiting for you to make a mistake, nor will they pamper your need for attention. They just want to get a job done: take part in a team effort.

Be yourself, and recognize that as adaptable, considerate, cooperative individuals, you do not have to depend on somebody else for decision making, tranquillity, or self-esteem.

SELF-MOTIVATION

Youth:

As a tot, the number 2 urge that the child feels is to be peaceful, friendly, and happy. When reprimanded, this child will become more upset than one would expect. Disharmony of any kind may bring the individual to the brink of tears. If surrounded by argumentative authorities, unsympathetic siblings, or unjust criticism, this child's school and social behavior will suffer. The number 2 youngster wants to give and receive love, helpfulness, and consideration.

Parents may describe their number 2 child as "soft, placid, or affable." Those words describe the individual when he is surrounded by flexible, genial, patient authorities. If the child's communications are considered to be timid, and parents are aggressive and impatient, the youngster may internalize his feelings into depression. Once this child, whose feelings are highly influential, is pushed into the background, he will magnify and build resentments. If this tension is prolonged, emotional turmoil erupts. The youngster reacts with a show of allergies, eyelid tics, intestinal disorders, stuttering—all manner and form of chronic nervous dysfunctions.

In an attempt to placate the sensitive 2, authorities may

become too attentive and truly spoil the youngster. The ideal solution is to allow him to do things for others. Authorities should show the appropriate appreciation of the child's gentle nature. A too standoffish or condescending influence on the youth may encourage him to establish self-effacing habits that linger into maturity.

The number 2 youngster wants to be appreciated for the little things he does. A supportive position from which he can be cautious, courteous, and tactful makes him comfortable. The individual may bask in the reflected glory of leaders and authorities, for example, and is adaptable and tolerant when involved in group activities. Moreover, music and rhythm are in his soul, and dance and music lessons—cello or bugle instruction—may prepare him to associate with peers, in cooperative ventures, where he can shine.

Number 2 teens should wait to observe the way the wind blows before giving their support to a new cause or leader. They should be aware of their own sensitivity and relate to the temperaments of others. Generally 2s wait for leadership and stay in the background. When in harmony with intimates, they excel. Recognition for cooperative efforts encourages them to be friendly and supportive. If the 2s' good manners and hospitable actions are not appreciated in childhood, teenagers will have a hard time building sufficient self-esteem. Furthermore, striking out on their own may become a problem.

As young adults, 2s usually perfect their natural gifts—keeping secrets, accumulating knowledge, and collecting alliances. They may have extended apprenticeships and are likely to be more outstanding after age twenty-eight. In addition, the receptive number 2 attracts good prospects, lovers, and jobs; these gems just seem to fall into their laps. In general, 2 youths are capable, easygoing, and content when working hand in glove with assertive, creative, progressive companions.
Maturity:

Number 2 adults want friends, love, and unpretentious comforts. They surround themselves with people who need them because they prefer doing things for others. Tight schedules, strict orders, and exacting authorities make them uncomfortable. These individuals enjoy confidences with intimates. Twos are confidants—closemouthed, helpful problem sharers. At the first blush of happiness or pain they will drip out a tear, listen, and, when appropriate, console. Balanced 2 adults never lose their considerate nature.

The number 2 desire for knowledge begins in childhood and intensifies as time goes on. Little-known facts and artfully detailed tiny miniatures generally fascinate them. Their pleasure in collecting confidants, hobbies, and information is reinforced by a talent for absorbing everything that comes into their lives. Within the number 2 soul, people and things take on emotional meaning.

More aggressive (and abrasive) friends, employers, and mates are attracted to people with the number 2 self-motivation, because the modest 2s pose no threat to their ambitions for leadership, status, or power. Twos do not object to being a support system for more assertive and dominant intimates and associates. In order to feel needed and loved, these gentle diplomats strive to maintain peaceful domestic and work environments. In their subtle way 2s get their points across. They get what they want and attract recognition for being the glue that binds marriages, families, and businesses together.

Self-discipline is not a prime mover for number 2s. These team players do not expect exactitude from the people whom they take into their hearts. Any kind of companionship or marriage is preferred to solitude. Twos feel incomplete alone. Too often an early marriage is sought in an effort to gain security and acceptance. Insecure number 2s then may become doormats for an inconsiderate or egocentric soulmate. Affectionate, bolstering, watchful 2s are a treasure for an ambitious, active, creative lover or partner.

Easily hurt and delicate, receptive 2s may be oversensitive. If overtired, overworked, or depressed, they often become caught up in their emotions and lose sight of practical major issues. Twos may also be timid—too shy to speak up when little slights bother them. As a result, minute problems accumulate, appearing to be mountains of unhappiness, and these detail-oriented individuals become overwhelmed. When frustrated or after patiently waiting for others to change, they become hostile.

An angry 2 can be very, very petty. If another person starts a discussion rudely or critically, the refined 2 may finish it with a cynical or shrewish flourish. He may act with indifference or commence with a list of every painful experience he has suffered over a period of years. Each little chink in another's armor has been observed and ingested by the detail-conscious number 2. One may be sure that if the number 2 decides to be unsupportive or reproachful during an emotional upheaval, nothing will be omitted.

Generally the number 2 self-motivation inclines these individuals to want peace and encourage harmony. Modest to a fault at times, 2s will rarely complicate situations by demanding recognition. It is not their natural instinct to be forceful. They are happiest when quietly persuasive. Thus 2s are not uncomfortable when others share their ideas. Material needs or status are not their prime concerns; instead, easygoing friendship, personal comfort, and intimate love are major focuses for the number 2 self-motivation.

Balanced 2s share or receive credit and recognition with humility. They are usually extremely thankful for small favors and take pleasure in reciprocating. These individuals are quite capable of being disgusted by impatient, loudmouthed movers and shakers. However, they may be intimidated by controlling leaders. In an effort to keep up with demands they may exhaust their energy. Twos are quite capable of denying themselves for the benefit of others. When their energies are spent, they may leave the scene—and the applause—to the people who depend upon it.

The marriage of one number 2 self-motivation to another will thrive in friendship but will probably not be sparked by scintillating sex. These individuals are sexually receptive. Who will initiate foreplay? The pairing of two number 2s is, nevertheless, an affectionate combination. Retiring number 2 individuals need self-disciplined, aggressive, assertive soulmates.

The partnership of two number 2 motivations will result in both sensitive helpers straining to find little things to do for each other. They will make gentle attempts to spark romance, and both parties will avoid aggressiveness. The result may be either charming or boring and unproductive. Business partnerships will display a "You first, Alphonse"—"No, you first, Gaston" tendency as well.

SELF-IMAGE

Youth:

When lying on the bed, listening to music, and imagining "What am I going to be like when I grow up? How will I walk, dress and talk?" the number 2 preteen visualizes himself becoming a responsive individual. He dreams of the perfect marriage in which he unobtrusively helps his mate, and, nested in a peaceful atmosphere together, they cautiously climb the ladder to comfort and happiness. The number 2 envisions himself cared for, secure, and cozy.

Children with the number 2 self-image picture themselves as partners, group leaders, and diplomats. They may settle household disputes between siblings and parents, learn to sew or iron, and delight in finding little treasures to accumulate and cherish. They are slow to initiate activities, preferring instead to contribute by observing details ignored by more daring or impatient playmates.

Number 2 individuals relate to comforting others and offering services and sensitivity. Studying or teaching may be more important than climbing trees or auditioning for the lead in a school play. Therefore number 2 teens must be encouraged to envisage themselves in assertive situations—not just following orders or making suggestions for which they allow others to take the credit.

As youths, 2s will dress to blend with their peers. They are joiners and offer to take the tedious jobs that keep them involved, while shrinking from those jobs that force them to make individual decisions or attract criticism. It is their choice to remain in the background. They envision themselves as careful, unobtrusive, subtle dressers and do not create their own designs. If asked what professional ambitions they may have, secretary, artist, or librarian may come to their minds. Any career depiction that includes a noncompetitive working atmosphere, peaceful surroundings, and an unhurried pace appeals to those with the number 2 self-image.

Maturity:

When walking out of an elevator or into a room—before personality or intellect come into play—number 2 adults send out cautious and unpretentious vibrations. Their attitude indicates courteousness, and they appear to be refined and unhurried. Clothing styles tend to be subdued, with a tendency toward neutral shades. Intending not to be individualistic, 2s are noted for their neatness and attention to delicate accessories.

It is not unusual for number 2s to unconsciously select tones of orange clothing. When wearing orange and its different shades, they reveal their self-image. During these times 2s feel more friendly. They are indicating that they offer consideration and hospitality.

Note: Howard Johnson, the highway restaurateur and innkeeper, has the number 2 self-expression, of which orange is the correspondent color. He uniformly constructed his businesses and built his career featuring welcoming orange roofs that are easily spotted from the freeway.

Number 2 adults perceive themselves as adaptable, genial, gracious people. When living up to their self-image, their first impression implies kindliness, sincerity, and tolerance.

The self-expression number may govern the first impression

if uniforms, stylized business dress codes, or fads are indicated by the career descriptions included in the meaning of the number.

The self-motivation number may influence the apparel of the bearer if he is relaxing and doing what he desires to do. However, when the individual is intent upon living up to his self-image, he should feature its correspondent color.

SELF-EXPRESSION

Youth:

It is obvious to adults when children have a number 2 self-expression number. In youth, number 2 talents are based in supportiveness. The youngsters follow the leader when game-playing. As they get older 2s discover that they are uncomfortable attracting the spotlight. They may decline to make suggestions and shy away from situations that single them out. At times they may appear to be disinterested and alienate their peers as well as enthusiastic adults. As retiring, patient, quiet little busybodies, 2s rarely lose concentration or miss observing the interactions of the group. These helpful, pliant tots may be a mother's delight—if they are not *too* submissive. They will be amenable to training and a conventional upbringing.

Number 2 talents put these children in the assistant's chair. They will be more capable adults if given opportunities to feel the accomplishment of doing things alone. Wise parents will therefore give them the responsibility and companionship of a pet. Twos are less likely than others to have to demand attention from their parents. Without the need to learn how to attract authorities at home, these gentle children may not know how to deal with competitiveness at school. They may thus be overlooked and underrated until they find their niche.

As teenagers and young adults, 2s should be good students. They have the talent to be diplomatic, detailed, and skillful organizers. Dance and music lessons are good outlets for their artistic abilities, and group activities bring them comfortable recognition. Twos may read a lot, become absorbed collecting alliances, or keep busy maintaining an orderly schedule. They are intent upon knowing every detail of their interest. These helpful, supportive youngsters will relate their talents to the instigations, leadership, and creative ideas of family, friends, and authorities.

Maturity:

Suggested Occupations: Secretary, teacher, diplomat, bookkeeper, accountant, librarian, statistician, biographer, bacteriologist, politician, civil servant, poet, columnist, technical writer, novelist, editor, group singer, dancer, musician, office worker, file clerk, keypunch operator, computer programmer, social organizer, astronomer, florist, landscaper, waiter/waitress, practical nurse, mechanic, housekeeper, mother's helper, repair specialist, astrologer, numerologist, tarot reader, tea leaf reader, biorhythm analyst, handwriting analyst, phrenologist, reflexologist, psychic, medium, psychologist, bank teller, building custodian, geographer, office machine operator, receptionist, stenographer, social worker, cashier, mail carrier, postal clerk, dental assistant, hospital orderly, companion.

Options:

Careers that are indicated by the meaning of the self-motivation number may not make use of readily available talents but will allow the individual to feel comfortable.

Careers indicated by the self-image number meanings will encourage the individual to live up to youthful dreams.

Careers indicated by the meaning of the destiny number, if it is not the same as the self-expression number, will require that the individual learn from incoming personalities and experiences.

If self-expression and destiny numbers are the same, the individual's talents will be recognized and utilized early in life.

Maturity: Self-expression Analysis

Number 2 individuals have a potential for financial rewards for their diplomacy, responsiveness, and attention to detail.

Recognition is possible for their ability to maintain personal orderliness in frantic environments. The basic ingredient of number 2s is their ability not to step on the toes of innovators or leaders—to be supportive, receptive, and cooperative. Twos know how to make someone else look good and how to get paid for doing it. In business or private life 2s are the world's best private secretaries.

Number 2 talents must recognize their own need and desire for harmony and time to do their tasks carefully. In a business environment they should put emotional judgments on the shelf and not allow sensitive reactions to color their attitudes. Twos are concerned with the opinions of others. Balanced number 2 talents prefer to be allied with partners and involved with jobs where minuteness is essential, as well as gentle persuasiveness rather than forcefulness.

Generally sweet, quiet, and reserved at work, these individuals must select jobs that allow them to interact one-to-one with individual executives and/or groups. They will earn advancements for knowledge and thoroughness. The ability to be competitive, meet deadlines, or create guidelines for others should not be a job requirement for the number 2. Number 2 talents must find a niche in which they are in accord with superiors and coworkers. Twos become the power behind the throne.

When following instructions or analyzing compromises with associates, careful 2s excel. They carry through assignments in a prescribed, precise manner. Friendly conditions where watchfulness, trustworthiness, and championing of leaders is needed are ideal. Twos attract promotions, and express themselves best in a cooperative partnership.

In selecting a career, the number 2 must be realistic about his abilities and interests. He may be surrounded by dynamic leaders, be expected to follow their example, and attempt to please by trying his wings in an insensitive or fast-paced world. If executive positions are the individual's objective, too much sensitivity, shyness, or lack of initiative may cause confusion.

The result will be disappointment for the 2 and his subordinates.

Artistically gifted number 2s may be expected to be more competitive. They may resort to covering their delicate egos by acting apathetic. It is best for number 2s to progress subtly. They should wait until singled out by authorities for promotion, not vie for supremacy. In short, they win through dependency.

Individuals with the number 2 as a self-expression number must be in control of their emotions in a business atmosphere. Twos must keep their cool! Career situations are desirable in which sensitive 2s are not overwhelmed by anxious coworkers or superiors whose lack of personal planning fills the number 2's days with emergencies.

DESTINY

WE ARE NOT BORN KNOWING WHAT LIFE HAS TO OFFER. INDIVIDUALS WITH THE NUMBER 2 DESTINY LEARN HOW TO BE MODEST AND COOPERATIVE IN RELATIONSHIPS AS THEY ENCOUNTER THE PEOPLE AND EXPERIENCES THAT TEACH THEM TO VALUE SENSITIVITY, PATIENCE, AND PEACE.

This destiny indicates a lifetime of giving and receiving. To make the most of numerology's ability to forecast, the number 2 must expect to be of service to others. The individual may choose to stay in the background in youth and is therefore placed in supportive positions. A bossy, authoritative or impatient attitude will repel the options and tenderness offered by this destiny. When the individual with the number 2 destiny realizes that he is here to learn to listen and comply, then loving, attentive, thoughtful people will offer him emotional and material security.

There are limits to the capabilities of this destiny. Children with the number 2 destiny do not rush out alone to greet new experiences, nor do they create their own opportunities. As time passes they become more flexible, intuitive, and receptive.

Opportunities will arise for 2s to consider the feelings and ambitions of others. These individuals learn to have patience and understanding and to put others before themselves. They will be required to be attentive in order to attract the love, material comforts, and companionship offered by the number 2 destiny.

It is essential that those with the number 2 destiny develop emotional control in order to maintain relationships. To progress, number 2s need to develop tact, diplomacy, and friendliness. Individuals with this destiny may form partnerships with either number 2 challenge holders or people with the same self-motivation or self-expression number. Number 2 destiny holders observe the traits of these others, from whom they intuitively know they must learn humility. Relationships with people who have the number 2 self-motivation or self-expression are helpful, because they know what the number 2 destiny must learn.

For the number 2, family or environmental expectations may be different from the opportunities that life will offer. It may be necessary for the 2s to wait for opportunities to drop in his lap. Authorities may not understand that the number 2 destiny does not respond to aggressiveness, self-reliance, or a fast pace. Two does respond to understanding, partnerships, and careful planning. In destiny, as in all numerological explanations, the individual has choice. After learning what life has in store, the number 2 destiny holder has to be reminded to place secondary importance upon personal ambitions and to have faith that everything he wants or needs will be offered.

BIRTHDAY INFLUENCES WITHIN THE DESTINY

February and November

Individuals born in February and November learn while young that they must depend upon others, provide services, and strive to compensate for the little things they observe are lacking. When situations arise that cause them to care for others, they learn that a sympathetic, hospitable, and cooperative response to another's problems has a positive influence on the opportunities they are offered.

Childhood's sensitive interactions and dependencies provide a training ground, and its lessons are not forgotten. Youth may be remembered as a time to learn, work with intimates, and assist others. The youngster wants harmony, so if there is disharmony and his quiet, happy nature is repressed, tears come easily. To learn to provide for himself, the youngster must collect knowledge and use it when it is requested or obviously needed by others.

Birthday: 2, 11, 20, 29

THE BIRTHDAY NUMBER HAS AN INFLUENCE ON PERSONALITY AND DESTINY. IT ATTRACTS PEOPLE AND EXPERIENCES DURING MID-LIFE THAT EXEMPLIFY THE NUMBER MEANING.

The mid-life productivity cycle begins with maturity. It lasts from approximately twenty-eight to fifty-five years of age and coordinates with the destiny during that time span. The birthday-number meaning adds character traits and experiences to an individual's numerology analysis.

People born on the second, eleventh, twentieth, or twenty-ninth of the month, in addition to the character traits outlined by the number meanings for the name, are helpmates and collectors. They may not be happy alone or comfortable with hyperactive intimates. Individuals born on these dates want early marriage or partnership.

Between approximately twenty-eight and fifty-five years of age—the twenty-seven-year productivity cycle within the destiny—life will offer additional opportunities for rewarding partnerships and marriage. Attention to little details and the sensitive feelings of family, friends, and associates will require their adaptability, diplomacy, and easygoing attitude. These individuals should develop interests that are harmonious with the lifestyle provided or offered.

PERSONAL YEAR

The number 2 year is the second year in the cycle of nine years of experience and results in a polish and skill of performance based upon goals set in the first year. It is the time to let last year's newly instigated actions gel. For most, the people and experiences encountered require both attention and assistance. For others, the year focuses upon learning the details of new interests and jobs. It may be a time of apprenticeship, when a little humility in the spring will attract practical rewards in November.

Love, intimate friendships, and petty problems tap emotional and physical energy. Planned times for rest, quiet, and mental meditation are musts after the previous year's activity. Key words for this year are patience, calm, and modesty. The people who are offered for growth relationships this year do not take kindly to impulsiveness, aggressive attitudes, and attention-getting power plays. Courteous approaches and a focus on details will encourage others to establish unions that will pay off in the future. This is a preparation period; the number 2 individual will not see results of last year's plans until the number 3 cycle next year.

One must not forge ahead or become impatient with intimates, subordinates, or superiors. This is a constructive, nurturing year, but it will attract petty annoyances and have slowdowns. In life's numerology cycles, seeds are planted in the number 1 personal year that must take root during the number 2 year. It takes more than water to nurture a seed. It is the manure in the soil that feeds the seedling as it lies hidden under the ground. The same idea applies to people living through the veiled growth of a number 2 year. The individual will grow when able to stay still: he should absorb information the way a seed absorbs the soil's nutrients—without rebeling when forced to mature, quietly accepting the touch of a little of life's manure.

During the number 2 personal year, one may find out who his true friends are and how to be a real friend to others. It is better to play Mona Lisa and smile mysteriously than to let petty annoyances cause major rifts. This is an inactive and receptive year, a time to be reminded that everyone cannot be a lion, as the lambs have to have a say, too.

Money comes in dollops, little problems come in by the truckload, and delays may get on one's nerves. The number 2 personal year is a time to observe, refine, and be willing to take responsibility for keeping the peace. Nothing new begins, but one must maintain friendly relationships with people who will be around for the next seven years.

PERSONAL MONTH

The number 2 personal month within any personal year offers an opportunity to make others happy. Interactions with friends and lovers take top priority while ambitious material changes should be put on the shelf. Last month was active and tiring; now is the time to rest and allow intimates time to ingest and adjust to things that may differ from their personal desires. Situations may arise that require tactful handling. Use this time to do the little things that were overlooked last month. Listen with an open mind for innuendos and constructive criticisms that may be helpful: be gracious, adaptable, and understanding as you await developments.

PERSONAL DAY

Wake up with an easygoing attitude. Whether you are heading for an office, a vacation day, or a Laundromat, take your time, observing and sensing the atmosphere. Use intuition when involved with other people. Responding with sensitivity to the needs of others will keep things peaceful. Be kind, understanding, and helpful. In return, expect to get assistance from family and coworkers today. Don't make waves; this isn't the time to push for results. Rather, it is the time to latch on to anything useful that comes your way.

You will be surprised to note that others want to do the talking, take the lead, and unload their assignments. Nit-picking is in the air, and it may not be easy to keep calm or cool. Avoid self-pity, attend to personal details, and get things out of the way that may slow you down tomorrow. This is a good day to sew, iron, or file the bills.

Make a personal commitment not to rush, show resentment, or undertake major jobs. Do not instigate anything. Let the phone ring. Incoming information will bring in benefits, but if you make a call, the party will be out to lunch either physically or mentally. Nothing will be accomplished and you may become annoyed. You will have to be the one to "turn the other cheek"—if someone steps on your foot, apologize for getting your foot under theirs. Avoid confrontations, and, above all, displace criticisms and angers with friendliness, understanding, and tact.

Take whatever comes in today and have faith that future benefits will follow if you do not attempt to alter plans or relationships. This inactive day has a purpose: it should be used to support yesterday's activities, absorb information, and reaffirm alliances.

CHAPTER SEVEN

NUMBER 3

Communication

Communication

ATTRIBUTES:
POSITIVE—Optimistic, Imaginative, Talented, Sociable, Amusing, Tasteful, Happy, Verbal, Youthful, Cordial, Eager
NEGATIVE—Inarticulate, Whining, Extravagant, Superficial, Gossipy, Narcissistic, Defeated, Withdrawn, Lying, Dull

CORRESPONDENTS:
LETTERS: C, L, U
ODD NUMBER: Aggressive
DISPOSITION: Cheerful; Personally Expressive
NUMBERS: 12, 21, 30, 39, 48, 57, 66, 75, 84, 93, 102
COLOR: Yellow
GEM: Topaz
CRYSTAL: Galena
VEGETATION: Daffodil, Honeysuckle, Orchid, Rose, Pansy, Elm, Mahogany, Redwood
FOODS: Romaine, Duck, Potatoes, Tomato, Pudding, Grapes
MUSICAL INSTRUMENTS/APPEAL: Cornet, Trombone; Band

MUSICAL NOTE: E (When Challenged: F)

LOCATIONS: State: Arizona, Arkansas, Iowa, New Mexico, New York, South Carolina, West Virginia

City: Asheville, Battle Creek, Billings, Charlotte, Grand Rapids, Hollywood, Nashville, New York, Providence, Rochester, Salt Lake City, Syracuse

PLANET: Venus

MONTHS: March, December

BIRTHDAYS: 3, 12, 21, 30

DAY OF THE WEEK: Wednesday

GENERAL COMPATIBILITY NUMBERS: 1, 3, 5, 6 (9 commercially)

INCOMPATIBILITY NUMBERS: 4, 7 (8 commercially)

Note: If an individual has the challenge to the number 3, these descriptions will swing from positive to negative until the challenge is balanced. Please be sure to read the challenge meaning.

CHALLENGE OF THE NUMBER 3

This is a challenge to the individual's communication skills, imagination, and sociability. It stems from too much or not enough parental focus on outward appearances during childhood. In particular, the mother and siblings together or the grandmother and mother as a unit made too much fuss over the child or cast him aside. The number 3 youngster is often an only child, the only boy, the only girl, the eldest, or the youngest in the family. As the favored or disfavored child, the 3 challenge holder becomes a socially self-conscious adult without understanding how he appears to others. He is unable to see beyond superficial judgments and mature gracefully.

As these children grow older they imagine themselves to be Cinderella or "the fairy prince." Number 3 challenge holders hide in the woodpile or preen before a mirror. Remembered punishments may be related to too much or too little talk—explanations being too extensive or nonexistent. These charming children may have been forgiven every transgression without the benefit of mature, constructive criticism. They may also have been punished with childish, adult penalties such as the silent treatment.

Authority figures likely showed the child unreasonable friendship or removed their companionship. Parents may have had a variety of interests, lacked concentration, or behaved like children themselves. They may never have played, teased, or joked. Thus, for the child the judgments of older siblings may have been paramount. The child was probably left alone— without mature authorities—to learn responsibility and to read between the lines. As a result, they use their unfettered imaginations, fibbing, making up playmates, and escaping from reality. Without adequate preparation or restrictions, the 3 can easily become irresponsible or overloaded with concerns.

The youngster grows to maturity fulfilling or relinquishing desires dramatically. Because he has to express his own personality yet had little or too much training, the 3 dotes upon or laughs at the social graces. Exposed to the limelight or hidden in the shadows, the 3 had no time to accumulate positive feedback on which to fall back. When feeling stress, he tends to become too withdrawn or too outgoing. The 3 grows too old too soon or resists growing up. He totally relies on personality to get by or fails to use it altogether.

The number 3 challenge can give a superior talent for friendliness, humor, artistic expression, and optimism or the tendency to be intolerant, cynical, wasteful, or pessimistic. In any case, 3s are born communicators; they can light up a room when expressing joy or make everyone uncomfortable when experiencing sadness. Number 3 children's facade is a mirror of their mind, emotions, and heart. When experiencing the emotional extremes of the 3 challenge, these children or adults may be filled with love or hate. These children are melodramatic and can play Sarah Bernhardt when the stage is set.

As teens, 3s emote at the drop of a hat, or they are tight-lipped. They are extravagant—either heroes or losers. Threes are overly concerned with clothes, popularity, and confidants, or perceive themselves as mousy wallflowers. In the latter case, they are unconcerned about fads or fashions, devoted instead to the one friend who they feel understands them, listens, and brings out their sense of humor.

When married, they are jealous or detached. When problems that are brought on by their jealousy become too painful, 3s play a game of aloofness. To a balanced 3 spouse, their actions are childish, attesting to the axiom that 3s are not consistently mature adults. When the challenge pendulates, it swings between wide-eyed wonder and squinting disbelief.

As adults, 3s perceive friendship as the key that opens their door to love—or they never reveal themselves or make a commitment in order to build an alliance. They trust too much—accepting words, gestures, and people without sensing underlying factors—or suspiciously refuse to accept anything at face value.

To the 3 the telephone is an extension of the arm and the pen is the sword. They either employ words as their major tool, or they keep their mouths closed. At one extreme, they are observing and reclusive stars of their imaginary scenarios. If absorbed in social activities, they scatter time, energy, and money; yet, when withdrawn, 3s criticize wastefulness in others. As children, they have often had too much freedom from ordinary worries and responsibilities—or borne extraordinary burdens. They placed too much importance on friendships—or suffered troublesome social encounters that made them uncomfortable. In youth, 3s felt social pressures that had no avenue for expression or were talked to death but remained unresolved. As adults, 3s may gossip or they may be unable to engage in small talk.

Number 3 challenge holders often have deep feelings of inferiority or superiority. They are depressed or exhilarated and express themselves accordingly. They are unable to build faith in communication or to have the confidence to reveal their feelings. To 3 challenge holders, things are either superficial or very serious. This attitude may prove to be a detriment to business or social ambitions. For example, when a job or a date depends on establishing a positive self-image 3s may feel compelled by an urge to expand upon assets—even to fib or lie—or they may be too uncomfortable to speak well of themselves at all.

Round-shouldered stances, speech impediments, and excessive throat clearings are common 3 challenge habits, balanced by the beautiful eyes, unforgettable voices, and commanding presences that are commonly their gifts.

The defensive habits that grow forth from stress during youth contribute to a confusing adult personality. Scattering interests and assuming superiority are especially nonproductive habits. The 3 gets an idea, talks up the project, imagines it completed, and, without completing it, goes on to another. His ability to visualize is extraordinary: he possesses artistic talents, elfish charms, and castle-building dreams that are overextended or ignored in childhood and cannot find groundedness in the adult personality.

Threes feel deprived and escape reality through drink, drugs, multiple hobbies, or whatever makes them like themselves. They get attention by acting like spoiled children or play the role of domestic dictator; they utilize any means to manipulate the people they love the most. For instance, when reproached or ignored, they take actions to indicate that they prefer to be alone or with strangers. After becoming bored with self-imposed austerity and their own company, the dam breaks and the challenge holders turn back to seek companionship in multiple interests that are, in retrospect, materially unproductive. But their memories are self-deluding, and the pattern repeats until eventually the 3s balance their antisocial or overly talkative extremes and learn subtlety.

The number 3 challenge may swing from one of the following extremes to another until the challenge holder learns how, when, and why it is necessary to be self-expressive.

Too fashionable or too frumpy.
Too irresponsible or too upright.
Too superficial or too earthy.
Too talkative or too quiet.
Too austere or too playful.
Too fun-loving or too serious.
Too vain or too downgraded.
Too wasteful or too careful.
Too brave or too scared.
Too honest or too hypocritical.
Too artistic or too practical.
Too imaginative or too dull.
Too sociable or too alone.
Too optimistic or too pessimistic.

PHYSICAL CHALLENGES OF THE NUMBER 3

Challenges can affect physical as well as mental health. Body chemistry changes when individuals are stressed, and when we do not know what is good for us, our minds trigger anxious, angry, or frustrated habits. When we are mean to ourselves, we get sick. Our attitude sends the brain a message, and the brain tells the body to scream for help.

To get attention for their dis-ease, often people get sick or form negative habits. Numerologists believe that illness and wellness depend upon attitude, and challenges indicate the attitudes that result from needy feelings. When we do not feel needy, we feel well and balanced and do not crave attention from others. Essentially, if the personality challenges are balanced, the body chemistry is in balance, too, and therefore there is little chance of mental or physical dis-ease.

Challenge numbers indicate the ways people subconsciously punish themselves for not being consciously good to themselves.

The following list of dis-eases and negative habits relate to the challenge of the number 3.

Addictions	Migraine Headaches
Agoraphobia	Mononucleosis
Boils	Night Blindness
Bruises	Paralysis
Fear	Paranoia
Gas Pains	Shingles
High and Low Blood Pressure	Shoulder Problem
	Throat Clearing
Insanity	Urinary Tract Infections
Liver Problem	Wrinkles

TO BALANCE THE CHALLENGE OF THE 3 AND BRING IT OUT AS A TALENT . . .

The first step to balancing the challenge is to feel comfortable about saying "I need attention." Organize your closet: buy and maintain clothes that are appropriate to the occasions in your lifestyle. Stop wearing the same pair of dungarees or tie until they walk to the cleaner. To the other extreme, change the blouse or skirt instead of the entire outfit each day. Stop being too frumpy or too fashionable! Put a smile on your face, and feel confident knowing that a happy approach will get you everywhere.

Go to a party willingly, and walk over to the most interesting and attractive group. You belong with them. You don't need a drink to be a sparkling conversationalist or a lamp shade on your head to get attention. You were born with the gifts of gab, charm, and humor. Recognize adult game playing, joking, and social contacts as essential parts of responsible maturity. Enjoy taking center stage and sharing intimacies when the time is right.

Use the phone appropriately. If your phone bills are too big or below average, let others call you or pick up the phone to maintain your contacts. Try writing a letter, get a ham radio, or add a modem to your computer. Try keeping a diary or journal. Read your prose; you will be astonished at your own eloquence when you are alone or gaining admirers in a crowd. You do not have to be too obvious or too inconspicuous to be distinguished from—or by—others.

If you identify with the extremes discussed, change your tactics. Focus on your means of self-expression. Enhance and enlarge your options. Recognize your social responsibilities, and you will attract loving relationships, gifts, and financial success. You are a magnet for your own pleasures and shed happiness on others.

SELF-MOTIVATION

Youth:

As a tot, the number 3 urge that these children feel is to be cheerful, content, and imaginative. When reprimanded, these children will mope for a moment and bounce back with a twinkle in their eye. Threes need people, sunshine, and toys. These youngsters are charming, talkative, and funny, but if they are surrounded by austere authorities, they wilt or become overly dramatic. Overall, it can be said that 3s want attention and will try to be seen and heard.

Parents may describe their number 3 child as creative, effervescent, and merry. These words describe the individual when he is surrounded by affable, loving, and sociable authorities. If, however, the child's communications are viewed as silly and the parents are brusque and disapproving, the youngster may become dispirited and withdrawn. Number 3 youngsters want to dress up, entertain, and be entertained. Once this child, who has his feelings rooted in love for everyone, is pushed into the background, he will not be subtle. In fact, he will go to any extreme to be noticed.

Number 3 children need constant artistic and creative stimulation so that their various talents can be explored. These children should focus on one or two of these talents until one captures their undivided attention, as scattering interests is likely to be a problem in both childhood and maturity. Threes are genuinely interested in everything and everybody, and since they are outgoing, sitting still and studying will not be appealing to them. They love the limelight, and creative, faddish, lighthearted diversions will capture their imagination. Serious conversations, in turn, make them uncomfortable.

The strong-willed number 3 wants to use words to his own advantage. He will attempt to joke, tease, and talk, talk, talk to get away from unpleasantness. If caught in a fib or hyperbole, he may clam up. When chastised, he appears to be wounded or makes every effort to charm the listener into forgetting about the unpleasant situation. The 3 is attracted to colorful, beautiful objects and shies away from ugliness. It is difficult to remain angry with the number 3 personality kid when he is disobedient.

Friends and an active social life are foremost in the minds of number 3 teenagers. They have an urge to talk, and it is best to begin teaching proper telephone etiquette to them as preteens to avoid later problems in the family. To encourage them to write, parents should give 3s personalized stationery. Writing letters will sharpen their talents and skills, and they will be drawn to writing if the paper is attractive to them.

When the number 3 is also a challenge number, parents should also help these children develop a variety of communication skills. Dancing, singing, painting, or acting lessons, or any such means of training for self-expression, will attract positive feedback. Threes need to take an interest in people and the social graces. Friendships will get them everywhere.

If 3s have more introverted number meanings (2 and 7) in other aspects of their charts, those meanings will affect their tolerance for constant companionship. Regardless of relative obstacles, however, they will find a means of expressing themselves. In solitude, less outgoing teens may communicate by using ham radios, computer telephone modems, and complex stereo equipment. In general, however, balanced 3 teens want to be carefree, happy, popular young adults. When comfortably following their natural instincts, 3s enjoy a variety of interests, concentrate on learning to do one thing professionally, and greet maturity with optimism.

Maturity:

These adults want to be popular, witty, and well dressed. Threes need to see and talk to people. They want to feel that everyone is friendly and every day is sunny. If that seems a bit naive . . . it is, and 3s are. However, they are also the cockeyed optimists of song and fable: they are capable of seeing some humor in the bad times and bouncing back when the going is tough. They worry, but not for long.

Number 3 people do not like to be alone or tied to one interest. Rarely disloyal or unfaithful friends or mates, they do feel the need to flirt. They must have the latest adult toys— any new gadget, fashion, or entertainment that is newly advertised will strike their fancy. These role-players may like to relax with charades or word games. They adore children and pets, and correspondingly other youngsters are drawn to the cheery, interested, and youthful number 3 because they are kindred spirits.

The heart rules over the number 3 head. They are creative, affectionate make-believers who often place lovers, business associates, or family members on a pedestal. Threes try to encourage and enhance the attributes they see in their soulmates. They are extraordinarily positive visualizers. Adult 3s identify with Peter Pan, because they believe that dreams can come true, and, as self-fulfilling prophecy would have it, Tinkerbell often comes through.

Threes get an idea and, without letting it gel, imagine that it is a reality. This is the root cause of their dispersed time, energy, and money. Threes may be irresponsible or impractical butterflies who talk about more projects than they can handle. As time goes on, however, these individuals will realize that they must clarify, develop, and budget an idea. To attract the cooperation of practical associates, they must learn to maintain interests before moving on to another. To intimates, fun-loving

3s may seem to be childlike, superficial, or frivolous individuals not to be taken seriously. To avoid being considered persons of little substance, then, 3s must learn to hold their tongues. It is wiser to speak up when a new interest is cultivated and, more importantly, secure.

A craving for decorative environments that fit each mood urges number 3s to spend money uncautiously. Their love of beauty often makes them impulsive. Threes want to appear up-to-date and different, too. When wearing various clothing styles, they strike a different pose; their attitudes change to accommodate the fashion. When comfortable with themselves—doing what they want to do—3s may be talented models. Just the way an actress appears different—plays a role—using the words of various characters, models strike a pose based upon the type of clothing they are showing. Those with the number 3 self-motivation have the soul and desires of the designer's model and the performing artist.

Threes make a game out of everything, particularly shopping. They will spend their last dollar for a yellow rose to match their yellow place mats to beautify a dinner table. Tomorrow's bread and butter may not be as important as today's cake and coffee. If number 3s decide to invite a few friends in for a chat, correspondingly, they may snack by candlelight, because the electric bill has not been paid. Overall, 3s do not want to worry, work without rewards, or live a cheerless lifestyle.

Those with a 3 self-motivation require opportunities to show off talents, charm, and stylish clothes. They are restless and try to joke their ways through adversity. They may be naive, but with compatible numbers in their own charts (1, 3, 5, 6, 9) or a destiny that brings in people and opportunities needing their optimism, 3s get what they want. Gifts, friends, travels, and a variety of social activities may all come their way.

Balanced number 3s will want to have many choices and may display difficulty in intuitively knowing when to grow up.

The knight on the white charger or the ruby-lipped princess may be just around the corner; however, 3s should remember that stories beginning with "Once upon a time" have a moral. In other words, all too often 3s fantasize a fairy-tale relationship and have difficulty accepting mundane responsibilities.

Thus marriage for the balanced number 3 may be wonderful, but its practical realities may be terrible. It provides him with a live-in audience and a friend for life, but if extravagant personal desires tax the family budget, even the lively 3 may not be able to get a laugh with jokes about poverty. The multifaceted 3 must therefore cultivate financial discipline to hold on to a lover's adoration and support.

It follows that the marriage of two number 3 motivations may not be practical. Two people who love to spend money, do not want to be troubled by unasked-for obligations, and gravitate toward the lighter side of life may create an irresponsible muddle out of their union. Threes will not want to worry about bills, unfinished projects, or tight schedules. Since the self-motivation number describes what we need to be comfortable, the partnership of two number 3 motivations may result in a happy-go-lucky, self-indulgent existence. This is so because as a unit they instinctively resist maturity and the practical need to grow worldly wise.

SELF-IMAGE

Youth:

When lying on the bed, listening to music, and imagining "What am I going to be like when I grow up? How will I walk, dress, and talk?" the number 3 preteens visualize themselves becoming stars. Babies look like dolls, tots are animated charmers, and kindergartners make friends the first day of school. Teens dream of receiving the Academy Award and see themselves upstaging Paul Newman or Meryl Streep. Children with the number 3 self-image picture themselves as scene stealers: fashion models, actors, artists, and writers.

Threes may be first to reach the hair dryer and last out of the bathroom. These noticeable individuals cannot pass up a mirror or a ringing telephone. They are always ready to tease or be teased. It is 3s' greatest joy to make others happy. When they are well dressed, groomed, and prepared to greet their public, they are happy.

The number 3 self-image relates intensely to getting attention. Accordingly, 3s may try every fashion and fad that comes along. They appear to be animated, popular, and amusing, and their youthful wish is to have the versatility to offer the world some expression of beauty, joy, or wit. At times, 3s may seem to overact and overreact, but when feeling in tune with their self-image, their personalities will alter to fit the environment or others' expectations.

As youths, 3s dress colorfully. They carry out trends, appreciate costumes, and have fashion sense. They also often succumb to peer pressures that influence them unduly. Threes may not realize their natural beauty, but when surrounded by people, they come to life. Balanced number 3s have an unforgettable presence, smile, and voice.

When living up to their self-image, number 3s will be witty, show uncommon poise, and lift the mood of any group. When out of balance, however, they may be too talkative, lack subtlety, and appear awkward. Yet again, if these number 3s are supported by a self-motivation or self-expression number 3, they are absolute traffic-stoppers.

Maturity:

When walking out of an elevator or into a room—before personality or intellect come into play—the number 3 adult sends out an attractive and friendly vibration. His attitude indicates a lively personality, he is brimming with cordiality. His first impression is one of welcome, and even if self-motivation and self-expression numbers are introverted or send out businesslike vibrations, the number 3 will still catch every eye. Clothing styles, posture, and attitude speak for him when he chooses silence.

When 3s are wearing the color yellow, the self-image is emphasized. Threes do not have to speak or move to make everyone notice them. In essence, number 3s possess the communication gifts of the model and the performing or creative artist. It is number 3s' greatest desire to have their dramatic fantasies come true. Correspondingly the first impression of number 3s may transport onlookers away from reality and into a world of the 3s' own fantasy.

Number 3 adults perceive themselves as highly sought-after people. When living up to their self-image, their first impression implies beauty, talent, and optimism.

The self-expression number may govern the first impression if uniforms, stylized business dress codes, or fads are indicated by the career descriptions included in the meaning of the number.

The self-motivation number may influence the apparel of the bearer if he is relaxing and doing what he desires to do. However, when the individual is intent upon living up to his self-image, he should feature its correspondent color.

SELF-EXPRESSION

Youth:

It is obvious to adults when children have a number 3 self-expression number, because in youth number 3 talents are based on friendliness, imaginativeness, and artistic talent. As they get older number 3s discover they can talk, dramatize, or joke their way into or out of practical work or appropriate responsibilities. When frustrated, they may appear to be too cute, silly, or theatrical. As charming, personable, and trusting little hams, it is difficult for them to stifle their imaginations or to quiet their chatter.

Without intending to lie, the dramatic number 3 may alter the facts, mimic, or playact. Threes strive to make themselves attractive or a story more interesting. To pragmatic, down-to-earth, unimaginative parents, they may appear to be too frivolous, long-winded, or fanciful. To outgoing, gregarious, creative adults, on the other hand, number 3 children are accepted as charmers and will likely be spoiled.

Number 3 talents put the child in the limelight. He will be a more fertile-minded, literate, and tasteful adult if encouraged to verbalize, paint, play an instrument, dance, or write. His flashes of artistic and creative talent will be noticed by authorities, and, once given praise, his blithe spirit will carry him to a broad, appreciative audience.

As teenagers and young adults, number 3s are lovable and responsive, and when well balanced, they are vivacious scene-stealers. These teens get the lead in a play, design the sets, or write the original script. They are natural performers and have a gift for memorizing and wearing costumes. These children of light shy away from solitude, intellectual analysis, and disapproval. Threes are ready to let the world know they have arrived. They invite companionship as an expression of their joy in life.

Self-expressive number 3 children may say whatever pops into their mind and may be intractable in a routine. They are the first to invent playmates if left alone as tots and usually talk before they can walk. These children should be encouraged to read, as books may be their door to vocabulary and the world if they are unable to socialize. Generally number 3s will learn by participating or watching. Tots, teens, and youths should therefore be encouraged to concentrate, complete commitments, and smile. A charming happy personality will be their key to success.

Maturity:

Suggested Occupations: Writing—and all means of self-expression with a focus on words. Entertainer, model, actor/actress, designer, artist, musician, singer, salesperson, decorator, lecturer, lyricist, cosmetologist, hairdresser, fashion stylist, jeweler, milliner, receptionist, social worker, kindergarten teacher, personnel director, recreation worker, professional game player, social secretary, boutique merchandise buyer,

bookshop owner, telephone operator, gift wrapper, evangelist, advertising account executive, promoter, trial lawyer, druggist, cartoonist, humorist, photojournalist, poet, photographer's assistant, plastic surgeon, electrologist, restaurant host/hostess.
Options:

Careers that are indicated by the meaning of the self-motivation number may not make use of readily available talents but will allow the individual to feel comfortable.

Careers indicated by the self-image number meanings will encourage the individual to live up to youthful dreams.

Careers indicated by the meaning of the destiny number, if it is not the same as the self-expression number, will require that the individual learn from incoming personalities and experiences.

If self-expression and destiny numbers are the same, the individual's talents will be recognized and utilized early in life.
Maturity: Self-expression Analysis

The 3 has a potential for financial rewards for his ability to express youthfulness, friendliness, beauty, charm, talent, and wit. Recognition is possible for his talent with words. The 3 draws people to him, using the basic ingredient of his personality—his ability to communicate. The animated 3 sends out a vibration that puts him in the limelight and brightens the lives of less expressive people.

Number 3 talents must recognize their own need for optimism and their desire for a variety of interests. In a business environment 3s should make an effort to adhere to routines and systems, as socializing and amusing diversions may or may not be part of the job. If their careers require a diversification of attitudes, number 3s have the cleverness to play the appropriate role at the right time. Balanced 3s may be depended upon to speak up and express their feelings. They are generally a fashionable, approachable, fertile-minded asset to any business.

Threes must select a job that allows them freedom to use their imaginations. An unattractive office or inhospitable associates may force number 3s to quit a lucrative job. Beauty and cheerfulness help them to maintain optimism and serenity; these are the ingredients that 3s need to further their ambitions. As people who attract people and who need interaction, 3s are uncomfortable working alone or going unnoticed. They have the ability to find something good about everyone and appreciate all efforts made in their behalf.

In selecting a career, cerebral number 3s may choose to write fiction, content with the attention that publication attracts. In contrast, the more emotional individuals will aim for theater, lecturing to receive immediate feedback. And finally, less disciplined number 3 communicators will play in the social whirl, finding careers as social secretaries, hairdressers, or fashion boutique salespeople.

Those with the number 3 self-expression should not have trouble talking themselves into a job. Because of their expressive talents, the telephone and mail will be important aspects of any trade they select. Career problems for the 3 may stem from a lack of concentration, from impracticality, or from temperament, while mixing business and social activity work well for balanced number 3s. Negative aspects of number 3 talents are their extravagance, moodiness, and superficial interests. Compliments and sales pitches are easy to come by and easily given; however, 3s may become victims of their own vanity or their extreme willingness to show appreciation. They may be duped by words or flimflam others *with words*.

Number 3 salespeople are the easiest people to sell something to, as they know the value of a good sales pitch. Self-promoting clients, auditioning producers, and judges of art will be quick to spot the 3s' talents. They bring their ideas to life by breaking down the barrier between imagination and reality. The result is that they sell themselves in any career they choose.

DESTINY

WE ARE NOT BORN KNOWING WHAT LIFE HAS TO
OFFER. INDIVIDUALS WITH THE NUMBER 3 DESTINY
LEARN TO DEVELOP IMAGINATION, ARTISTIC ABILI-
TIES, AND PERSONALITY. THEY ENCOUNTER THE
PEOPLE AND EXPERIENCES THAT TEACH THEM TO
ENJOY LIFE AND TO VALUE BEAUTY, CHARM, AND
WIT.

This destiny appears to be the easiest of all to learn. It
implies a lifetime of seeking self-expression, companionship,
and artistic creativity. To make the most of numerology's ability to forecast, the number 3 must be sociable, fashionable,
and optimistic.

The number 3 individual may be a late bloomer. He may
be born with a charming personality but take half a lifetime
to develop his talents. When 3 learns that friendships open
doors, a sense of humor helps through the rough spots, and
an attractive personality greases his path, he attracts the people
who will ultimately relate to him. The number 3 destiny should
seek out an appropriate lifestyle that includes emotional, artistically creative, and self-expressive people.

Number 3 destiny holders must learn to keep up with the
times and stay youthful. People with attention-getting ideas
and a love of beauty are the companions to help further this
destiny's purpose. Threes should therefore focus on cultivating
contacts, talents, and pleasures. People who laugh eagerly,
play easily, and live on the lighter side of life exemplify the
3 destiny. Negative 3s may start out being antisocial, serious,
or suffocatingly responsible, but life experiences will change
that perspective over time.

There are no limits to the possibilities that a charming,
cordial, amusing personality will attract for those with a number 3 destiny. They may create opportunities by dressing fash-
ionably, being responsive, and doing a variety of currently

interesting things. If 3s do not let the vicissitudes of life make them cynical, critical, and mercenary, optimistic people with the number 3 self-motivation or -expression number will show them the way to enjoy whatever comes to them.

Children with the 3 destiny are not necessarily self-expressive unless their self-motivation or self-expression numbers are 3s, too. As time passes they create beautiful surroundings and look for imaginative companions. Opportunities will arise for them to meet "the beautiful people," and eventually 3s will be prepared to take center stage. They recognize their ability to help others live more happily. Number 3 destiny holders also learn to heal their own and others' sunken spirits by giving a token of love, sharing a joke, or responding with a kind word.

It is essential that those with the number 3 destiny find a way to shine in society. To progress, they must relate to all people, communicate with them, and share their purposes. Threes should not appear bored, snobbish, or cocky; brusqueness, gloominess, and inarticulateness push away the multifaceted, vivacious, and amicable strangers who are in the same destiny and who will want to become friends and boosters.

Individuals with the number 3 destiny should form partnerships or marry people with the number 3 as a self-expression or self-motivation number, who know what the number 3 destiny is intended to learn. The marriage or partnership of two number 3 destinies will make a game out of life, but will not promise material security. Such a relationship will never be dull—life will offer few heavy responsibilities and a kaleidoscope of experiences. The success of the union will hinge on the necessity for spouses to join together in a concentration and to learn to be good friends and a responsible unit. This union may make solo self-expression a problem, but as a duet, the partners may make beautiful music.

BIRTHDAY INFLUENCES
WITHIN THE DESTINY

March and December

Individuals born in March and December learn to get along with people in youth. Situations arise to teach them to be articulate, up-to-date, and personable. They may not be geared to academic concentrations, looking instead for opportunities to express their artistic talents. They learn to be entertaining, friendly, and socially ambitious, and their early years offer opportunities to encounter clever, talented, entertaining, and attractive people.

Childhood exposure to various experiences may lead to instability or confusion as to which career choice to make. If they did not find a concentration in youth, people born in March or December may bring frivolous interests into maturity. If these children are too scattered and self-indulgent, or un-disciplined, basic adult responsibilities may appear to be road-blocks to happiness. Youngsters born in March and December learn to make themselves desirable companions instead of ac-ademic whiz kids. They have a sense of humor, speak their mind, and make friends easily.

Birthday: 3, 12, 21, 30

THE BIRTHDAY NUMBER HAS AN INFLUENCE ON PERSONALITY AND DESTINY. IT ATTRACTS PEOPLE AND EXPERIENCES DURING MID-LIFE THAT EXEM-PLIFY THE NUMBER MEANING.

The mid-life productivity cycle begins with maturity. It lasts from approximately twenty-eight to fifty-five years of age and coordinates with the destiny during that time span. The birthday-number meaning adds its character traits and expe-riences to an individual's numerology analysis.

People born on the third, twelfth, twenty-first, and thir-tieth of the month, in addition to the character traits outlined by the number meanings for the name, are imaginative, optimistic, and inspired by life. They will be unhappy alone or without a means of self-expression. Individuals born on these dates are communicators; they must be seen and heard.

Between approximately twenty-eight and fifty-five years of age—the twenty-seven-year productivity cycle within the destiny—life will offer additional opportunities to be successful in the creative arts, decorating, entertaining, or any industry that uses words as a primary medium. People born on these dates have memorable speaking or singing voices and extremely expressive eyes. Attention to clothes, grooming, and social contacts compete with a love of children, pets, and a variety of fashion-related interests. People born on these dates should stifle restlessness and avoid squandering time, energy, and money. Through a talent for attracting gifts and the limelight even as adults, people born on the third, twelfth, twenty-first, and thirtieth have a childlike belief that "everyone lives happily ever after," or if that does not work out, Tinkerbell or Nana will save the day.

PERSONAL YEAR

The number 3 is the third year in the cycle of nine years of experience and results in a polish and skill of performance based upon goals set in the first year. It is the time to see ideas and instigations that began two years before come to fruition. For most, it is a welcome change from the preceding year's petty problems, delays, and emotional concerns. It is a year offering opportunities to enjoy lighter interests and increase social contacts. The 3 personal year requires attention to fashions, fads, and fancies. Shop for clothes. Do some home decorating. Create an atmosphere that attracts fun.

Love and happiness are offered with few strings attached. The focus is on telephone and mail contacts to activate social and commercial opportunities. This is a year to ease work loads, take time to play, and vacation. Parties, artistic skills, and delightful people should be the focus. Friends open the door to business, fun, and gifts.

Most months are lively, April and August being the exceptions. Old and new relationships should be encouraged. Talk may be all that is accomplished until October, but the subjects for discussion will bring in work and material assets for the following year. For people with a 3 destiny, this year's opportunities will be unforgettable; however, they must keep major goals in mind and avoid wasting time and money while exploring and expanding avenues of self-expression.

This is a year for pleasure. Romance may flourish and should be viewed with youthful zest. Associates may need a listening ear, and the number 3 should be ready with a joke, uplifting advice, and positive attitudes, making his presence felt and prepared to greet each day with a smile. A happy, gracious, eager attitude will attract the people and experiences that make this year worthwhile.

During the number 3 personal year, contacts will be made that bring in social activity or attract responses for creative endeavors. The number 4 work year that follows will not be geared to impractical or unconstructive activities. This year has a purpose—to relieve tensions and burdens. It allows time to watch others entertain or to improve creative methods. The year revivifies interest in and understanding of the joys one may feel when relating to other people. It sparks humor and reminds one that life can be beautiful. Part of the purpose of the number 3 personal year is to remind adults that the child within still lives.

PERSONAL MONTH

The number 3 personal month within any personal year gives one an opportunity to feel lighthearted, playful, and self-expressive. Lively companions, parties, and all forms of communication are important now. This is not the time to pout and become reclusive. After last month's slowdowns, seize this month to get out to be seen and heard. The projects begun two months ago will blossom now. This is the time to talk them out. Situations arise that require an attractive appearance and a happy facade. Call old friends. Take a phone number at a party and be sure to call to make a new contact. Shop for clothes and decorative household items. Be primed to entertain and be entertained. Use this month to verbalize ideas, show off talents, and have fun interacting with friends and loved ones.

PERSONAL DAY

Wake up with a happy, lively, and friendly attitude. Whether you are heading for an office, a vacation day, or the Laundromat, sing a lilting tune on the way. Call a friend for dinner, or expect an invitation. Make this day cheerful and maintain an optimistic attitude. Work may feel like play, and if that is the case, your frame of mind will be contagious. Spread good news or a joke, and dress to get attention. Latch onto enjoyment, and give others the pleasure of your company.

You may note a lot of talk yet very little getting done. This is the day that sets the stage for tomorrow's self-discipline and practical approach. Use today to make someone smile. Do not let doom-predictors or gloom-spreaders dampen anyone's spirit.

Hobby and conversation time are available now. Go to the theater. Play with children and pets. Snuggle up with a humorous lover or book and enjoy a good laugh. Ease up on routines, and relax material objectives. Be the one to pick up the phone, and make time to listen and respond. Above all, stay on the sunny side, and stifle talk about personal troubles and anxieties.

Take whatever comes in today with a grain of salt, and realize that what may seem to be concerns are really just superficial and will not materialize. Some conversations will involve projects requiring tomorrow's opportunities for practical planning. This active day should be used to relax, kid around, and brainstorm with positive thinkers.

CHAPTER EIGHT

NUMBER 4

Practicality

Practicality

ATTRIBUTES:
POSITIVE—Practical, Disciplined, Loyal, Organized, Orderly, Factual, Frank, Constructive, Cautious
NEGATIVE—Unproductive, Incompetent, Lax, Inflexible, Careless, Crude, Penurious, Rigid, Plodding

CORRESPONDENTS:
LETTERS: D, M, V
EVEN NUMBER: Receptive
DISPOSITION: Sensible; Down-to-Earth.
NUMBERS: 13, 22, 31, 40, 49, 58, 67, 76, 85, 94, 103
COLOR: Green
GEMS: Emerald, Green Jade
CRYSTAL: Cassiterite (Tinstone)
VEGETATION: Sweet Pea, Pepper, Bean
FOODS: Grapefruit, Oysters, Veal, Ham, Cod, Yams, Carrots, Pumpkin Pie, Strawberries, Pretzels, Honey, Coffee.
MUSICAL INSTRUMENTS/APPEAL: Fiddle, Guitar, Lute; Instrumental.

MUSICAL NOTE: F#
LOCATIONS: State: Alabama, Mississippi, New Hampshire, North Carolina, Oklahoma, Washington
City: Birmingham, Boston, Canton, Dallas, Danbury, Des Moines, Houston, Jersey City, Reading, St. Joseph, Tallahassee
PLANET: Saturn
MONTH: April
BIRTHDAYS: 4, 13, 22, 31
DAY OF THE WEEK: Thursday
GENERAL COMPATIBILITY NUMBERS: 2, 6, 8
INCOMPATIBILITY NUMBERS: 3, 5, 7, 9

Note: If an individual has the challenge to the number 4, these descriptions will swing from positive to negative until the challenge is balanced. Please be sure to read the challenge meaning.

CHALLENGE OF THE NUMBER 4

This is a challenge to the individual's attention to traditions, organizational abilities, and understanding of practical realities. It stems from a childhood that focused on material objectives and controls rather than creativity. Often the child lacked contact with people who were responsive to his needs. Parents strove to give the child a routine, externals, and a proper upbringing—or the child's environment lacked conventional planning, practical necessities, and stability. As a result, the child becomes an extremely organized, self-disciplined, and conservative—or unindustrious, careless, and shiftless—adult.

The child may have been toilet trained with a whip. Schedules and specifics were detailed by authorities before the 4 even had the emotional or physical capacity to comply with demands. Or the number 4 may not have repeated many routines, and his authorities may not have expected great accomplishments or instilled in him the importance of maintaining schedules. Either extreme causes a child frustration and prompts him to look for ways to plan and structure the future. He either develops preventive methods and controls, or he abhors systems.

As adults, 4s often concentrate too much on the details and system. They plan and customize everything and find it difficult to produce a product without straining themselves. Often 4 working parents, in their need to manage children and a job, choose parochial or military schools as an ideal secondary training ground. If these children are individualistic, creative, and imaginative, these rigid educational systems may make them feel like fish out of water. Conversely, if they are spared the rod and standards, they may not learn that leadership and artistry require concentration and discipline, too. For the challenge 4 holders there are either too many rules and guidelines or a lack thereof, which limit these children's ability to bend or toughen up when there is a practical necessity to do so.

The teenager who is given a fair proportion of chores, adequate clothing, and free time to let the imagination roam, will not have this challenge. The youngster who only perceives emotional sensitivity and receives recognition when conventionally living up to parental ambitions will rebel in time. He will conceal his excursions into nonconformity in youth and become an adult who fights the system surreptitiously.

Number 4 challenge holders are either scrupulously honest or underhandedly dishonest. They may chase someone for blocks who has dropped a penny or keep the extra ten dollars in change that a cashier accidentally gives them. They are wedded to custom, preach the work ethic, or unconventionally have children without the formality of marriage. They may refuse to cross at the green, ridicule the bureaucrats, or conventionally marry because they have conceived a child. Either they are lazy and undisciplined, or they work eight days a week. They may plan twenty-eight hours of accomplishment for each day but must get sick to allow themselves a vacation.

These are the children who went to school at their own discretion or were not allowed to take a day off unless they were
very sick.

When challenge 4 people are chided into taking a vacation,
they rationalize its necessity. They may combine business with
a peer-pressured cultural accomplishment, the planning and
execution of which may be a job in itself. Either economy is
foremost or concern about cost is thrown to the winds. Vacation usually follows a crisis, as 4s must have an excuse to
take a rest. Fun for fun's sake and relaxation of schedules has
to be earned—if acknowledged at all. After a few days of
forced leisure, these workaholic vacationers are on edge and
ready to repeat the pattern again.

Large sums of money are never readily available, and yet
when number 4 challenge holders buy something they want
or think is required to maintain the standards of their peers,
they unreasonably spend top dollar to get the highest quality.
Fours save money and wear and tear on the car or furniture
religiously or they rarely keep a bankbook, buy a new car, or
wipe their feet before lying on a sofa. They either do not
concern themselves with pensions for later years, or continue
to focus unrealistically on the rainy days ahead even when they
are financially secure.

Most number 4 challenge holders have *very* kinky or *very*
traditional sensual tendencies. When they discover that ordinary foreplay does not turn them on, they seek unconventional methods that release self-imposed daily pressures—or
they do only what is expected. The wife of a number 4 challenge holder once said, "It is difficult to hug a machine." Many
number 4 challenge holders may want affection but repel shows
of affection with their austerity. Sex, love, marriage, and material ambitions are either calculated or disregarded. To a future
mother-in-law, 4s are the perfect or the worst possible candidates for provider or homemaker.

Intolerance of different customs, methods, and lifestyles

may incline the number 4 challenge bearer to be a social bore, an Archie Bunker. He is often too bigoted to be placed in a position of leadership. To an impersonal observer, he may appear to be a prudent, hardworking, practical achiever, and he is; however, a too traditional or too unconventional background has not prepared such a child for experimentation. The result is that he does not understand that circumstances may arise in which rules must be bent or broken. The challenge 4 holder interprets everything practical through a black-or-white filter. He has no point of reference for changing or bending, so it is difficult for him not to get into a rut when he can only conceive personal plans for the future by past performances. The challenge number 4 holder is a firm believer and often dogmatic communicator. He must learn to observe innovators, try things himself, and adjust his rules. His talent for self-discipline either goes unrecognized or is a crutch that limits his options.

The number 4 challenge may swing from one of the following extremes to another until the challenge holder's behavior is recognized and new habits are initiated that update his practical assessments of himself.

Too disciplined or too lackadaisical.
Too austere or too informal.
Too forceful or too limited.
Too practical or too impractical.
Too economical or too wasteful.
Too managerial or too unprepared.
Too thorough or too careless.
Too rigid or too loose.
Too puritanical or too kinky.
Too stubborn or too flexible.
Too ritual or too nonhabitual.
Too lazy or too busy.
Too intolerant or too open.
Too repressed or too free.

PHYSICAL CHALLENGES OF
THE NUMBER 4

Challenges can affect physical as well as mental health. Body chemistry changes when individuals are stressed, and when we do not know what is good for us, our minds trigger anxious, angry, or frustrated habits. When we are mean to ourselves, we get sick. One's attitude sends the brain a message, and the brain tells the body to scream for help.

To get attention for their dis-ease, often people get sick or form negative habits. Numerologists believe that illness and wellness depend upon attitude, and challenges indicate the attitudes that result from needy feelings. When we do not feel needy, we feel well and balanced and do not crave attention from others. Essentially, if the personality challenges are balanced, the body chemistry is in balance, too, and therefore there is little chance of mental or physical dis-ease.

Challenge numbers indicate the ways people subconsciously punish themselves for not being consciously good to themselves.

The following list of dis-eases and negative habits relate to the challenge of the number 4.

Abortion	Hypoglycemia
Blood Problems	Insomnia
Car Sickness	Jaundice
Cataract	Liver Problems
Cyst	Migraine Headaches
Foot Tapping	Rickets
Gas Pains	Shoulder Problems
Genital Herpes	Teeth Problem
Halitosis	Thumb Sucking

TO BALANCE THE CHALLENGE OF THE 4 AND BRING IT OUT AS A TALENT . . .

The first step to balancing the challenge is to feel comfortable about saying "I need security." Forget the approach that is too serious or too free. Only place those restrictions on yourself that enable you to live today, and plan as if you were going to live a thousand years. You have a choice. Listen to your feelings. Hug an acquaintance. Try loosening up— you may like it.

Apply yourself to a sensible work load and schedule. Work five days a week, and save your weekends for play. Keep appointments, maintain a daily planner, and keep track of business and social limitations. You will be able to maintain a slow but stable lifestyle that will give you long-term security. Spend money on necessities, and save for pleasures.

Cut down on detail work if the routines seem unending. Reschedule plans that keep you from experiencing the enjoyable emotional reactions and receiving the affection you deserve. Think about easing up on restrictions that you can relax and strengthening those that are required. Be practical, but not to the point of losing emotional contacts.

If you are always doing "the right thing," ask yourself if you are enjoying it, too. You will be surprised to learn that many people find you acceptable—even more likable—when you let down your hair.

You may find yourself planning carefully for your retirement instead of playing just a little. Make room for serendipity . . . as well as accidents. When you leave the post office box on the day you receive your first pension check, a flowerpot may fall on your head. It is prudent to plan, but plans can always change. You recognize yourself as a sensible, hardworking, conventional, material achiever. But a solid person such as you certainly has the right to take a break from routines. You must exercise free will, take a few risks, and make a few mistakes along the way.

SELF-MOTIVATION

Youth:

As a tot, the number 4 urge that these children feel is to be careful, consistent, and dutiful. When reprimanded, these children will grope for the rule or routine that will put them back on firm footing. These tots need straightforward instructions and discipline. Number 4 youngsters are conforming, conscientious, and earnest. If surrounded by disorganized authorities, they will become negligent or stubborn. They need and crave coolheaded, constructive, and principled leadership.

Parents may describe their number 4 child as dependable, determined, and methodical; these words describe the individual when he is surrounded by controlled, sober, and trustworthy authorities. But if parents consider the child's industriousness unnecessary and disregard the need to provide him with painstaking service, the child may become impassive and contradictory. The number 4 youngster wants to organize, manage, and build. Once this child, whose feelings are rooted in law-abiding devotion, is pushed into uncertainty or narrow-mindedness, he will not be aggressive; instead he will become thick-skinned and perverse.

Number 4 children need to exhibit their preparedness, endurance, and ability to turn detailed directions into tangible results. Their various abilities should be channeled in a way that employs their awareness of thrift and efficiency. Piano, guitar, or sports instruction can put to good use their ability to coordinate mind and body. Fours will constantly practice because they understand the role of repetition in achieving and maintaining their goals.

Fours are genuinely interested in maintaining conventions and traditions. Since they are so dignified, gushing shows of love and intimacy may not appeal to them. They love respectability, regularity, and unpretentiousness; family, community, and national pride will capture their loyalty. However, too much self-discipline may prove problematic in maturity if these children do not receive warmth and affection.

The strong-willed number 4 wants to employ proved methods. He is attracted to building blocks, sculpting clays, and constructive toys. He may shy away from creative paints, choosing to collect materials for collages instead. New games and relationships must be studied. If caught being wasteful or disobedient, the 4 may be indifferent and react with submission or stiffness. It is difficult for the number 4 child to be innovative or totally independent until a stable behavior pattern is established with and for him.

Friends and an active social life may not be foremost in the minds of number 4 teenagers. They may be pragmatic conversationalists, and frank, honest, controlled peer relationships tend to attract them. Fours have an urge to apply themselves to a task and finish it before they take time to relax. It is best to teach them to plan for vacations and entertainments. Baby-sitting, paper routes, and neighborhood jobs will satisfy the number 4 teens' need to have the money to accumulate the products they want. They should be encouraged to patiently work and save to own the things that make them comfortable. If the number 4 is also a challenge number, material rewards and unexpected gifts may be the only signs of love they understand.

Impractical number meanings in other aspects of the 4 youth's chart will affect his productivity negatively. He will nevertheless find a means of expressing his need for security and systemization in projects such as auto repairs, woodworking, and school managerial projects. In order to be a systematic young adult, a 4 should enjoy having a definite plan, for which he will want to organize the priorities and meticulously carry out the details.

Maturity:

Number 4 adults want to be deliberate, industrious, and reliable. They need to painstakingly structure and manage jobs or goals and to feel solid, constant, and proper. If this posture seems a bit inflexible and resistant to novelties, it is. But 4s are often the loyal disciplinarians and patriots who serve our country and love law and order. They are capable of profound self-sacrifice and feel that without principles or commitment, stability is an impossible dream. Fours work toward an orderly, unwavering prosperity.

Number 4 people do not like to be discourteous or compromising. Rarely unrefined or crude friends or lovers, they do need to know what is expected of them to provide for another's wishes. Fours must have their duties outlined, and any reliable convention, dependable leader, or practical tool will command their attention. These individuals prefer prudent objectives and have reasonable expectations. Youngsters in their care are taught to obey and to be self-possessed and thorough. When able to follow their natural instincts, adults motivated by the 4 are imperturbable, firm, and practical parents.

Fours want material objectives and are most comfortable with people who labor to provide traditional necessities and help them build for the future. Lovers and mates can expect down-to-earth assessments and impartial judgments. In return, 4s want expressiveness, support, and integrity. These self-restrained individuals may appear to be oblivious of outpourings of affection; however, they do need and appreciate love. One may expect 4 spouses to celebrate a birthday with a new dishwasher or an automatic garage door opener.

One problem for those with a number 4 self-motivation is a fear of altering routines. They imagine that loosening up will cause confusion, problems, and loss of control. Fours may therefore have to learn to let go of outdated methods and to upgrade others. These individuals are businesslike achievers, and over time accomplish most of their social and material objectives. Yet 4s must develop an open mind and focus on progressive changes.

To modernize their foundation and maintain a progressively stable lifestyle, people motivated by the number 4 should not allow themselves to be inundated by preventative details. They can avoid overdoing the "I will do what has to be done" tendency by learning to respect intuitive feelings and taking actions based on urges rather than reason.

An obsession with paid-up bills and a good reputation make the 4s careful investors. Fours want to appear creditworthy and in accordance with society. They are most comfortable in conservative colors, durable fabrics, and traditional clothing styles. They save fuel and invest in classic cars that have resale value, and they prefer expanding, suburban environments where property values safely grow.

Fours do not like to pay for services, interest rates, or frills. Tenacious number 4s are only content when they are rid of car payments, children's college tuition payments, and the home mortgage. Only then will they begin to check out the merits of investing in a retirement travel-camper—that will hopefully appreciate—and to plan on retirement.

Economical 4s who want bargains and value for their money are careful shoppers. They will never spend their last dollar. The truly precautionary extremists have their first paycheck in the bank or invested in a burial plot. Tomorrow's cloudy day is always expected, and today's momentary feelings to get out of a rut are either put on the shelf or rationalized away as momentary madness. Fours want to work and live with the assurance that they have covered all bases and can stay in the game.

Balanced number 4s will realistically analyze the future. Desires are saved for, and impulsiveness is frowned upon. They establish a logical time to marry and do not condone or relate to Elizabeth Taylor's or George Hamilton's lifestyle. Too often they wed or form partnerships with equally methodical people. Such practical alliances make them feel that their orderly existence will go undisturbed.

Marriage for the number 4 can be wonderful with a less rigid and more expressive mate. However, if his austerity and economical habits limit spontaneous ideas, the relationship will be limited by a lack of shared feelings. Eventually a creative or unconventional mate may either look to others for emotional excitement—or become uncomfortably reconciled to a relationship based upon financial necessity.

The marriage of two number 4 motivations may be very good for business and friendship. They will be loyal, dedicated, and trustworthy. However, the union will be limited by the shared goals of maintaining routines, saving for rainy days, and accounting for family stability. This may be a boring combination, and the union may result unhappily in a plodding lifestyle. If hamburgers and french fries are the family favorite, family members may never try veal scaloppine or potatoes au gratin.

Two 4s in love should focus on finding new points of view, with one taking the executive leadership role. One partner must fight the natural instinct to polish the furniture or the car and occasionally lead the other out the door for a second honeymoon. In a long-term relationship it is worthwhile to remember that feelings must be tended to as much as the most treasured of possessions. Experiences should be counted as money in the bank. Feelings should be acknowledged, and joint investigations into physical fitness projects, investment plans, and vacation spots may keep a 4 x 4 relationship from becoming too square.

SELF-IMAGE

Youth:

When lying on the bed, listening to music, and imagining "What am I going to be like when I grow up?" number 4s visualize themselves as solid citizens. They dream of living well-ordered, respected, and appreciated lives. Little boys see themselves as national protectors receiving their countries' highest awards for duty. Little girls see themselves owning and diligently maintaining a white house with a green lawn, safely secured by a traditional picket fence. Children with the number 4 self-image picture themselves as industrious, dignified, and orderly self-disciplinarians.

Fours may appear to be studious, quiet, and reserved children who are manually dexterous and enjoy fixing things. When number 4s say they want to join the army, police force, or fire department, they envision themselves in the appropriate uniform with their work cut out for them. When living up to their self-image, 4s will be the first to apply themselves to a practical problem, do the detail work, and figure out a system to avoid the same problem in the future. They depend only on things they can touch, smell, spend, hear, or feel.

Youngsters with dreams based upon the meaning of the number 4 may be blunt and straightforward. They will often actively assert themselves in order to maintain their security. Fours' overall appearance is neat and natural, sturdy and classically attractive. Not ones to overdo first impressions, they are uncluttered, utilitarian dressers who prefer neutral or earth tones. When they are in tune with their self-image, 4 style is focused on the proper attire for a given activity or social occasion.

Rarely time or energy wasters, 4s put one foot in front of the other with an athlete's sense of balance and the caution to walk along a designated path. Only an emergency could excite them enough to ignore a DO NOT STEP ON THE GRASS sign, park a bike without locking it, or show gratitude with a smothering bear hug. They can be counted on to follow protocol, and they expect the same from others.

As youths, 4s are not concerned about trends, fads, or short-lived fashions. When surrounded by lively, enthusiastic peers, they may appear slow or exacting. It is their dream to be in control of the people and situations they encounter, as excitable people make them uncomfortable and they balk when hurried or unsettled. The number 4 self-image indicates a sturdy body and a dignified presence. These individuals tend to concentrate on good posture, which makes them appear to be taller than they really are. When defensive, disorganized, or undecided, their faces appear drawn and serious.

When living up to their self-image, 4s surround themselves with equals. They frown upon dishonesty, superficiality, and cowardice, and when out of balance, they may be disorganized, critical, obstinate, or caught in a fruitless maze of precautionary measures. Those whose 4 self-image is supported by a self-motivation or self-expression number 4 may be too self-limiting. Often they lock themselves into complicated procedures that have them forget their main objectives. Therefore frustrated number 4 youths should be encouraged to establish priorities, make realistic decisions, and assume short-term leadership positions. Fours should excel as organizers when experienced at their job and secure enough to allow others to carry out their directions.

Maturity:

When walking out of an elevator or into a room—before personality or intellect come into play—number 4 adults send out a carefully groomed and conservative vibration. Their attitude indicates a businesslike personality, and they appear controlled and attentive. The first impression they give is reliable and sometimes rustic, but always down-to-earth. If their self-motivation and self-expression numbers are extroverted or culturally expansive, number 4s will look custom-made and well-traveled. Clothing styles, posture, and attitude will not indicate their thrifty or conforming self-image.

When 4s are wearing the color green, the self-image is emphasized. Green implies an earnest quality. Generally 4 adults will not stand out in a crowd unless the crowd is overly bejeweled, outlandishly costumed, or quarrelsome and rowdy. In public they present a sensible, traditional, well-behaved facade. It is the 4 heart's desire to give an imperturbable, moderate, and capable impression. At first blush, number 4s will never seem gregarious, flashy, or undisciplined; instead, they will appear solid and ready to work.

Number 4 adults perceive themselves as administrators. When living up to their self-image, their first impression implies a knack for practical problem solving.

The self-expression number may govern the first impression if formal, faddish, or extravagant dress codes are indicated by the career descriptions included in the meaning of the number.

The self-motivation number may influence the apparel of the bearers if they are relaxing and doing what they desire to do. However, when 4s live up to their self-image, they will not feature correspondent colors indicated by a number in another part of their numerology chart.

SELF-EXPRESSION

Youth:

It is obvious to adults when children have a number 4 self-expression number, because in youth the number 4 talents are based on attentiveness, conscientiousness, and orderliness. As they get older, 4s discover they can follow instructions, prepare for activities, and make or fix things to gain recognition. When frustrated, they may be servile, insensitive, and resistant to routines. As cautious, serious, methodical little helpers, they are happiest when contributing to a family project. It is difficult to stifle one's surprise at 4s' indefatigable practical energy.

Without intending to be bossy, the precautionary number 4 may humorlessly and rigidly set rules and regulations for grown-ups and playmates alike. Each detail and routine may be outlined carefully and viewed as very necessary. To unconventional, playful, individualistic parents, 4s may appear to be too fixed, obstinate, and rule-bound. To precise, industrious, systematic adults, number 4 children are accepted as "chips off the old block" and will probably be given tangible rewards for productivity.

Number 4 talents lead these children to willingly accept instructions, carry them out, and organize playmates to see a plan through. They will be more confident, compliant, definite adults if encouraged to make their own plans known. Fours should share opinions with others and realistically assess priorities. Too often 4 youths try to put everything in motion at once and become drained by overwork. Their thoroughness may be an asset or a liability. However, 4s' self-discipline and orderliness will no doubt be noted by authorities, and once given praise, they apply their perseverance to consistently productive efforts.

As teenagers and young adults, 4s will maintain an established routine and concentrate on things requiring hands-on attention to detail. These teens are not social butterflies or intellectual wizards. They are natural planners, upkeepers, and producers of useful products or materials. Fours need and will labor for material possessions. Carpentry, automobile mechanics, knitting, and sewing may keep them occupied. They are not idlers and will study, practice a sport, or find an after-school job. Number 4 children provide services willingly and are healthiest when busy. They are capable of fulfilling obligations and enjoy seeing the fruits of their labor.

Orderly number 4 youths may be direct and have strong likes and dislikes. Once they get into a routine or discover something they like, it is difficult to introduce them to changes. Fours often want to personally select the things they eat and wear; it's not surprising that they may consistently choose the same foods or the same style of clothes in a few subdued colors. Generally number 4 young adults find placements in fields requiring a uniform or a standard dress code, and find structure efficient and agreeable.

As teens, 4s want to be neat, reasonable, and moderate. It pleases them to look appropriate, so if they are dressed to function efficiently, they are comfortable. Predictably, they prefer not to have to waste time and energy shopping for fads or fashions. Number 4 teens should be encouraged to practice a trade and to have hands-on experiences, as they are suited to skilled crafts, building trades, and office management. Furthermore, their endurance, patience, and self-discipline make them excellent technicians, accountants, and professional sports participants. Among their keys to success are a desire to see clear-cut results, unwavering preparedness, and steadfast dedication.

Maturity:

Suggested Occupations: Construction, real estate, and all businesses that relate to products of the earth. Bricklayer, gardener, landscaper, builder, pipe fitter, construction painter, machinist, mechanic, architect, plumber, electrician, real estate broker, farmer, rancher, forest ranger, instructor, military officer, baseball, tennis, football, hockey, soccer, etc., professional athlete, gymnast, weight lifter, physical fitness teacher, dentist, doctor, practical or registered nurse, engraver, printer, tailor/seamstress, cashier, produce and merchandise buyer, economist, accountant, statistician, technical writer, musician, office manager, bookkeeper, hospital or school administrator, fire fighter, police officer, road machinery operator, chauffeur, gas station attendant, telephone installer, assembler, packer and wrapper, building custodian, security guard, manufacturing chemist, keypunch operator, computer service technician, mining, agricultural, civil, industrial, mechanical, petroleum, or ceramic engineer, merchant marine sailor, truck driver, urban planner, playground supervisor, recreation worker, sculptor.

Options:

Careers indicated by the meaning of the self-motivation number may not make use of readily available talents but will allow the individual to feel comfortable.

Careers indicated by the self-image number meanings will encourage the individual to live up to youthful dreams.

Careers indicated by the meaning of the destiny number, if it is not the same as the self-expression number, will require that the individual learn from incoming personalities and experiences.

If self-expression and destiny numbers are the same, the individual's talents will be recognized and utilized early in life.

Maturity: Self-expression Analysis

Fours have the potential to reap financial rewards for their ability to produce practical results from organized, systematized, painstaking work, and they may also earn recognition for their administrative efficiency. Fours attract positions requiring detail work, reliability, precision, prudence, honesty, self-discipline, obedience, and endurance. Their communications are direct, pragmatic, and firm, and their approach is slow, sure, and coolheaded. Often they earn the limelight when solving problems for others.

Fours rarely give or get anything for nothing. They preach and teach economy of time and effort. Therefore these individuals are frugal, cautious, and scrupulous when handling another's finances. Day-to-day routines are a must, and they pride themselves on trustworthiness and meticulous accuracy. Beating around the bush to get to a problem is not the 4 style. In a business environment, number 4 workers may be incorruptible and will make every effort to be law-abiding and productive. The bottom line is that 4s are down-to-earth.

The balanced number 4 talent knows when to stop and take a rest. When challenged by the number 4 or out of control, the individual may become an uncompromising, dogmatic, stuffy workaholic. Thus, if a career requires a diversification of attitudes, the number 4 may have a problem letting go of the taskmaster within. He never asks more from a coworker than he asks from himself—which is a lot, as his labors are diligent, devoted, and exacting. Number 4 managers are a tough act to follow.

Routinized jobs often make the responsible 4 a dull workmate. Fours should try to experiment occasionally, or they will risk becoming plodding drones. These stable, systematic, definite procedure addicts do not leave much time to give something new a whirl. If self-motivation and/or destiny number meanings indicate unconventional, intellectual, or money-making activity, the number 4 self-expression will strain to be multifaceted. Number 4 achievers supported by compatible numbers

2, 6, and 8 in other parts of their chart will not struggle with constancy. Number 4s' progress is materially rewarded for a job they usually do themselves. Unaccustomed to innovations, speculations, or nonconformity, 4s may sweat to gain promotions while others perspire delicately and mail their ideas to the office.

Generally number 4s are not envious or jealous. However, since their talent number indicates long, hard hours of both mental and physical work, they may covet others' playtime. Fours should take weekend freedom or vacations seriously in order to avoid physical or mental burnout. Why put in one day too many, only to have it end in exhaustion or frustration? That day may be the restricting, self-limiting straw that breaks the camel's back and causes conscientious 4s to leave steady jobs. One of the hardest lessons number 4 self-expressions must learn is when to quit.

DESTINY

WE ARE NOT BORN KNOWING WHAT LIFE HAS TO OFFER. INDIVIDUALS WITH THE NUMBER 4 DESTINY LEARN TO DEVELOP CRAFTSMANSHIP, INDUSTRIOUSNESS, AND SELF-DISCIPLINE. THEY COME IN CONTACT WITH THE PEOPLE AND EXPERIENCES THAT TEACH THEM TO VALUE WORK, ECONOMY, AND STEADFASTNESS.

This destiny implies a lifetime of determined effort and slow, sure, practical work that results in material security. To make the most of numerology's ability to forecast, number 4s must be realistic, systematized, and conscientious. Fours may be the ones to break the child labor laws by applying for a paper route while in first grade. Overall, they need to be productive. This need may begin with financially restrictive limitations and the desire to emulate hardworking parents. A tendency for practical problem solving and a strong financial need may cause 4 youngsters to work through college, apprentice a trade, or learn on the job. Number 4 destinies will never get anything without planning, stick-to-it-iveness, and work.

People with a number 4 destiny may labor with their bodies or their minds. The prime example of steady, routined, constructive effort implied by this destiny is the bricklayer who patiently lays one brick at a time until a sound structure is completed. Fours should plan and have a concrete purpose. The people who make single deals for megabucks or entertain for their supper are not examples to follow for the conventional, sensible, controlled 4 destiny.

Law-abiding, dependable, and businesslike acceptance of the limitations of this orderly life path will earn 4s a beautiful, stable, and dignified lifestyle. While others may speculate to accelerate, 4s may be disappointed to find that their rewards are obtained and anchored only when an incorruptible, faithful, solid foundation is prepared and maintained. Life will offer significant accomplishments as long as they do not include expansive travels. As time passes, respect, recognition, and material accomplishments will satisfy the number 4s' restlessness and fill the gaps of unexplored experiences.

There are limits to the freedoms offered by this destiny. To make the most of the number 4's options, he must not live life in the fast lane. His is a deliberate and principled path requiring individual balance, moderation, and conventionality. The 4 needs to be straightforward in communications, and he prospers when methodical, accurate, and prudent in investments of time and money. He stabilizes when serious about and devoted to family, job, and community. He may not want to be cautious, controlled, or obedient in youth, but this straight and narrow path makes an individual self-possessed early. The result is that the 4 grows up learning to be reasonable and productive.

People who have conservative tastes, ideas, and pursuits set the example for 4s to follow. Number 4s should focus upon the tried-and-true friendships of school chums, coworkers, and

neighbors; they may create the opportunities for these bond-
ings by joining service organizations such as volunteer fire
fighters, parent-teacher groups, the Rotary Club, the Kiwanis,
the Lions, etc. Other 4s who take pride in their work, know
where their duty lies, and see a commitment through to its
worthwhile conclusion will recognize their number 4 destiny
bearer counterparts among them.

In time, 4s make order out of chaos. They face difficult
problems and handle them better than they do less strenuous
jobs. One of number 4s' drawbacks is that too strong a sense
of right and wrong may make them too critical or straitlaced
to maintain harmonious relationships. By stubbornly concentrating on petty issues or short-lived details, number 4s lock
themselves into Archie Bunkerisms or view the world in much
too generalized terms. Fours must learn just how much they
may physically, mentally, socially, and materially accomplish
without limiting their adaptability.

One with a 4 destiny must realize that the train of life is
not passing him by when he may just be looking out the wrong
window or missing one of the stations. Generally the bearer
of this destiny will not look into millionaires' windows, though
he may well envy his more successful peers. The 4 should
recognize that success, like beauty, is in the eye of the be-
holder. It is just as likely that the number 4 destiny's peers
may be envious of his quality of life.

BIRTHDAY INFLUENCES WITHIN
THE DESTINY

April

Individuals born in April learn in youth that they cannot
be apathetic or discourteous or make a game out of life. They
are exposed to routines, traditions, and practical values. Situations arise that cause them to appreciate the rewards of work
and devote their time and energy to productive pursuits. There
may be financial or intellectual shortcomings in these youths'

environments that place limits on their freedom or self-expression. Down-to-earth authorities set the example.

Interactions with straightforward, hardworking, thrifty people with productive expectations of number 4s provide a disciplined training ground in childhood with lessons that are not forgotten. Youth may be remembered as a time to learn how to be coolheaded, dependable, and honest. April–born want security. If there is uncertainty or a lack of traditions or disciplines, they may become sluggish, dishonest, and unrefined. To learn to provide for themselves, these youngsters must work or study, organize themselves efficiently, practice economy, and lay a serviceable foundation for future material security. Above all, April youths must learn practicality.

Birthday: 4, 13, 22, 31

THE BIRTHDAY NUMBER HAS AN INFLUENCE ON PERSONALITY AND DESTINY. IT ATTRACTS PEOPLE AND EXPERIENCES DURING MID-LIFE THAT EXEMPLIFY THE NUMBER MEANING.

The mid-life productivity cycle begins with maturity. It lasts from approximately twenty-eight to fifty-five years of age and coordinates with the destiny during that time span. The birthday-number meaning adds its character traits and experiences to an individual's numerology analysis.

People born on the fourth, thirteenth, twenty-second and thirty-first of the month, in addition to the character traits outlined by the number meanings for the name, are organizers and tireless workers. They may not be happy when unproductive nor comfortable with time-wasters. Individuals born on these dates know that they have their work cut out for them in their struggle to gain stability and security under down-to-earth conditions.

Between approximately twenty-eight and fifty-five years of age—the twenty-seven-year productivity cycle within the destiny—life will offer additional opportunities to strive for a dignified lifestyle, one in which duty to home, family, and community is always essential. Attention to accuracy, trustworthiness, and reasonable principles of right and wrong will require one's dedication. The individual should provide service to others and develop conventional interests that build a firm foundation for his future. Someone born on the fourth, thirteenth, twenty-second or thirty-first can expect to work and prosper.

PERSONAL YEAR

The number 4 is the fourth year in the cycle of nine years of experiences and results in polish and skill of performance based on goals set in the first year. It is time to work and let the previous year's variety of interests and friendships bring in social activity. For most, this is a down-to-earth year to correct material mistakes made over the past three. For others, the year focuses on taking and giving orders, curbing impulsiveness, and paying attention to a basic routine and work schedule. It is a year to persevere and save and accumulate assets. The projects begun three years ago finally begin to produce material rewards.

Self-discipline, moderation, and endurance will be required to make the most of options open this year. Careful planning, conscientiousness, and a businesslike attitude are musts after the preceding year's scattering. Key words for this year are caution, dignity, and orderliness. The people who are offered for growth relationships this year are not creative, romantic, or broad-minded. They are practical bottom-liners who do not appreciate apathy, incompetence, or frivolity. Faithfulness and reliability will have their rewards, and dedication to work will additionally attract supporters. This is a year to be sane and rational to correct misconceptions and cultivate long-term goals.

One must often forgo vacations, party times, or unscheduled expenditures. One should keep an eye on future payoffs. This is the year to buy a new house, fix the roof on an old one, or invest in other real estate. To get the best from this year, one must be patient, coolheaded, and practical. A methodical approach to everyday details and commitments is a must. Don't allow yourself to feel restricted by duties and physical demands. Recognize opportunities to put your affairs and your body in working order. For instance, prepare yourself to take advantage of vacations, sensual pleasures, and the chance to break from routine, which are all offered in the number 5 personal year, next year. Prepare to enjoy freedom, changes, and adventure by saving money and being constructive at this time.

The number 4 year will test the value of plans and clarify self-imposed or real limitations. It is best to acknowledge mistakes, balance budgets, and not to chance experiments that may crack the concrete of a foundation. Problem-solvers are available; use their input to eliminate deadwood, recognize the inevitable, and adopt a different point of view, if necessary.

Take time to take care of your health and organize a daily regimen that includes personal physical fitness. Your body is the house of your soul and should be considered just as important as money in the bank. This is the time to reconstruct the material and practical aspects of life, if necessary, and diligently work toward solving immediate problems. Sustained efforts made at this time will determine the stability of the following five years.

PERSONAL MONTH

The number 4 personal month within any personal year gives one an opportunity to produce tangible results. Serious application to economy, routines, and physical fitness should take top priority. Laziness, disorganization, and impracticality should be put on the shelf. The previous month was not filled with responsibilities, and there was time for friends, but now is the time to reconstruct plans or projects and square up mistakes in finance or judgment.

Situations may arise demanding a straightforward approach. Use this time to be realistic. Work instead of talking about what should or could be done. Be efficient, meticulous, and scrupulous in stabilizing finances. Organize time, do not waste energy, and follow through on commitments. Pie-in-the-sky notions go out the window, and practical ideas come in.

PERSONAL DAY

Wake up early and organize plans with a determined attitude. Reevaluate details and schedule to get mundane jobs out of the way. Control impulses and keep schedules. Be faithful to your objectives. Use patience, perseverance, and reasonable judgment to put your house, job, and social obligations in order. Do not become innovative or changeable. Follow procedures, depend upon yourself, and keep your dignity. This is not the time to experiment or be lazy. Plans made today for tomorrow will likely be altered or canceled, so attend to details that may curtail tomorrow's freedoms.

You will note that others are delegating responsibilities and examining budgets. Mistakes may be corrected and improvements made at this time. Avoid becoming discourteous, insensitive, or pigheaded. Creative juices may be flowing, but there is no outlet or cooperation in today's methodical, mundane, controlled options.

Make a personal commitment to persevere until things get done. Do not become slipshod or unadaptable. Let the necessities of the moment guide today's actions. Use elbow grease and planning, and do whatever must be done to maintain conventions, discipline, and durability. Be frank and obedient in dealings with superiors; maintain composure and be reasonable. Nothing will be accomplished unless you make a scrupulous, prudent, steady effort. This is a good day to weed the garden, clean closets, or balance the checkbook. Tomorrow's sensual pleasures may be pursued if work is done today.

CHAPTER NINE

Number 5

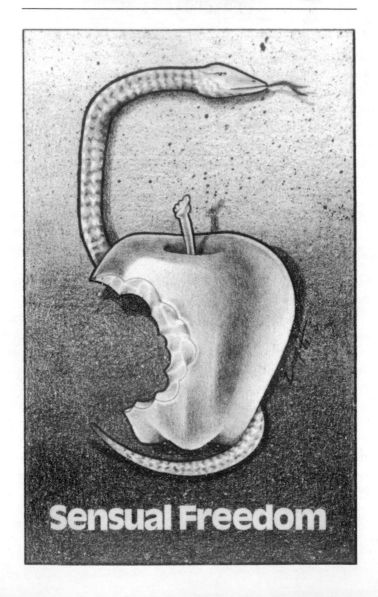

Sensual Freedom

◄◄◄

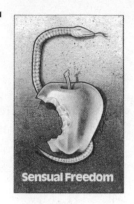

Sensual Freedom

►►►

ATTRIBUTES:
POSITIVE—Enterprising, Enthusiastic, Active, Versatile, Clever, Freedom-loving, Prolific, Sensual, Adventurous
NEGATIVE—Irresponsible, Rash, Passionless, Forgetful, Oversexed, Purposeless, Overindulgent, Dull, Old-fashioned

CORRESPONDENTS:
LETTERS: E, N, W
ODD NUMBER: Aggressive
DISPOSITION: Sensual; Spontaneous, Unconventional
NUMBERS: 14, 23, 32, 41, 50, 59, 68, 77, 86, 95, 104
COLOR: Turquoise
GEM: Turquoise, Aquamarine
CRYSTALS: Muscovite, Hornblende
VEGETATION: Carnation, Gardenia, Primrose
FOODS: Lettuce, Celery, Cucumber, Endive, Beet, Broccoli, Bass, Apple, Cherry, Raspberry, Melon, Custard, Almond
MUSICAL INSTRUMENTS/APPEAL: Bells, Trumpet, Viola; Rhythmic

MUSICAL NOTE: G (When Challenged, G#)
LOCATIONS: State: Utah
    City: Akron, Baltimore, Chicago, Denver, Fresno, Kansas
    City, Pensacola, Pittsburgh, Provo, Salem, San Antonio,
    San Francisco, Scranton, Topeka
PLANET: Mars
MONTH: May
BIRTHDAYS: 5, 14, 23
DAY OF WEEK: Tuesday
GENERAL COMPATIBILITY NUMBERS: 1, 3, 7, 9
INCOMPATIBILITY NUMBERS: 2, 4, 6 (8 in business)

Note: If an individual has the challenge to the number 5, these descriptions will swing from positive to negative until the challenge is balanced. Please be sure to read the challenge number meaning.

CHALLENGE OF THE NUMBER 5

This is a challenge to the individuals' understanding of life's physical aspects. It deals with freedom, restlessness, and sexuality. As children, the challenge holders are exposed to too much or too little loyalty. They do not learn when to adhere or when to change. Too many confusing experiences tax the tots' adaptability, or adult cautions anchor them too much. This challenge centers on the bearers' expectations of pleasure and pain, which have been influenced by too much curiosity or too few questions asked.

Having parents who do not live conventionally may cause these teenagers to focus on sex, stimulants, and speculations or avoid excitement and escape the temptations of puberty. Fives may have witnessed or experienced sexual, emotional, or mental abuses in youth. As a result, they try to forget and cannot learn from past experiences.

Number 5 challenge holders are attracted to sensible, traditional, obviously dependable people—or the opposite. They think that anyone who is unlike themselves is interesting. Relationships are usually short-lived or painfully dragged on, and after 5s understand a person or situation, boredom often sets in. Because of a confused sense of loyalty, challenged 5s will dispassionately hold on or enthusiastically find a new interest.

Commitments may be held long past their desired result or let go before the original purpose is accomplished. Holders of the number 5 challenge tend not to learn from experience; therefore they get stuck in a rut in order not to repeat an unsettling episode. As tots, they might have had parents who unreasonably insisted upon acceptance of their judgments or inappropriately left judgments to these youngsters.

Childhood exposures made sex a taboo or too inviting. Parents may have flaunted their bodies provocatively or shamefully hidden natural exposure of bodily functions. As adults, sex and sensuality are either all-important or ignored.

These children may be too conditioned to changes or fear the unexpected. Thus they may fail to test their curiosity or be forced by circumstance to absorb things only from experience. As teenagers, they are too adaptable—always the good sport—or too fearful of the unexpected—lacking the sporting instinct. As adults, they may marry to satisfy a sex drive and divorce when they come to their senses.

Number 5 challenge holders usually marry more than one time or not at all. It is difficult to turn them on, but once sexually active, they cannot get enough. Basic responsibilities are forgotten. Bills do not get paid. Clothes are left uncleaned. Money is spent lavishly. Fives maintain momentum until something extreme happens to bring them back to reality. People unchallenged by the number 5 accept sex, sensuality, and stimulations as part of the natural course of events. Number 5 challenges make too much or too little of the importance of these pleasures: sensuality, impulsiveness, and stimulants become pitfalls diverting them from the path of their ambitions.

Fives either touch, taste, smell, and feel everything that life has to offer or live vicariously. It is difficult for number 5

challenge holders to know how or when to modify enthusiasms. They investigate unknowns too carefully or embrace
them on the spot. They seek variety or hold on to commitments
long after having proved unworthy of their loyalty.

As tots, they may have seen judgments made quickly. As
adults, they play hunches or investigate too carefully before
getting into new situations. It is difficult for challenged 5s to
sense who is worthy of their allegiance. Their intuitive talent
for knowing when to change or what to change has been
warped. Although they are immediate diagnosticians for others, number 5 challenge holders cannot spontaneously do the
right thing for themselves.

This challenge results in a fear of taking chances or a lust
for living. These challenge holders may be vestal virgins or
active, seductive swingers. They are entrepreneurs or cynical
observers. For them, life may become an escape from one
responsibility to another—or a series of unconsciously undertaken and cloistering commitments. Fives imagine that they
themselves can stabilize when involved with conventional people—instead the result is stagnation. They are either enthusiastic about everything or their catalyst talents are squelched
by tedium.

Drugs, drink, travel—anything that offers nirvana—is a
temptation either to be seized greedily or pushed hurriedly
away. The challenge of the number 5 sometimes causes the
holder to appear irresponsible and undependable, although this
is not really the case. In reality, the appearance is just a result
of unguarded curiosity, unconventional expectations, and the
inappropriate glossing over of imperfections.

Number 5 talents are based in cleverness, eagerness, and
an adaptability to those aspects of life unknown to conventional
thinkers. The 5's early lifestyle may have been unstable. This
situation causes the youngster to expect to live by his wits.
Perhaps exposures were too limiting to allow the youngster to
use his quick mind. The result is a temperamental personality—
he is often a scrapper or a coward.

Broken engagements, short-term marriages, or businesslike social relationships are 5 common denominators. Lifestyles may change repeatedly. Money comes in or goes out unexpectedly. Physical problems with the reproductive organs are not uncommon. It is difficult to mentally, emotionally, or physically balance this challenge. These challenge holders seek steady relationships with stabilized people who will not be comfortable with the 5s' restlessness. Often they attract their counterparts: people who overcompensate sensually or sexually.

This challenge is usually understood and channeled when the holder is between fifty and sixty years old. Up until that time, self-discipline, self-awareness, and a willingness to remember hasty judgments are necessary. Fives must remember that old loves and friends are part of life experience. They should not be discarded like old shoes once they are understood. Number 5 challenge holders generally want what they do not have at the moment and forget what they do not want to remember.

The number 5 challenge may swing from one of the following extremes to another until the challenge holder's behavior is recognized and new habits are initiated that stabilize his restlessness, curiosity, and sensuality.

Too free or too chained.
Too versatile or too unadaptable.
Too self-indulgent or too unhappy.
Too irresponsible or too caring.
Too understanding or too mean.
Too excitable or too calm.
Too adaptable or too firm.
Too curious or too inactive.
Too clever or too slow.
Too loyal or too fickle.
Too sensual or too cerebral.
Too busy or too bored.
Too impatient or too cool.
Too lucky or too unlucky.

PHYSICAL CHALLENGES OF
THE NUMBER 5

Challenges can affect physical as well as mental health. Body chemistry changes when individuals are stressed, and when we do not know what is good for us, our minds trigger anxious, angry, or frustrated habits. When we are mean to ourselves, we get sick. One's attitude sends the brain a message, and the brain tells the body to scream for help.

To get attention for their dis-ease, often people get sick or form negative habits. Numerologists believe that illness and wellness depend upon attitude, and challenges indicate the attitudes that result from needy feelings. When we do not feel needy, we feel well and balanced and do not crave attention from others. Essentially, if the personality challenges are balanced, the body chemistry is in balance, too, and therefore there is little chance of mental or physical dis-ease.

Challenge numbers indicate the ways people subconsciously punish themselves for not being consciously good to themselves.

The following list of dis-eases and negative habits relate to the challenge of the number 5.

Abortions	Gum Problem
Abscess	Hemorrhoid
Accidents	Infections
Acne	Kidney Problem
Anxiety	Mouth Problem
Arthritis	MS
Brain Tumor	Obesity
Cataracts	Pessimism
Cysts	Recovering Alcoholic
Drug Problems	Stomach Problem
Earache	Temper Tantrums
Eye Blinking	Ulcer

TO BALANCE THE CHALLENGE OF THE 5 AND BRING IT OUT AS A TALENT . . .

The first step to balancing the challenge is to feel comfortable about saying "I need to be free." Hold fast to one materially productive purpose. Forget the inconsistencies or unconventional disappointments of childhood, and remember how adaptable you are. Use your mind to observe, learn, and explore. Stay with one person or job until you get into the details and gain expertise. Bring your enthusiasm to the attention of less curious souls, for you have the ability to be a catalyst for change in the lives of others. Open new vistas for people, and encourage new relationships and allow them to grow.

If you are contemplating a new long-term commitment, ask yourself whether you will be comfortable when the natural course of events requires compromise and routines. Are you focused on sexual attraction? Are you putting down sensual preferences, background differences, or financial needs because you imagine that a lover's sense of responsibility will provide you with stability? Are you rationalizing a move because you are restless? Sit still and think!

Contemplating divorce? Ask yourself different questions: Are you stuck in your momentary desires? Have you forgotten the reasons that attracted you to marriage in the first place? You may want freedom now, but you may be looking in all the wrong places; instead, look inside yourself. Points of reference from childhood may make you "want to be alone"— unhampered by responsibilities to family or lovers—for all the wrong reasons, *or* you may realize that you've made your initial commitment for all the wrong reasons.

When you are offered a new job, check health, pension, and vacation benefits. Before you are tempted to give up the security you have worked for, reflect and plan. You may not actually have to reseed or cultivate a new position.

Visualize yourself as an enthusiastic, versatile, and adaptable wildflower, recognizing at the same time that your attitude can make you feel like a weed. Throughout, remember that a weed is only a flower in the wrong environment. Pick your flower beds carefully!

SELF-MOTIVATION

Youth:

As tots, the number 5 urge that these children feel is to be curious, active, and free from restrictions. When reprimanded, these children will become bored or temperamental. Number 5 tots need mentally and physically stimulating applications for their enthusiasm and energy. These youngsters are nonconforming, impatient, and daring. Consequently, if surrounded by pragmatic, routine-fixated, sober authorities, they will become unpredictable or wild. Fives want progressive, imaginative, broad-minded leadership.

Parents may describe their number 5 child as eager, exuberant, and spontaneous. These words describe the youngster when he is surrounded by multifaceted, adaptable, alert authorities. If the 5's inquisitiveness is considered bothersome and the parents disregard his need to learn by trial and error, the child may conform and fear taking risks. The number 5 youngster wants to venture out, seize every opportunity to experiment, and demonstrate his latest interest. Once this child— who has his feelings rooted in sensuality—is pushed into exacting disciplines, he will become purposeless. In other words, the restricted 5 will indicate unreasonable restlessness.

Number 5 children need outlets to exhibit their flexibility, promotional abilities, and gregarious nature(s). They have many sides to their personality, so they are able to do a number of things at one time. Their natural skills should be channeled to employ and complement their keen perceptions of people. Activities such as walking or auto trips, trumpet, bell, or viola lessons, or changes in any routine will put their eager minds to good use.

Fives absorb knowledge from every experience, but once

they understand something, they become bored with it. Fives will not want to practice or rehearse to attain or maintain a goal. If these children are not shown thrift, discrimination, and temperance, they may have the problem of accepting too little responsibility in maturity.

Fives are genuinely interested in trying everything at least once. Since they are demonstrative, formal, or uptight, expressions of approval may not satisfy their need to give and receive warmth. They love pranks, jokes, carnivals, and surprises. Plain-spoken people, new ideas, and excursions into the unknown will tempt their concentration.

The strong-willed number 5 wants to feel emancipated. The individual is inclined to invent methods or use an existing toy or tool for other purposes. He may shy away from rigid educational systems, rule-bound games, or following the leader, choosing instead to explore less boring activities. Unconfining and up-to-date recreations will occupy him temporarily. If caught bending regulations or straying far from his normal play area, he will apologize with a wondrous tale that may enrapture the unsuspecting listener. The 5 promotes himself with a flair that is hard to resist and finds it difficult to wait for permission when he gets an idea. A number 5 youth or adult cannot be locked into structured thinking or environments.

Sports, school politics, journalism, science, or the arts may be first today and second tomorrow in the mind of the number 5 teenager. A member of the opposite sex may vie with a variety of interests for supremacy. The 5 may be the class macho man or sex goddess. A venture into horseback riding, motorcycling, or challenging the great outdoors may add to his storehouse of life experiences. The 5 has a continual urge to go from one fascinating unknown to another, and he rarely relaxes his need for expansion.

It is best to teach 5 youths to expect the unexpected and save their money for traveling. Only fast-paced trips, short-term jobs, and unconventional hobbies will satisfy the need of number 5 teenagers to take a chance. They discover the world by the hunt-and-peck method and should be encouraged to investigate. However, if the number 5 is also a challenge number, they will become involved in projects before they think things through. Number 5 challenge holders rarely learn from reading books, past mistakes, or by observing another's experiences. Conversely, the balanced 5 will investigate or learn from past mistakes.

If number 5 youths have more practical number meanings in other aspects of their chart, these number meanings will affect their unpredictability. Despite this, they will nevertheless find means of expressing their desire for freedom and untraditional interests through unconventional means. As teens, number 5s hurry from one interest to another; as changeable adults, 5s may not want or need an academic education or a definite plan. Alert parents will understand that these clever promoters will be able to learn and/or make money doing a variety of things that interest them. When 5s decide that an academic specialty is necessary, they whiz through it; however, a lack of formal training will never stop 5s from accomplishing their goals. They are clever!

Maturity

Adult 5s want to remain youthful, exciting, and on the move. Fives are entrepreneurs—they need to find outlets for their curiosity and use their enthusiasm to inspire others to try unknowns or to probe the depths. They want to feel footloose, free of responsibility, open-minded, and just a little improper. If that seems a bit unconventional, it is, as are number 5s themselves. Fives are often catalysts for change in other people's lives. They try anything that is new to them and profit from speculations.

After quickly and cleverly assessing all they want to know, 5s build everyone's enthusiasm, become bored, and move on. They are the doers who open the eyes of the watchers. Their ability to think and act untraditionally has made advertising, motion-picture, and political history.

Number 5 people do not like to be old-fashioned, colorless,

or stagnant. Rarely dull or passionless lovers or mates, they just need to know that nothing is expected of them and they will provide excitement. Fives must not have their duties outlined, and they will not be regimented. Any new diet, fitness plan, self-improvement seminar, or foreign intrigue will command their interest. When balanced, these individuals adapt to any situation, absorb knowledge easily, and foster daring expectations. When in their care, youngsters are taught to be fearless, friendly, and flexible. Able to follow their natural instincts, number 5 adults are spontaneous, energetic, and informal parents.

Material objectives do not rule number 5s. High on their list of necessities, money usually comes and goes spontaneously. Fives are comfortable with people who labor in untraditional occupations and are "easy come–easy go," exuberant spenders. Numbers 5s are friendly, sporting, prolific idea people who will investigate when prompted by intuition.

When asked for help, number 5s respond to lovers, mates, and business associates with straight talk, skillful assessments, and progressive advice. Fives enjoy mental challenges, sensual enticements, and physical competitions. Often oblivious of procedures, schedules, and domestic obligations, they have their own time clock. To compensate for this tendency, 5s prefer to marry practical people and expect others to be flexible and understand their unquenchable curiosity. One may expect caring and sharing 5s to surprise loved ones with tickets for a trip to Tahiti or a heart-shaped Jacuzzi. Fives do not need a reason to give a gift.

One problem for number 5 self-motivations is a fear of being pinned down. They imagine that settling conventionally will cramp their style. Business, social, intimate, and family relationships must adapt to their fast pace and changeable ideas. As time goes by, a variety of people and experience strike their fancy. Anything or anyone that cannot be absorbed or figured out is retained while unpleasant experiences are easily forgotten. Balanced 5s live in the "now."

Number 5s do not worry, complain, or mope about paying bills on time. Nor do they care what others may think. Fives never get old; they stay young by being involved and constantly move on to new and progressive interests. They rarely stay in one place long enough to establish a reputation unless they become known for turning up and disappearing unexpectedly. Witty, sensual, mind-boggling people make them sit up and take notice. Fives enjoy people, and they fit in anywhere. Generally flamboyant clothing styles, fast cars, and encounters with the unpredictable opposite sex keep them feeling sensual and lively. Fives are attracted to hotels, boats, and planes. They pride themselves on living out of a suitcase or an automobile trunk. Fives love to travel and keep their passport up-to-date. They are nonconformists who rebel at certainty.

Number 5 individualists do not have the patience to commute from suburbia, will pay for mundane services, and prefer cash purchases, to avoid monthly bills. They may not be concerned about pensions, profit sharing, or health insurance. Because of carelessness or the unavailability of security owing to job changes, 5s may not have to think about early or late retirement.

Money comes and goes for pleasures and self-promotion. Fives will spend their last dollar gambling on something in order to pay the bills. They do not cover all bases consistently: they may cleverly manipulate rewarding situations, grasp a short-term opportunity, and look forward to the next lucky break.

Marriage for the sometimes thoughtless and temperamental 5 may be of short duration. For a sensitive or very disciplined partner, the number 5's desire for freedom will cause problems. The bonds of fidelity are elusive when one is restless, emotionally excitable, and unconsciously selfish. It takes a tolerant, self-confident, and responsive person to maintain a long-term relationship with the number 5. To maintain balance, however, there may be other domestically rooted number meanings in the number 5's chart that add the ability to make stable commitments. Before contracting for life, the number 5 should note and compare his own numbers with the basic numbers in his lover's chart.

The marriage of two 5 motivations will begin and end with sensual adventures. There may be multiple partings and wild, wonderful reconciliations. The union of two people who are not comfortable with responsibility, are accident-prone from spontaneous decisions, and have a passion for excitement may be too frenzied to last. This dynamic duo will be eccentric, overly indulgent, and imprudent. They both will want and instinctively lean toward freethinking, whimsy, and changeable investigations. If one of the two tries to compromise, they will both be bored. This combination, then, is definitely not a good bet for the long haul, either in business or monkey business.

SELF-IMAGE

Youth:

When lying on the bed, listening to music, and imagining "What am I going to be like when I grow up? How will I walk, dress, and talk?", number 5 youths visualize madcap daredevils. They dream of living an unencumbered, serendipitous, and unconventional life. Little boys see themselves winning the nation's biggest lottery and spending it all on pleasures. Little girls see themselves traveling the world, meeting mystifying strangers, and attracting attention wherever their wanderlust leads them. Children with the 5 self-image may picture themselves as free-spirited, fearless, multilingual adventurers and intriguing sex symbols.

Fives may appear to be eager, natural, daring children who have the cleverness to get along with friends and authorities. When 5s say they want to be merchant seamen, pilots, or advertising account executives, they see themselves in the appropriate position to use their versatility, creativity, and progressive ideas. When living up to their self-image, these individuals will be first to try new foods, jump into a pool to see how deep it is, or make friends with strangers. They appear ready to touch, taste, feel, hear, and smell everything that life has to offer.

Youngsters with dreams based upon the meaning of the number 5 may be too venturesome and get into trouble. They will assert themselves in order to have freedom of choice and action. Their overall appearance is out-of-the-ordinary: they are out to stop traffic. Number 5s may wear unconventional, futuristic, multi-styled outfits and prefer electric colors or dynamic combinations. When in tune with their self-image, 5s' style sense is focused upon anything that allows them to appear entertaining, unconfined, and ready for action. Rarely dedicated to disciplines or restrained conversationally and physically, youthful 5 expectations change often. The young 5s seem to relate to everyone they meet . . . and they usually do. *Maturity:*

When walking out of an elevator or into a room—before personality or intellect come into play—the number 5 adult sends out a provocative, untraditional, and sociable vibration. His attitude indicates a vibrant personality, and he appears to be ready for anything. The first impression he gives is energetic, sometimes animated, and always decided. If self-motivation and self-expression numbers are introverted or conventional, 5s will look carefully costumed and colorful. Clothing styles, posture, and attitude will not necessarily indicate his sexy or adventurous self-image.

When 5s are wearing the color turquoise, the self-image is emphasized, as turquoise implies restlessness and stimulation. Generally a number 5 will stand out in a crowd, in essence presenting an unconventional, aggressive, sensual facade to be observed by the public. It is the 5 heart's desire to give an enticing, open-minded impression. The number 5 will never look like everyone else: appearing ready to embark on an exciting adventure, he thrives on anything new or fast-moving.

Number 5 adults perceive themselves as swashbucklers. When living up to their self-image, their first impression implies a knack for getting folksy with everyone.

The self-expression number may govern the first impression if conservative or uniform dress codes are indicated by the career descriptions included in the meaning of the number.

The self-motivation number may influence the apparel of the bearer if he is relaxing and doing what he desires to do. However, when the individual is living up to his self-image, he will not feature correspondent colors or styles indicated by numbers in another part of his numerology chart.

SELF-EXPRESSION

Youth:

It is obvious to adults when children have a number 5 self-expression. As tots, number 5 talents are based in curiosity: they kick through restraints, become animated early, and will touch the stove to see if it is hot. Because 5s will often only learn from experience and get bored quickly, they keep parents physically active and mentally alert.

As they get older 5s will not follow instructions, sit still, or accept a rigid routine. They will charm disciplinarians and teachers to wiggle out of trouble. As unbridled, mischief-making, resourceful little helpers, they are eager to add enthusiasm to family projects. It is difficult to stifle one's surprise at their cleverness, inventiveness, and adaptability.

Without intending to be imprudent, the enterprising number 5 may resourcefully and gregariously entice peers and adults to alter or break rules and regulations. Each original and complex idea may be carefully promoted and skillfully sold. To serious, routine-oriented, practical parents, the 5 may appear too changeable, questioning, and ungovernable; to experience-seeking, spontaneous, pliant adults, on the other hand, the number 5 is accepted as a welcome traveler and will probably be given leeway to take a few risks.

Number 5 talents may lead these children to fight the conventional educational system and attempt to make each day different. They have the sales ability and charisma to lead friends to explore nonscholastic interests with them. They will be more stable, less frustrated adults if encouraged early on to have multiple challenges in addition to school and domestic duties. Too often number 5s try to conform and do not sustain or complete commitments. When attempting to be traditional, the unique number 5s become bored jacks-of-all-trades who may or may not master any of them.

As teenagers, these rugged individualists may be called underachievers. They will not concentrate for long and may cut classes. However, authorities will note that they are clever, spontaneous problem-solvers and warmhearted do-gooders. When encouraged to set their own pace, they are capable of being anything they want to be. In other words, 5s excel when interested.

Fives are opportunists in a positive sense—they should seize every chance to accumulate experiences. School vacations spent traveling in situations where they are able to meet people from various backgrounds will open vistas for their inquiring minds. Sports, art, and technical interests may not be enduring enthusiasms, but while they last, 5s will be passionately competitive.

Fives are not planners, upkeepers, or self-controlled material producers; rather, they become proficient or productive when a colorful idea strikes them. They are capable of fulfilling obligations, but may appear irresponsible, self-indulgent, or extravagant when larded with controls or responsibilities. Fives need mental and physical freedoms.

Go-getting number 5 youths will not be hesitant and will demonstrate leadership ability, although they may not use it if pushed. They prove themselves when they find a career interest that offers daily changes, stimulation, and an opportunity to show their talent for understanding how others think and act.

Number 5 youths change eating and clothing habits with each new experience. Repeating foods or establishing one mode of dress is rare. Generally number 5 young adults try various restaurants, fads, and fashions. They are comfortable in businesses that allow them to dress comfortably, naturally, and interestingly. They may not be neat, appropriate, or turned out to function efficiently, but they will always attract comments.

Tots, teens, and youths should be given time and autonomy to discover how they will function on a mental, physical, or emotional career level. Fives may run the gamut of experiences to become outstanding psychologists, entertainers, or civic leaders. Their multifaceted personalities, quick minds, and natural ability to promote daring ideas can be awesome.

Maturity:

Suggested Occupations: Entertainer, lecturer, writer, theatrical producer, promoter, publicist, traveling sales representative, public relations specialist, booking agent, politician, advertising account executive, lawyer, psychologist, personnel director, design engineer, inventor, investigator, detective, insurance claims adjuster, newspaper reporter, photojournalist, pilot, test pilot, flight attendant, travel agent, tour guide, cruise director, merchant marine sailor, explorer, marine, automobile or aviation electrical specialist, locomotive engineer, gourmet chef, wine expert, bartender, waiter-waitress, long-distance truck driver, rancher, rodeo performer, chemist, circus owner or performer, professional blackjack or craps dealer-player, gambling-casino owner, burlesque performer, taxi-limousine-bus driver or owner, stock or bond broker-agent, entrepreneur, beachcomber, surfer, gambler, tramp, or bum.

Options:

Careers indicated by the meaning of the self-motivation number may not make use of readily available talents but will allow the individual to feel comfortable.

Careers indicated by the self-image number meanings will encourage the individual to live up to youthful dreams.

Careers indicated by the meaning of the destiny number, if it is not the same as the self-expression number, will require that the individual learn from incoming personalities and experiences.

If self-expression and destiny numbers are the same, the individual's talents will be recognized and utilized early in life.

Maturity: Self-Expression Analysis

Number 5 individuals have the potential for financial rewards for their ability to capitalize on spontaneous, unconventional, and changing opportunities, and they may achieve recognition for their talent in determining the causes of existing problems. Fives understand the nature of missing links and the needs of all types of people. They attract positions where sensuality, personality, and divergent hours and/or opportunities are offered. Communications are friendly, unpremeditated, inquisitive, and exuberant. Fives are quick, expansive, and many-sided. They find that they are in the limelight when promoting themselves or any product.

Number 5 talents are troubleshooters. They rarely get involved with mundane careers or businesses. Fives accept people and experiences on the spot. These dashing individuals are not frugal, cautious, or behind the times when promoting themselves or others. Talented speculators, 5s know that it takes money to make money. Usually prolific idea people, they may leapfrog from one job to another. Always on the lookout for adventure, 5s will take a challenging promise of large commissions to a guaranteed yearly income. Day-to-day routines drive them crazy, and they will quit a job that is too predictable. In a business environment these imaginative, clever, talented charmers will strike when the iron is hot.

Balanced number 5 talents know how to make work appear to be play. They are energetic when interested and ready to take a vacation when there is no action. When challenged by the number 5 or fenced in by traditional thinkers or obligations, these individuals may become extravagant, irresponsible, and indiscriminate. If a career requires steady, conservative, formal attitudes, number 5s may have a problem taking it seriously. Fives are most successful when interacting with challenging people. They never know what they will do next and can never be depended upon to be systematized or second-guessed. They are affable, freethinking, go-getting employees and employers who respond with wit and a direct approach.

Unconventional jobs make changeable number 5s vague about future security. Fives should try to stay in one field in order to build experience and a responsible reputation, as progressive, footloose, spontaneous travel addicts do not build a risk-free future. If self-motivation and/or destiny number meanings indicate orderly, self-sacrificing, unworldly activity, those with the number 5 self-expression will strain to endure confinements. Number 5 achievers supported by compatible numbers 1, 3, and 9 in other parts of their chart will not struggle with their need for freedom. Unaccustomed to plodding, carrying a heavy load, or supporting others' claim to fame, number 5 talents will change horses in midstream and ride the currents to a more promising personal shore.

Generally 5s will not overindulge in drugs, drinking, or sensuality, although some do. The negative aspects of this number require self-discipline to avoid forgetting past blunders, and negative 5s tend to hold on to losing propositions, getting caught up in momentary interests and not investigating or gambling on long shots. Talents who inspire exciting, frequent, questionable launchings have cause for more bon voyage parties—or hit bottom more—than most. Those with a number 5 self-expression must know how to retain enthusiasm, humor, and adaptability without going overboard.

DESTINY

WE ARE NOT BORN KNOWING WHAT LIFE HAS TO OFFER. INDIVIDUALS WITH THE NUMBER 5 DESTINY

LEARN TO DEVELOP FLEXIBILITY AND VERSATILITY AND TO PROFIT FROM SPECULATIONS. THEY EN-COUNTER THE PEOPLE AND EXPERIENCES THAT TEACH THEM TO VALUE UNCONVENTIONAL LIFE-STYLES AND UNEXPECTED OPPORTUNITIES AND HOW TO RECOGNIZE THE DIFFERENCE BETWEEN CON-STRUCTIVE AND UNPRODUCTIVE RESTLESSNESS.

This destiny implies a lifetime of change, sensual curiosity, and untraditional work or play. The result is a late bloomer who is youthful, enthusiastic, and eager to try everything at least once. To make the most of numerology's ability to fore-cast, the number 5 must be broad-minded, multifaceted, and free to experiment.

Fives may have multiple careers or marriages before the age of thirty-six. They may be born to nonconforming parents who shun formal education and learn from the school of hard knocks, or life may be filled with exciting adventures that may cause the youngster to become impatient with conventional progressive methods. Number 5 destinies will never hold on to material things or people without feeling limited by duties or responsibilities.

Fives may not find success working traditional hours or in conventional careers. They may find that opportunities come in the back door or pop up from unlikely sources. They should plan to prosper from self-promotion, flexible ideas, and on-the-spot methods. Unlimited possibilities are offered during 5s' lifetime. Some examples of individuals with this erratic destiny are traveling salesmen, Ian Fleming's James Bond, Agent 007, or sensual, attention-getting wit Johnny Carson. Mr. Carson's many talents and flair for making money—and losing it to divorce—are a common pattern for the number 5 destiny. Eventually 5s learn to enjoy changing experiences but become precautionary about finances in being free to travel or playing the field.

Fives must be willing to take each opportunity as it comes. They should make the most of surprises and enthusiastically

tell the world about each new venture. The number 5 unquenchable curiosity will earn this destiny holder a reputation
for being a catalyst for change in other people's lives. Positive
5s never get think-stuck or old. They may choose to play it
safe, allowing compelling people and situations to keep them
on a roller coaster ride. Any interest may bring fame, fortune,
and fun if it is tackled with resourcefulness.

There are no limitations to the freedom offered by this
destiny. Only stagnating and the fear of taking chances will
delay its positive progress. Number 5 destiny holders are best
suited to becoming opportunists in a world that is their oyster.
Stylish, up-to-date, freethinking people open doors for broad-
minded 5s, while plainspoken, rustic, vigorous, sexy people
add color and warmth to 5s' experiences. Fives are spared
tedious, plodding lifestyles through emancipation from mundane responsibilities, and their lives are sparked by whimsy,
merriment, and offbeat passions. Number 5s may character-
istically live life in the fast lane; certainly their overwhelming
possibilities may make them become self-indulgent or develop
insatiable tastes for excitement. When number 5s realize they
can handle any and all uncertainties, they will pace themselves
appropriately.

One should never tell balanced number 5s that something
is impossible. They are capable of doing or having anything
they set their sights on. However, one love, one career, one
job, is impossible to imagine for these curious, ardent lovers
of life. Fives should not focus on maintaining childhood relationships, buying lifetime health club memberships, or form-
ing emotional attachments to material possessions. Fives are
intended to experience things that are unfamiliar.

Number 5 people are consistently undergoing transitions.
They create costly or delaying problems by signing long-term
leases, collecting material assets, or acting possessive. It is
difficult for them to own anything permanently or to have
anyone own them. Fives should follow a lively interest, become
skillful, complete a goal, and move on to new challenges.

Without intending to be free and easy, they will discover that destiny will not allow commitments or responsibilities to tie them down.

If a number 5 tries to stabilize on his given lifepath, he will find that hesitancy, escapist habits, or a nine-to-five job will not eliminate surprises and inconsistencies. Time spent attempting to frustrate life's changes will only result in feelings of inadequacy.

Generally the bearer of this destiny wonders why others are able to live in the same home for a lifetime, plan for vacations, and become pensioned senior citizens. Actually the expansive number 5 may be envied by more grounded, less adventurous destiny bearers. In a balanced number 5 destiny the bearer takes risks in order to learn about freedom. As time goes by the number 5 learns to depend upon his talents and versatility to be what he needs to be—he may be a bum, a bandit, or a businessman. Having freedom is easy; knowing how to cope with it or profit from it is the problem.

BIRTHDAY INFLUENCES
WITHIN THE DESTINY

May

Individuals born in May learn in youth that they cannot be conventional, tied down, or materialistic. They are exposed to nonroutine situations, changes, and fluctuating values. Situations arise that cause them to learn from experience and to discipline their restlessness. There may be travels, financial ups and downs, or sensual temptations in youth to teach number 5 destiny holders to live by their wits.

Unconventional freedoms and interactions in childhood with a variety of resourceful, adaptable, daring people provide for the 5 an unconfined training ground whose lessons are not forgotten. This time may be remembered as a period of learning to be broad-minded, inventive, and flexible. The youngster wants to satisfy his curiosity, so if he suffers from inactivity or his questioning, clever nature is too focused, he may become passionless and purposeless. To learn to provide for himself, the number 5 youngster must be a go-getter, one who adapts to spontaneous opportunities and promotes talents or ideas. People born in May rarely lay a foundation that guarantees future stability. They do learn to understand human nature and to be delightful, alert, fun-loving companions.

Birthday: 5, 14, 23

THE BIRTHDAY NUMBER HAS AN INFLUENCE ON PERSONALITY AND DESTINY. IT ATTRACTS PEOPLE AND EXPERIENCES DURING MID-LIFE THAT EXEMPLIFY THE NUMBER MEANING.

The mid-life productivity cycle begins with maturity. It lasts from approximately twenty-eight to fifty-five years of age and coordinates with the destiny during that time span. The birthday-number meaning adds its character traits and experiences to an individual's numerology analysis.

People born on the fifth, fourteenth, and twenty-third of the month, in addition to the character traits outlined by the number meanings for the name, are multifaceted, on-the-spot, nonconforming enthusiasts. They may not be happy when confined, or comfortable with spiritless or stagnant traditionalists. Individuals born on these dates want freedom, independence, and opportunities to progress.

Between approximately twenty-eight and fifty-five years of age—the twenty-seven-year productivity cycle within the destiny—life will offer additional opportunities to strive for a reduction of limitations and to travel mentally or physically. Attention to unknown lifestyles, people, and experiences will keep one expanding abilities to analyze character and make oneself at home in any environment. The individual should not condemn anything because it is different, but should try everything, absorb the experience, tell others about it, and make taking risks worthwhile.

PERSONAL YEAR

The number 5 is the fifth year in the cycle of nine years of experience that results in a polish and skill of performance based upon the goals set in the first year. It is a time to get away from routines, simultaneously keeping last year's practical assessments in mind when May begins a time for vacations, sensual pleasures, and transitions. For most, this is a fast-paced time—filled with new people and scenery—that is intended to spark curiosity, add versatility, and result in a broader perspective. For others, the year focuses on accommodating a restless feeling that began in October of the preceding year. It is an energetic year to learn from experience, discard old ideas, and consider looking at long-term goals from a different angle.

One should keep material ambitions in mind while gambling on a new approach to business, home, and lifestyle. One ought to take a chance on unknowns and not fear making spontaneous decisions. This is not the year to buy a house or otherwise add to responsibilities. To get the best from this year, one must ease up on workaday obligations and let go of practical and emotional burdens. A willing, vigorous, and original approach to the many possibilities offered should make this a lively year.

Do not fear experimenting with up-to-date clothing styles, foods, or fancies. Recognize this once-in-nine-year chance to be a bit self-indulgent, informal, and gregarious. Go anywhere. Do anything. Attract attention. Do not plan too much or expect to maintain a tight schedule. Plans will be altered, and schedules will change. Expect only the unexpected. Welcome this golden opportunity to work less and progress anyway. Strike while the iron is hot. This year includes a few strokes of good luck for the person who is ready to make room for unusual methods, ideas, and philosophies.

The 5 year will test one's ability to feel free and easy yet remain constructive. Understand that progress depends on exhibiting tolerance and profiting from new experiences, and don't anticipate the end result or preconceive how people will interact. Attitude is very significant: it is best to go with the flow. Social activities will lead to contacts with impulsive, freewheeling, dynamic people who will indicate the availability of new directions. Residential, family, or business moves may come out of the blue or manifest themselves as the result of last year's planning. Whether you think the changes are good or bad, breaks from everyday role-playing or the natural course of events should be viewed as transitions that lead to growth.

If married, expect a rekindling of the focus on sensuality. If single, expect to meet titillating, provocative, extraordinary strangers. If a lover or friend remains in the picture through April of the following year, they are potential marriage partners. In school, expect extracurricular interests to break concentration on studies. In business, expect to advertise, to attract publicity, and to make changes. This is a time to bend the rules. People who thrive on system, order, and responsibilities will feel threatened. The open-minded will have a ball! Efforts made this year will determine the scope of the ambitions harvested during the following four years.

PERSONAL MONTH

The number 5 personal month within any personal year provides an opportunity to make transitions and changes. Whimsical ideas, travel, and a drive toward less responsibility should take top priority. A narrow point of view, rigidity, and sustained efforts should be put on the shelf. The previous month was filled with practical realities and limitations and there was little time for experimentation. Now is the time to take a chance on love and luck. Enjoy excitements, new people, and burgeoning opportunities. Situations may arise requiring one to follow a hunch. Use this month to be venturesome: try something different, attention-getting, and spontaneous. Be flexible, enterprising, and broad-minded when face-to-face with unexpected possibilities.

PERSONAL DAY

Wake up early or late and approach each hour's unconventional opportunities with an open mind. Whether you are heading for the office, a vacation day, or the grocery store, do it differently. Experiment and change perspectives. Dress to stop traffic, take a long lunch, and meet whatever comes with enthusiasm. Be responsible when necessary, but allow yourself to feel restless, sociable, and sexy. In other words, expect to be flexible. Show the world a skillful switch-hitter, ready to go to bat when plans are altered or changed.

On their 5 personal day, people are attracted to physical attributes, enthusiastic promotions, and adventurous touches. This is the day to make a blind date, go to the racetrack, or spontaneously take a prospective client to lunch. Avoid becoming too practical, inconsiderate, or determined to see tangible work results. Risks, freedom, and good times are in the air. Outlets for experimentation await, and potentials are ripe for future long-term commitments.

Make a personal resolution to do something on the spur of the moment. Bowl someone over with charm, wit, and adventurous ideas, but allow time for unanticipated socializing or accidents. In haste to get many things done, you may break a dish or trip on your own feet. Be careful and slow down if nerves get frayed, and be resourceful when commencing new projects. Nothing will be accomplished today unless you release structures and get a new point of view. Turn to tomorrow's added responsibilities, conventional duties, and the priority of emotional relationships to bring back routines and make time to finish commitments.

CHAPTER TEN

NUMBER 6

Nurturing

◄◄◄

▶▶▶

Nurturing

ATTRIBUTES:
POSITIVE—Conscientious, Peacemaking, Kind, Stable, Devoted, Idealistic, Wise, Congenial, Domestically Concerned.
NEGATIVE—Smothering, Opinionated, Worried, Unforgiving, Intolerant, Unconcerned, Unreliable, Sacrificing, Discontented.

CORRESPONDENTS:
LETTERS: F, O, X
EVEN NUMBER: Receptive
DISPOSITION: Parental, Responsible
NUMBERS: 15, 24, 33, 42, 51, 60, 69, 78, 87, 96, 105
COLOR: Blue
GEMS: Blue Sapphire, Blue-White Pearl, Diamond
CRYSTAL: Indicolite (Blue Tourmaline)
VEGETATION: Chrysanthemum, Dandelion, Laurel, Tulip, Palm, Poplar, Rosewood.

FOODS: Potatoes, Spaghetti, Sweet Potato, Pork, Fish, Crab, Rye Bread, Parsley, Orange, Banana, Peach.

MUSICAL INSTRUMENTS/APPEAL: Banjo, Mouth Organ, Concert, Hymn, Musical.

MUSICAL NOTE: G (When Challenged, G#)

LOCATIONS: State: Delaware, Hawaii, Maine, Massachusetts, Montana, Texas

City: Altoona, Anaheim, Atlanta, Bridgeport, Cincinnati, Cleveland, Raleigh, Stamford, Tampa

PLANET: Jupiter

MONTH: June

BIRTHDAYS: 6, 15, 24

DAYS OF THE WEEK: Sunday, Monday, Friday

GENERAL COMPATIBILITY NUMBERS: 2, 3, 4, 9 (8 IN LOVE)

INCOMPATIBILITY NUMBERS: 1, 5, 7, 8

Note: If an individual has the challenge to the number 6, these descriptions will swing from positive to negative until the challenge is balanced. Please be sure to read the challenge number meaning.

CHALLENGE OF THE NUMBER 6

This is the challenge of responsibility, obligations to personal relationships, and emotional judgments. It stems from too much or too little family and community focus in childhood. Parents, siblings, and the older generations may have contributed too forcefully to the child's morals, ethics, and standards. Perhaps there was a lack of domestic responsibility and unity early on. The child may have been encouraged to be too mature or may have been too protected.

The 6 challenge holder may feel selfish if unwilling to assume unnaturally heavy burdens. The adult with this challenge may volunteer too much, be opinionated, and take everything to heart. He may be unable to sense who really needs sympathy or how much to give. If the 6 challenge holder sacrifices too much, he becomes selfish and argumentative, and feels like the martyr. Under such circumstances, his talent for encouraging loving, peaceful, nurturing relationships is lost.

The challenge holder may not be able to express himself creatively if he is surrounded by leaners in a domestic environment. It is too difficult for a 6 challenge holder to assess which burdens and responsibilities are solely his own. As a preteen he may have been left to care for siblings—cooking, cleaning, and marketing—excluding school chums and youthful diversions. He may have felt resentment and ultimately guilt for his attempts to care for others when he could barely care for himself.

As teenagers, 6s may refuse to share household responsibilities. Challenged 6s either resent self-sacrifice or assume parental obligations. They are required to make either too many or too few personal/domestic adjustments. Too much or too little nurturing causes the challenge holder to become too sympathetic and involved—or too uninterested in another's emotional pressures.

As adults, these challenge holders seek out the needy or are sought out by the needy. They send out vibrations that encourage dependency and rebel when they find themselves in servitude. They are the office or hobby club volunteers who teach and help before being asked. Yet when they assume responsibility for the whole project and take on more than they can handle, they feel used. The result is that no one says thank you. The overbearing challenge holders inadvertently cause the "users" to feel guilty. The challenge holders are convinced that they have the thankless jobs and only get ridiculed or taken for granted. For them, volunteering becomes a difficult habit to break. The challenge holders will likely repeat this pattern until they are emotionally drained and exhausted. After they recover, they repeat the pattern.

When 6s are invited to a dinner party, they become "Mr. or Mrs. Full-charge." They check the hors d'oeuvres trays, the bar, and the table arrangements. If things are not up to their standards, they rush into the kitchen to personally right all wrongs. They will rearrange the seating because the host's seating plan was thoughtless or "a terrible mistake." The other side of the challenge places the 6 bearers' noses in the air. People at this extreme do not pitch in, even if a need becomes obvious. In their opinion the party would have been a success *if* they had been invited to participate in the planning and execution.

The physical strains induced by this challenge of intolerance and personal idealism make for a tight spinal cord, emotionally induced chronic problems, and an overly stressed heart. It is not unusual for the number 6 challenge holder to forever be fighting fat, as they eat their way from frustration to emotional calm.

The "live and let live" attitude expressed by others only serves to alienate the number 6 challenge holder. He has a hard time learning that obligations or justice mean one thing to him and something else to others. He becomes angry after relentlessly making a slave of himself for loved ones while striving to uphold his own standards.

The number 6 challenge holder either cherishes or disdains an opulent and comfortable home. He may either go to artistic extremes or ignore the decor. If home life is disrupted, he may find it too emotionally painful to rebuild another. He may be envious, jealous, and spiteful *or* equally generous, loving, and peacemaking. Often the challenge holder's emotions will pendulate. Family ties will be either too close or too distant. Strained relationships will be the result until the challenge holder chooses to take a less personal attitude and turns his broad-minded perspective on himself as well as others.

The number 6 challenge may swing from one of the following extremes to another until the challenge holder recognizes his behavior and new habits that stabilize his opinions are initiated.

Too smug or too unsure.

Too firm or too weak.
Too cynical or too loving.
Too judgmental or too unconcerned.
Too anxious or too calm.
Too family-focused or too alone.
Too obstinate or too yielding.
Too intractable or too adjusting.
Too harmonious or too disruptive.
Too protective or too suspicious.
Too burden-loving or too selfish.
Too all-knowing or too dependent.
Too concerned or too irresponsible.
Too parental or too immature.

PHYSICAL CHALLENGES OF THE NUMBER 6

Challenges can affect physical as well as mental health. Body chemistry changes when individuals are stressed, and when we do not know what is good for us, our minds trigger anxious, angry, or frustrated habits. When we are mean to ourselves, we get sick. One's attitude sends the brain a message, and the brain tells the body to scream for help.

To get attention for their dis-ease, often people get sick or form negative habits. Numerologists believe that illness and wellness depend upon attitude, and challenges indicate the attitudes that result from needy feelings. When we do not feel needy, we feel well and balanced and do not crave attention from others. Essentially, if the personality challenges are balanced, the body chemistry is in balance, too, and therefore there is little chance of mental or physical dis-ease.

Challenge numbers indicate the ways people subconsciously punish themselves for not being consciously good to themselves.

The following list of dis-eases and negative habits relate to the challenge of the number 6.

Breast Cyst	Kidney Problems
Colitis	Leg Problem
Cramp	Menstrual Problem
Dowager's Hump	Mouth Problems
Drug Problems	Neck Problem
Fatigue	Overweight
Gallstone	Pants wetting
Gum Problems	Prostate Problem
Hemophilia	Stomach Problems
Hemorrhoids	Tumor
Hip Problem	Ulcers
Hypertension	

TO BALANCE THE CHALLENGE OF THE 6 AND BRING IT OUT AS A TALENT . . .

The first step to balancing the challenge is to feel comfortable about saying "I need harmony." Allow the people in your immediate environment to do their own jobs, have their own opinions, and assume their own obligations. You are not responsible for the family, the neighborhood, the office staff, the community, or the world.

Being conscientious in everything you do makes you feel good. Invite people to see your lovely home, and if it is not up to your standards physically, cook a good meal and make guests and family feel welcome; this will make you feel good, too.

Take on obligations *when* you are invited. If you see the need to volunteer, ask if the person who needs assistance wants your contributions—sometimes temporary loan or a minute of your time is all that is necessary. Most needy people will speak up, but if you think they are unable, ask them how you may be of assistance. This step should eliminate an overextension of your capacities and answer your need to help, teach, and counsel.

If marriage and parenting are causing you stress, you may feel the responsibilities too deeply. Inadvertently or purposely you may indicate pressure when caring for others because you have not put time aside for your personal needs. It is your responsibility to yourself to adjust wrongs in your own life; allow others to learn from your example. You may attract dependency because you unconsciously build your self-esteem on others' inability to take care of themselves. Think about that.

If you are the one everyone comes to when in need, ask yourself why. You will be surprised to learn that things run smoothly even when you are not running the show. In reality, everyone can assume responsibility for himself. When you have learned to live and let live, people may display surprising generosity and resourcefulness. Your desire to feel pride in relationships will be fulfilled. You will have time for yourself and appear to be less pressured. You will change and see that change reflected in the happiness of loved ones.

Recognize yourself as a socially conscious, artistic, loving, protective person. You deserve to have respect, a comfortable lifestyle, and a peaceful environment.

SELF-MOTIVATION

Youth:

As tots, these children feel the number 6 urge to be involved, loving, and responsive. When reprimanded, they will try to appease authorities or act as if their hearts are broken. These tots need emotionally and physically comforting relationships to maintain a peaceful feeling. Number 6 youngsters are not prone to starting arguments; in fact, they are instead unobtrusive, uncomplaining, affectionate little accommodators. If surrounded by aloof or domestically negligent authorities, they will become protective and anxious. They want and need compassionate, congenial, instructional leadership.

Parents may describe their number 6 children as dependable, earnest, and trustworthy. These words describe these individuals when surrounded by kind, honorable, indulgent authorities. If the 6 children's conscientiousness is considered bothersome and the parents disregard their need to assume responsibility, these children may become disheartened and sullen. Number 6 youngsters want to serve, share, and indulge loved ones. Once 6s, who have their feelings rooted in devotion to home, family, and community, are overwhelmed by hostility and discouragement, they will become cranky and unreasonable, or will indicate indifference by becoming uncooperative.

Number 6 children need opportunities to exhibit their supportive nature in order to utilize their maturity and resourcefulness. Their desires should be channeled to employ their disarming, softhearted, amiable natural instincts and selflessness. Drama lessons, household chores, caring for more dependent oldsters or youngsters, or offering heartfelt advice will put their sensible minds to good use. Too little emotional security may prove a problem in maturity if these number 6 children are not shown firm judgments and assertiveness. One result may be that they will not want to be alone or to act unconventionally.

If there is disharmony in the family, peace-loving 6s are genuinely upset. They will attempt to get involved, pacify, and show an interest in maintaining a harmonious environment. Since 6s are volunteers, they will feel unappreciated if others take their generosity for granted or forget to say thank you. When their willingness to contribute is repressed or they are asked to sacrifice without eventual recognition, they will become resentful. However, these youths are generally principled and conscious of justice—they can usually be counted on to be tolerant and wise.

Ethical 6 youths enjoy promoting happiness and friendship, and they want to rectify all mistakes. Specifically, needy, personally idealistic, and artistic people will get them involved with little effort. It is best that parents teach them not to overdo their cordiality, or when school is out, they may find a kitchenful of their children's hungry playmates sampling the evening's dessert. Moreover, underachieving chums who attract number 6s' sympathy may also benefit from their urge to teach. As a result, parents may end up feeling as if they are running the neighborhood asylum for needy, hungry waifs who have sparked their children's benevolent instincts.

If number 6s have more self-absorbed number meanings in other aspects of their chart, these meanings will temper their altruistic urges. They will nevertheless find other means of demonstrating their desire to be well intentioned and protective.

As teens, 6s will want to be surrounded by beauty, comfort, and means by which to feel important. Their maturity begins early and they can actually be sensible counselors for peers and adults alike. Although the number 6 children may not be intellectual probers because they tend to do what is expected of them, their school grades should be average or better. Alert parents will soon find that these conscientious and respectable managers will be happy to earn money serving personal, domestic, and/or public needs.

Maturity:

Number 6 adults want to be settled, dependable, and judicious. They need to find outlets for good taste and put their understanding nature to use in uplifting or comforting others. Largely they want to feel wanted, loved, and respected. If this goal seems a bit conventional—it is, and 6s are; however, number 6 adults should be able to create stability out of irresponsibility. After assessing the problems, they are capable of managing people's lives. They are the contributors who willingly deny themselves so others may benefit. Their heartfelt impulses to advise, see justice done, and follow through on commitments make them superb therapists, teachers, and nurses.

Number 6 people do not like to be footloose or fancy-free. Rarely unresponsive or self-seeking lovers or mates, they just need to know that they are depended upon and they will provide. In much the same vein, 6s should have their duties outlined or they will take on too much. A lost pet, troubled stranger, or hospitalized friend will generally command their interest, indicating that when balanced, these individuals are emotionally receptive, creatively artistic, and strongly focused on home and family. When in their care, youngsters are taught to be accountable, constant, and tolerant. Able to follow their natural instincts, number 6 adults are unselfish, personally idealistic, and dutiful parents.

Material objectives are important to number 6s, but do not rule their decisions. An opulent home with a full refrigerator and comfortable furnishings is high on their list of priorities. Sixes are at ease with artistic, sociable, tranquil people who want solid, steady lifestyles. Above all, number 6 people want to be decent, humanitarian, moral citizens.

When asked for help, 6s respond with their interpretation of right and wrong, sometimes expecting others to live up to their standards and insisting upon the "law," as they view it. Too tenderhearted to send anyone away, they may feel overwhelmed by another's problems, find fault with his honesty or integrity, and generally become dismayed with him. Sincere and virtuous number 6s are likely to report a felon—or advise the felon to report himself to the police. One way or another, they find a way to balance the scales of justice.

One problem for those with the number 6 self-motivation is understanding why others need solitude. They imagine that life would be intolerable without social interactions and a safe place to nest. Their close ties to family may make one wonder if they ever prefer to be alone. Accordingly, business ambitions may come second to family obligations. As time goes by, many people and experiences fall under their parental gaze, and anything or anyone that may be assimilated and soothed is invited to share their home and affection. Even heedless or uncooperative recipients of their good deeds are not left stranded, because when balanced, 6s will be obliging and stay with a problem until it is solved.

Number 6s worry about paying bills, decorating a home, and making the right impression on loved ones. Their greatest goal is to stay in one place and establish a reputation for dependability, and to interact with solid, romantic, considerate people. Sixes want to love, and they give it generously. Usually creatures of comfort, they prefer utilitarian clothing styles, four-door sedans, and a stable, appreciative, significant love relationship. Sixes strive to maintain a conventional lifestyle in which they watch their families grow and prosper.

Number 6 individuals will commute from suburbia, do their own repairs, and build credit by paying off loans. They are concerned about children's college funds, a daughter's wedding arrangements, and retirement benefits. As worriers and careful planners, they have a deep sense of obligation and responsibility, and when guided by instincts, they earn and allocate money for family, home, and community improvements. These individuals try to cover all practical and emotional bases, often spending their last dollar to educate their children. When emotionally touched by a family member's problems or desires, they will sacrifice and expect their partners to agree with their decision.

For the balanced, indulgent, and sentimental number 6, marriage will be of long duration. The bonds of fidelity can be strong for dutiful, ethical, and resolute 6s. It takes greedy, nasty, unreasoning people to make number 6s take off their blinders once they have fallen in love; however, there may be other less responsible, restless, and unconventional number meanings in the chart to add instability to these 6s' character. Before contracting for life, 6s should always note and compare their own numbers and the basic numbers within their lover's chart.

The marriage of two number 6 motivations will be good if both can live up to the same morals, ethics, and standards. If they differ, both idealists will try to remake each other. Marriage may result in faultfinding, interfering, possessive disillusionment. Sixes need someone to care for, and they prefer giving what they feel the other should want. If wants are not the same, the recipient will not be appreciative. If desires are the same, in time, boredom may add confusing tensions.

The number 6 often tends to think that a washing machine, garbage compactor, or refrigerator makes a terrific birthday gift for a spouse; that's fine if the other 6 agrees that diamonds or Porsches are not trappings that he or she wants to own. If one partner tries to compromise, the other will be responsive once attitudes toward family, community, and material objectives are solidly established. Neither will want to lose a steadfast love or to be uprooted.

SELF-IMAGE

Youth:

When lying on the bed, listening to music, and imagining "What am I going to be like when I grow up? How will I walk, dress, and talk?" number 6 youths visualize homebodies. They dream of living a comfortable, hospitable, and responsible life. Little boys see themselves in well-respected positions in which they capably serve or comfort others and bring home the bacon to an adoring, appreciative family. Little girls see themselves as supportive friends and mates, always there when needed and devoted to marriage or a responsible position. Children with the number 6 self-image may picture themselves as affectionate fatherly or motherly types who nurture family ties, express artistic interests, and contribute to the community welfare.

They may appear to be quiet, refined, sturdy children who display more maturity than one would expect. When 6s say they want to be teachers, social workers, or parents, they envision themselves in these positions because they employ their compassion, helpfulness, and well-intentioned ideas. When living up to their self-image, these individuals will be first to show concern and place themselves in jeopardy to save others, and they appear ever ready to share their personal ideals, passionate hopes, and altruistic dreams.

Youngsters with dreams based upon the meaning of the number 6 may be self-sacrificing; because they extend their emotional responsiveness in this way, they are often overwhelmed by their attraction to and for dependent people. They will often assert themselves in order to rectify situations that cause problems for people they love or want to help. They seem able to create harmony in their own lives and the lives of their family members and community. Correspondingly, their overall appearance is comfortable and comforting, and they may wear durable clothes and soothing colors. They prefer loose, comfortable garments to stylish discomfort, and when living up to their self-image, 6s want to wear clothes that make them appear easy to approach and willing to listen. Rarely uncaring or irresponsible, youthful number 6s strive for steady, mature, secure relationships and a peaceful lifestyle.

Maturity:

When walking out of an elevator or into a room—before personality or intellect come into play—number 6 adults send out a sturdy, sedate, and comforting vibration. Their attitude indicates a sympathetic personality and a genuine responsiveness. The first impression 6s give is solid, sometimes artistic, and always warm. If self-motivation and self-expression numbers are mental or introverted number 6s will look quiet and unruffled. Clothing styles, posture, and attitude will not indicate their emotional or protective self-image.

When 6s are wearing the color blue, the self-image is emphasized, as blue implies surety, strength, and stability. It is powerful without bowling people over. Generally number 6s will not stand out in a crowd; in essence, they present a traditional, dependable, parental facade to the public. At first blush number 6s will harmonize with a group and appear willing to pitch in—making personal adjustments if necessary—when they observe the needs of people or situations.

Number 6 adults perceive themselves to be mature. When

living up to their self-image, their first impression implies a knack for assuming other people's burdens.

The self-expression number may govern the first impression if faddish or uniform dress codes are indicated by the career descriptions outlined in the number meaning.

The self-motivation number may influence the apparel of the bearers if they are relaxing and doing what they desire to do; however, when individuals are living up to their self-image, they will not feature correspondent colors or styles indicated by numbers in any other part of their numerology chart.

SELF-EXPRESSION

Youth:

It is obvious to adults when children have a number 6 self-expression. In youth, number 6 talents are based in willingness to volunteer for responsibilities and to assume a role in family obligations. Because they initially give devotion and try to maintain balance within the family unit, parents find little resentment when assigning chores to their number 6 children. As they get older, these children will be careful, detail-conscious, and diplomatic. They will delight authorities with their thoughtfulness, kindness, and maturity. As little know-it-alls, they may try the patience of adults; however, this annoyance is easily compensated by their judiciousness, sympathetic attitude, and dependability.

Without intending to be nosy, helpful number 6s may conscientiously and obligingly become too concerned about everyone's problems or business—the result being that each earnest, considerate gesture may lead to complications or confusions. To undemonstrative, businesslike parents, 6s may appear to be too troubled, interfering, and officious. On the other hand, to affectionate, sharing adults, they are accepted as welcome contributors to the family. Parents will probably pacify these children with additional domestic responsibilities.

Number 6 talents may lead these children to participate in musical, artistic, or theatrical interests. They have a need to feel useful and important and will initiate charitable activities in addition to fulfilling basic obligations. Happiest when environments are peaceful, they will try to avoid arguments and fulfill scholastic and social expectations. One personal fault is that too often number 6s try to find time and energy to uplift and comfort everyone crossing their path. Number 6 children will even attempt to counsel adults and peers, and when balanced, their wisdom is tempered with the openhearted understanding and honesty that enables them to hold an office staff or family together.

As teenagers, these community-minded improvers are often given positions of responsibility and trust. They are successful diplomats and will attempt to reorganize or make adjustments when they feel people or things do not meet their personal standards. Sixes are rarely noncommital and have passionate opinions and dramatic deliveries that will be heard. When frustrated or hurt by disloyalty, intolerance, or pessimism, they may eat too much, lose themselves in work for others, or smother pets with affection. They are faithful when appreciated, but when disheartened, they may be envious, troublemaking malcontents.

Loving number 6 youths will not be afraid to show tenderness or offer compliments freely. They may overflow with demonstrations of generosity, sincerity, and accountability. In general, number 6 individuals will seek or create an environment that nurtures their talents for providing answers. Once they find a career interest that offers the opportunity to serve family or community, they command respect and demonstrate their reliability.

Proponents of comfort and control, number 6 youths enjoy cooking, home beautification, and household improvements. Correspondingly, they will establish comfortable eating, sleeping, and work habits. Number 6 young adults prefer to dine out to discover new recipes and styles of decor, will be first to volunteer to paint or wallpaper, taking pride in their family or personal residence, and are uncomfortable in unbalanced groups or surroundings. If there is confusion in any arena, 6s will attempt to stabilize or tranquilize.

These youths should be encouraged to seek a job or career in which they can put to use their dependability, communication gifts, and personal instincts. They may become outstanding theatrical producers, teachers, or restaurateurs. Their awesome sense of responsibility and knack for harmonizing complex groups of people may extend far beyond the most doting parents' expectations.

Maturity:

Suggested Occupations: Sociologist, interior decorator, guidance counselor, academic advisor, practical or registered nurse, doctor, veterinarian, hospital administrator, student, teacher, teacher's aide, social service worker, costume designer, greeting card designer, poet, writer, songwriter, actor/actress, artist, musician, theatrical agent, hotel manager-clerk, restaurant owner-employee, caterer, party designer, bartender, hotel/motel owner-employee, professional housekeeper, butler, cook, chef, home products retailer or distributor, clothing store owner-employee, banking trust officer, insurance services manager, civil servant, hospitalization career adviser, judge, receptionist, nursing home owner-employee, cosmetician, playground director, zookeeper, youth group leader, homemaker.

Options:

Careers indicated by the meaning of the self-motivation number may not make use of readily available talents but will allow the individual to feel comfortable.

Careers indicated by the self-image number meanings will encourage the individual to live up to youthful dreams.

Careers indicated by the meaning of the destiny number, if it is not the same as the self-expression number, will require that the individual learn from incoming personalities and experiences.

If self-expression and destiny numbers are the same, the individual's talents will be recognized and utilized early in life.
Maturity: Self-Expression Analysis

Sixes have the potential to reap financial rewards for their ability to provide services, assume responsibilities, and be trustworthy employees and fair employers. In addition, they may receive recognition for their talent in providing comfort, integrity, and showmanship when needed or requested. In particular, they attract positions in which conscientiousness, trustworthiness, and congeniality are required.

Resolute, sincere, and supportive communicators, 6s are not afraid to let their feelings be known. These individuals are protective, devoted, and emotional, and earn the limelight by acting as peacemaking intermediaries.

Number 6 talents are rarely noncommittal or slipshod. They have strong personal ideals and constantly strive to bring others up to their standards. These passionate individuals are rarely argumentative, self-seeking, or unaccountable when teaching or uplifting others. Talented advisers, they know it takes tolerance to teach tolerance. Often imaginative artists, they bring their talents to both office and home. Always on the lookout for stability, they crave a guaranteed salary with retirement benefits and long-lasting security. Day-to-day routines satisfy their need to balance business and domestic commitments and their preference for a steady pace.

Balanced number 6 talents may be disarmingly blunt. They are well intentioned and moral romantics, but their responses may sometimes be inappropriately personal. When also having the challenge of the number 6 or in an interfering mood, 6 individuals may become smothering and possessive. If number 6s' career requires them to work alone, it is likely that the job will be of short duration, for 6s are most successful when interacting with groups, caring for the welfare of others, and creating harmonious environments. They know what is good for everyone and will volunteer to be part of a team effort or make personal adjustments for friends. They are loyal, sacrificing, and demonstrative employees and employers who respond to everyone with compassion and ethical rectitude.

Sixes may be too trusting, however. When volunteering or being called upon, they must avoid getting into a self-sacrificing rut. These responsible, dutiful, and temperate workers usually build a risk-free future; however, they often have latent artistic or communication talents. Therefore hobbies may sometimes lead to commercial prospects. Sixes often become professional home decorators, caterers, or college students late in life.

If self-motivation and/or destiny number meanings indicate unconventional, changeable, or self-promotional activity, those with the number 6 self-expression will strain to maintain their serious commitment to home, family, and community security. Number 6 home-lovers supported by compatible numbers 2, 3, 4, and 9 in other parts of their chart will not have to struggle with their need for job and domestic harmony. Unaccustomed to frequent changes, venturesome ambitions, or going it alone, number 6 talents will neither change horses in midstream nor attempt to shoot the rapids.

Generally number 6s will not indulge in complaining or suspiciousness, or allow themselves to be victimized. However, the negative aspects of this number require a balancing discipline to prevent overresponsibility and drudgery. Talents who inspire love, harmony, and appreciation have cause to expect long-lasting relationships, but 6s must relate to others, give service, and stay involved without becoming trapped by their own conscientiousness.

DESTINY

WE ARE NOT BORN KNOWING WHAT LIFE HAS TO OFFER. INDIVIDUALS WITH THE NUMBER 6 DESTINY LEARN TO DEVELOP RESPONSIBILITY, BALANCE, AND LOVING RELATIONSHIPS. THEY ENCOUNTER THE PEOPLE AND EXPERIENCES THAT TEACH THEM TO

VALUE STABILITY, UNSELFISHNESS, AND DOMESTIC-ITY.

This destiny implies a lifetime of congeniality, involvement, and emotional generosity: the result is an early bloomer who is sensible, dependable, and considerate. To make the most of numerology's ability to forecast, number 6s must be accommodating, earnest, and honorable. Sixes generally have one career or marriage during their lifetime, and they are on a protected road, paved by family ties, love of home, and community obligations.

The number 6 may be born to conventional, indulgent parents who insist upon a solid foundation and focus on responsibilities, in which case life may be filled with artistic interests that lead to expectations for an attractive, opulent home and a hospitable lifestyle. The number 6 destiny is interdependent: an individual learns to be a mainstay and is almost always surrounded by supporters. Within this lifestyle, the number 6 will strive to better personal and home conditions while maintaining harmony under problematic situations.

People with a number 6 destiny will not find success by escaping responsibilities or being insincere; instead, they find that opportunities come in when they put their hand out to help another, and often they themselves prosper from teaching others to stand on their own two feet.

Sixes work steadily to make material, domestic, and artistic improvements: the prime examples of this service-oriented destiny are dedicated teachers, theatrical producers, or anyone who stays single to care for an aged parent. Sixes learn to be responsive to the needs of weaker or less fortunate individuals without feeling resentment or becoming overprotective.

A willingness to be kind, sympathetic, and instructional will earn these destiny holders a reputation for being a volunteer, a pussycat, and a lover. Sixes are never childish. They may choose to be too trusting, however, and find that they must assume personal responsibility for the outcome of things. When they relax their standards or insist that their plans be carried out, 6s will find that either too little commitment or too much concern will disrupt their peaceful existence. Therefore, attempts at family or community uplift may bring them respect and add to their tranquillity only if done with discretion and earnestness. An emphasis on individual ambitions will not bring number 6 destiny holders happiness.

There are personal limitations to the obligations offered by this destiny. Only selfishness, irresponsibility, and unconventional behavior will delay its holders' right to find contentment while demonstrating and receiving love. Number 6 destiny holders are best suited to communication fields in careers that entertain or demonstrate concern for the welfare of others. Parental, conventional, and creative people open doors for these sentimental do-gooders, while dependents provide reasons for them to give advice. Children, pets, and self-destructive associates spark concerns, and life is peppered with other people's problems. Often crises arise demanding that this destiny holder respond with compassion and mature guidance.

Number 6s may not live life in the fast lane; however, they will reflect upon many quiet successes as time goes by. Sixes become capable of patient, tender, and protective love and build inner resources in order to sacrifice pleasures. They learn to promote equality and growth, which alerts marriage and business partners alike that these individuals are assets. Sixes are protected throughout life by the people they marry, by family background, or through job security; however, faultfinding and juggling many loves, careers, or jobs will probably make these destiny holders blind to the need to balance family and finances. The result is that 6 destiny holders must learn to maintain personal stability in order to render beneficial services to their family and environment.

Sixes grow wise quickly. They build everyday wisdom, which makes them likable business associates and friends. It is difficult for them to say no or to soothe their occasional feelings of restlessness, because they must be dependable. Sixes should follow their hearts, become involved when needed, and lead decent lives. People who are biased or intolerant may cross their path, for 6s will meet tests of both virtue and vice. Without intending to concentrate their energies on family and community, they nurture and balance until outside interests become less comfortable or appealing.

On the lifepath of the number 6, greed, impassivity, or unresponsiveness will never eliminate opportunities to take on commitments or drown out cries for help from the old, young, or frenzied. Yet time spent attempting to ignore lifestyle limitations will only result in feelings of inferiority, inundation, or melancholy.

Generally the bearer of this destiny wonders why others are free to follow their curiosity or be spontaneous and self-absorbed when actually the stable number 6 may be envied by more emancipated and nonconforming destiny bearers. In a balanced destiny the number 6 must learn not to take risks in order to be secure when others need him. As time goes by he learns to depend upon his ethics and resourcefulness to be what he needs to be. He may be a homemaker, a teacher, or a personnel director. Having demanding responsibilities may not be easy, but knowing how to provide for, shape, and guide others into a wiser and stronger independence is a labor of love.

BIRTHDAY INFLUENCES
WITHIN THE DESTINY

June

Individuals born in June learn in youth that they cannot be unreliable, indifferent, or selfish. They are exposed to close domestic situations, advisory authorities, and solid values. Situations arise that cause them to pitch in, study wisely, and understand the necessity for team effort. There may be restrictions, responsibilities, and family concerns in youth that teach June–born children to fulfill duties conscientiously.

Childhood's protective influences, artistic explorations, and focus on family provide the 6 with a traditional training ground whose lessons are not easily forgotten. Youth may be remembered as a time to learn to be considerate, creative, and trustworthy. The youngster wants to be loved and to show affection. If he feels insecurity or his concerned, imaginative nature is too uneasy, the child may become distant and self-seeking. To learn to provide for himself, the youngster must be willing to make personal adjustments and maintain friendly relationships.

People born in June rarely leave the family before they have secured another home. They do learn to share their wisdom, comfort those less fortunate, and serve other worthwhile purposes. June–born are surrounded in youth by well-intentioned, respected parental counselors.

Birthday: 6, 15, 24

THE BIRTHDAY NUMBER HAS AN INFLUENCE ON PERSONALITY AND DESTINY. IT ATTRACTS PEOPLE AND EXPERIENCES DURING MID-LIFE THAT EXEMPLIFY THE NUMBER MEANING.

The mid-life productivity cycle begins with maturity. It lasts from approximately twenty-eight to fifty-five years of age and coordinates with the destiny during that time span. The birthday-number meaning adds its character traits and experiences to an individual's numerology analysis.

People born on the sixth, fifteenth, and twenty-fourth of the month, in addition to the character traits outlined by the number meanings for the name, are responsible, accommodating, and supportive teachers. They may not be happy when alone, or comfortable with unreliable or unethical cynics. Individuals born on these dates want domestic tranquillity, material advantages, and a conventional lifestyle.

Between approximately twenty-eight and fifty-five years of age—the twenty-seven-year productivity cycle within the destiny—life will offer responsibilities and personal limitations. Attention to needy or dependent people will keep these protective people close to home and accountable. These individuals should never be insincere. They should try to improve the living standards and expectations for younger, older, weaker, or less fortunate dependents.

PERSONAL YEAR

The number 6 is the sixth year in the cycle of nine years of experience that results in a polish and skill of performance based upon the goals set in the first year. It is a time to focus upon home, family, and community responsibilities. The individual should keep the previous year's freedom in mind when April begins new projects and conscientiously accommodate loved ones and associates when demands are made. This is a receptive time span filled with household maintenance chores and obligations. It is best to take things as they come. "What goes around, comes around," and this year one cannot expect to be self-absorbed or receive love without giving it. This year will center on comforting others, and personal adjustments should be made to the tempo changes that last October brought on. It is a year when progress is calculated by emotional generosity, and in November, bread cast upon the waters will return.

The number 6 should keep romantic notions and peaceful relationships in mind when called upon to make personal sacrifices for others. A charitable, tolerant approach and a forgive and forget attitude will help. This is not the year to seek solitude or be noncommittal. To get the best from this year, the individual must be satisfied, concerned over another's problems, demonstrative of devotion to less able associates, and earnestly sympathetic. A considerate, faithful, indulgent approach to traditional obligations should make this year a stable one.

Do not object to staying home, supporting a loved one's desires, or devoting time to listen to someone else. Recognize the once-in-nine-year chance to be a conscientious copemate and adviser. Help to improve community relations, and cultivate artistic, genial, faithful friendships. Do not shirk work or make spontaneous changes. Expect to find problems waiting to be solved at home if you travel or are self-absorbed and immature. Welcome the golden opportunity to work out differences and be part of a team, and remain careful and patient. February, August, and November will be memorable if you are ready to dole out understanding and quietly serve when help is needed.

The number 6 personal year is called the year of marriage. Whether one marries a person or a job, commitments made now must be given top priority. One should plan for the future, live each day as if it were the last, and not fall asleep angry. One should make a resolution to settle differences at the end of a day and greet the morning free of hostility. An unselfish attitude is very significant; although it is best to wait to be asked, one may give assistance when needed. Social activities or travel should be centered around family and community projects, as no new directions are indicated. This is a time to deepen ties and maintain assets. Whether one thinks that focusing on the immediate neighborhood is pleasurable or boring, this year's break from commercial ambitions or whimsical explorations should be viewed as part of the natural course of events.

If married, expect to make home improvements and share precious moments with family and friends. If single, a lover or friend who came into the picture the previous year may be a candidate for a long-term relationship. If in school, be cooperative at home, expect to take on more responsibility, and take this opportunity to stabilize grades. In business or practical affairs, expect to be resourceful and resolute and to stand up for personal beliefs. This is a time to solve problems while maintaining personal integrity. Unselfish efforts and obligations undertaken this year will be appreciated and provide experiences that make one wiser. Dependents and people who are given assistance during this demanding time span will bolster ambitions harvested during the next three years.

PERSONAL MONTH

The number 6 personal month within any personal year gives one an opportunity to focus upon loved ones and home or community responsibilities. Travel is not advisable unless it is to visit family. Emotional responsiveness, domestic improvements, and maintenance of peaceful relationships should take top priority. An intellectual, intolerant, or self-seeking point of view should be put on the shelf. The preceding month offered a chance to get out of the rut, so now is the time to settle down to deepen love and create harmony. Enjoying sharing chores and old friends, and indulging in shows of affection is the order of this month. Situations may arise that require the sacrifice of personal desires. One should use this month to be accommodating—to teach, pacify, and indicate approval. It will best serve to be mature, devoted, and trustworthy when involved in emotional relationships.

PERSONAL DAY

Wake up early and approach each hour's responsibilities with a demonstration of integrity. Accomplish each task willingly and conscientiously. Do not experiment. Dress to get things done and to be comfortable. Be prepared to be accountable for all actions and remarks, but remember that this is also a day to show love and affection while taking on burdens for weaker or needier associates. Expect to make personal adjustments when necessary without making drudgery out of work. Let the world see a realistic, responsive, and dependable lover, partner, or friend.

People are subject to emotional outbursts and may make unfair demands on you. This is the day to be understanding, advisory, and indulgent. In these cases, avoid becoming argumentative, overinvolved, or unsympathetic. Domestic projects, creative ideas, and personally idealistic thoughts are in the air, and there are outlets for good deeds and potentials for long-term contentments to be tapped.

Make a personal commitment to go wherever help is needed. Hug someone. Bowl them over with sincere concern and practical advice. Allow time to shop for domestic purchases and for visiting family or a sick friend. Be fair and honest with everyone, and take care to clear up current misunderstandings or past discomforts in all areas. Don't go to sleep angry or force issues. This is a day to concentrate on making others happy. Tomorrow's communication delays and lowered physical energy give you a chance to analyze past or future goals and use private time for self-appraisal.

NUMBER 7

Mental Analysis

◄◄

►►►

ATTRIBUTES:
POSITIVE—Analytical, Authoritative, Mystical, Meticulous, Introspective, Aristocratic, Logical, Poised, Investigative, Wise
NEGATIVE—Aloof, Caustic, Cynical, Unrefined, Tactless, Opinionated, Faultfinding, Superficial, Joyless, Moody, Fussy

CORRESPONDENTS:
LETTERS: G, P, Y
ODD NUMBER: Intellectually Aggressive, Materially Receptive
DISPOSITION: Inquisitive, Contemplative, Discriminating
NUMBERS: 16, 25, 34, 43, 52, 61, 70, 79, 88, 97, 106
COLOR: Purple (Violet)
GEM: Alexandrite (Amethyst)
CRYSTALS: Amethyst, Violet Rutile
VEGETATION: Crocus, Geranium, Marigold, Poppy, Fern
FOODS: Herring, Omelet, Spinach, Roast Pork, Goose, Blackberry
MUSICAL INSTRUMENT/APPEAL: Harp, Ballet

MUSICAL NOTE: B (When Challenged A#)
LOCATIONS: State: California, Indiana, Maryland, New
Jersey, Tennessee, Wyoming
City: Alexandria, Columbus, Corpus Christi, Flint, Lin-
coln, Lowell, Oklahoma City, Orlando, Reno, Roanoke,
Tacoma, Trenton
PLANET: Mercury
MONTH: July
BIRTHDAYS: 7, 16, 25
DAYS OF THE WEEK: Saturday, Sunday
GENERAL COMPATIBILITY NUMBERS: 2, 4, 7 (Friend-
ship), 5 (Business)
INCOMPATIBILITY NUMBERS: 1, 3, 6, 8, 9

Note: If an individual has the challenge to the number 7, these
descriptions will swing from positive to negative until the challenge is balanced. Please be sure to read the challenge number
meaning.

CHALLENGE OF THE NUMBER 7

This is the challenge to the individual's ability to accept mundane realities and maintain faith in himself. It stems from a
childhood environment that did not recognize the tot's intellectual curiosity or could not finance a formal education. The
parents may have felt socially insecure, or the youngster may
have intuitively sensed that there were secrets surrounding the
family or its birthright, in which case legal papers and their
fine print are involved. Health, sensual, and commercial facts
were elusive or cloudy, and emotional responses were rationed.
Information lurked beneath the surface, and for the youngster
everything resulted in loneliness, disillusionment, and disappointment.

Parents and authorities may have based their values on
superficial or commercial accomplishments, whereas the child's
value system was based upon a thirst for investigation, quality,

and wisdom. The child with a number 7 challenge responds to stress by turning inward, becoming a secretive loner who consistently either reads between the lines or takes things too literally.

In youth, the individual is likely to make his relationships difficult on account of a reserved, emotionally unexpressive, and critical attitude. As an adult, the number 7 challenge bearer must learn to accept the earthiness, aggressiveness, and openness of others. He must learn to live in a world where everyone burps, occasionally eats with the wrong fork, and the average person lacks the patience to search for hidden truths.

As children, individuals with the number 7 challenge, left to their own devices, become bookworms or are inclined to join a select intellectual group. They may be "brains" or bores—complaining and doing nothing to build faith in themselves. As adults, they may feel hopeless, fighting bouts of moodiness and melancholy with liquor, drugs, and/or reclusiveness. They see themselves as a minority of one against the vulgar herd, and feel rebellious, secretive, and aloof when exposed to rustic, unrefined, or unenlightened people who do not understand their different wavelength.

Perhaps practical survival needs, importance placed upon beauty alone, or emotional judgments took precedence over education, technical facility, or genius during their nurturing years. Or they may have had parents who were too preoccupied or ill-equipped intellectually to be appropriate authorities. Pragmatic teachers or emotionally detached authorities may have led individual number 7s to feel different, unloved, or wrong to want more than mediocrity. Children with a number 7 challenge therefore often have unrealistic guilts and erroneous ideas that linger into maturity.

Challenged 7s may be unaware of the ordinary activities of their peers, and it is entirely possible that if they do not encourage intimacy or share their thoughts, they are in essence too aloof to have secrets shared with them.

As marriage partners, challenge holders are usually attracted to someone who has professionalism, accumulated wisdom, or a socially elevated status. They may marry much older or younger traditionalists beneath their own social or intellectual levels. Additionally they seek out elders, youngsters, or undeveloped individuals who make little or no demands on them. There are mornings when challenged individuals do not want to see another physical body, smell its animal smells, feel the need to communicate, or make contact with the human community; yet 7 challenge holders often feel lonely and want intimacy at all costs.

The number 7 challenge holder guards a secret self that is padlocked against intruders, nurturing a fear of merging with or losing himself to passionate alliances even after letting someone prick his heart to get under his skin. A challenge holder may marry, but if he tells his secrets to another, it is usually to the wrong listener. The challenged individual may stifle communication by acting too aloof or authoritative. He may retreat into meditation or subtly hide his emotions in material interests. In other words, the 7 can get into a mood that guarantees him privacy.

Until these individuals recognize a desire to better their circumstances, they may not be absorbed with the quality of life. Sevens balance their challenge when they communicate thoughts to associates, develop a sense of material self-worth, and have enough faith to follow their intuition. Commercial growth has its disappointing starts and stops until the 7s become specialists or authorities.

These challenge holders have the unique talent for playing mental games that may suggest to them an out-of-body experience. Additionally, in seeking to perfect themselves, these individuals observe their own actions and behavior and often think they are the only ones entitled to criticize. They either prefer to interpret their own successes or will accept anyone's word for their failures.

Letting down defenses, shedding isolating mannerisms, and letting go of erroneous, self-depreciating ideas is more difficult for this challenge holder than any other. The challenge holder's habit is to inappropriately fear loneliness and poverty, and his escapist devices often render him helpless, his own bogeyman. These and other introspective habits stop the challenge holder from being part of the activities outside his own enclosure. This challenge holder is required to replace imagined fears and skepticism with faith in himself and humanity. The challenge of the number 7 implies that the individual's handicaps are self-imposed and unwarranted; in truth, the 7 is intellectually and spiritually gifted.

The number 7 challenge may swing from one of the following extremes to another until it is recognized and new habits are initiated that stabilize the repression experienced by the challenge holder.

Too critical or too incompetent.
Too probing or too unenlightened.
Too fussy or too unconcerned.
Too naive or too skeptical.
Too authoritative or too gullible.
Too secretive or too open.
Too uncertain or too sure.
Too bookish or too unschooled.
Too cunning or too mystified.
Too aristocratic or too unrefined.
Too patient or too hasty.
Too deep or too unthinking.
Too withdrawn or too eager.
Too complex or too simple.
Too rational or too silly.
Too quick or too slow.

PHYSICAL CHALLENGES OF
THE NUMBER 7

Challenges can affect physical as well as mental health. Body chemistry changes when individuals are stressed, and when we do not know what is good for us, our minds trigger anxious, angry, or frustrated habits. When we are mean to ourselves, we get sick. One's attitude sends the brain a message, and the brain tells the body to scream for help.

To get attention for their dis-ease, often people get sick or form negative habits. Numerologists believe that illness and wellness depend upon attitude, and challenges indicate the attitudes that result from needy feelings. When we do not feel needy, we feel well and balanced and do not crave attention from others. Essentially, if the personality challenges are balanced, the body chemistry is in balance, too, and therefore there is little chance of mental or physical dis-ease.

Challenge numbers indicate the ways people subconsciously punish themselves for not being consciously good to themselves.

The following list of dis-eases and negative habits relate to the challenge of the number 7.

Addiction	Heart Problem
Adenoids	Hip Problems
Alcoholic Personality	Itching
Allergies	Leg Problems
Anemia	Menstrual Problems
Arteriosclerosis	Nail Biting
Blood Pressure	Nausea
Breast Cysts	Neck Problems
Cold	Prostate Problems
Cramps	Smoking
Depression	Stroke
Difficult to Diagnose	Tumors
Finger Tapping	Underweight
Gallstones	Varicose Vein

TO BALANCE THE CHALLENGE OF THE 7 AND
BRING IT OUT AS A TALENT . . .

The first step to balancing the challenge is to feel comfortable about saying "I need to have faith." Find an area of concentration to delve into and in which to achieve expertise. Academic credits are fine, but they do not constitute the only road to mastery.

The best way to build faith in yourself and others is to wake up every morning with an eye toward doing a job you love. With a willingness to serve an apprenticeship or investigation and time and integrity invested in your purpose, you will become skillful. Your talent for accuracy, originality, and investigation will attract other tasteful and discriminating professionals. If you make a commitment you will find friends among peers.

To balance this challenge, it is necessary to follow what is termed your intuition, first thought, or hunch. This is an important part of your special ability to draw from your inner resources. Do not be intimidated by titles, doctorates, or others' self-promotion. Consider the advice of carefully chosen professionals and then do what you sense is best. Remember that you do not have to answer to anyone but yourself, so if there is conflict between your hunch and logic, follow your hunch. You will discover that you are your own best friend and guide.

Aim to take a part of your day for reflection and analysis. In metaphysical circles quiet time to refresh your calm, poise, and dignity is called meditation. Do not stifle your spiritual nature with commercial or material ambitions and concerns: you will gain financially and accumulate material possessions as your reputation gains momentum, and quality-conscious seekers will find you wherever you may hide out.

Look beneath surface values, and use your perceptive gifts to read between the lines. Do not get caught up in analysis and forget practical goals. Give yourself a sound education, if possible, as your fine mind absorbs technical, scientific, legal, psychological, and metaphysical information. When you take time to smell the roses, you will discover the beauty of your own intellect.

Moodiness, melancholy, and escapes from reality are habits that can be broken. When these challenge holders accomplish goals, people will pop up who share their thoughts, and distrust, suppressions, and denunciations disappear and take with them the stress induced by negativism. The 7 challenge holders may build faith in humanity when they share insights and abilities. The feedback bolsters self-confidence and the resulting personality changes may be miraculous. Nothing works better for number 7 challenge holders than a combination of their sixth sense and common sense. By ceasing to expect perfection from themselves and humankind, doors open to self-esteem and self-help. The challenge will abate when these individuals realize that perfection may only be found on another cosmic plane. Nobody here is perfect!

Recognize yourself as an accurate, analytical, and inquisitive visionary who has the inner wisdom to put theories, research, and good taste to work for you.

SELF-MOTIVATION

Youth:

For number 7 tots the greatest urge is to be observant, quiet, and questioning. When reprimanded, these children will become reclusive, hide, and cry alone. Number 7 youngsters are trusting, intuitive, and solitary. If surrounded by superficial, gregarious, or overemotional authorities, they will shut them out. They want calm, refined, rational leadership, and need intellectually stimulating toys to satisfy their curious minds.

Parents may describe their number 7 children as deliberate, reasoning, and studious. These words describe these individuals when they are surrounded by learned, observant, and mature authorities. If the number 7s' introspective personality

is considered odd and the parents disregard their need to med-
itate, these children may become reticent and reluctant to
reveal their thoughts. Number 7 youngsters want to probe,
read books, and discuss their observations on a technical level—
if they talk about their perceptions at all. Once these children,
who have difficulty expressing their feelings, are given demonstrations of affection and love, they will become more animated and authoritative. In general, however, these youngsters
are secretive, particularly about their sensitivity and emotional
reactions.

Number 7 children need to be allowed to create their own
world: their innate wisdom should be taken seriously and channeled into mental activities. Trips to the library, harp lessons,
and opportunities to listen to classical music will stimulate their
already eager intellects. Sevens gain knowledge from investigating subjects that interest them. They will not have a large
group of friends or socialize spontaneously, and too few peer
relationships in youth may be a problem. Number 7 children
are discriminating and prefer solitude to boring companionship. Since they are geared to spiritual or intellectual pursuits,
quiet, inspirational, or theoretical conversations with well-read
elders should satisfy any desire they may have for social in-
tercourse.

Strong-willed number 7s enjoy silence, peace, and solitude.
These individuals may be ahead of their class scholastically,
but socially immature. Sevens may be shy, self-conscious, or
guarded when with classmates, preferring to leave unprogres-
sive educational procedures behind, shun parties, and invent
their own mind games. Overall, intimacy makes them uncomfortable.

Sevens are aristocratic loners who become melancholy if
surrounded by crudeness or people who pressure them to have
materialistic priorities. Surprisingly they fear loneliness yet
make it difficult for others to get to know them. Only when
7s are sure of their facts will they contribute to a conversation.
Parents should expose them to the complexities of photogra-

phy, computers, and the world of metaphysics to command their interest and keep them busy.

Number 7 youths need percale sheets, sweaters that do not itch, and contact with only the best of everything. If there are ten dresses on a store rack, number 7s little girl will unwittingly select the most expensive and best tailored garment. Shopping for a school notebook, little boys will automatically choose the most efficient and well-manufactured product. These children are at home with quality and prefer to have one perfectly fulfilled desire to a quantity of compromises.

It is best to teach number 7 youths to accept human frailty and their own imperfections early on. Fast talkers, manual labor, and physically demanding sports are not appealing to them, and they tend to be cerebral researchers who perceive the world with reserve and think long and hard before tackling any job. A technical, scientific, or classically academic education will serve these children well, and any specialization will provide them with the clout they need to be comfortable. Number 7s fit in with many professional, refined, reserved groups of people.

Sevens are perfectionists who grow to maturity studiously dissecting each detail in their lives before going on to another. If 7s have more conventional number meanings in other aspects of their chart, they may not be introverted; however, they will likely find a way to maintain respect for their privacy.

As teens, 7s will skillfully do one thing at a time. As truth-seeking adults, they will want all the information available before making a decision. Alert parents will understand that these sedentary analyzers are actually listening to the music of the spheres. Number 7s rarely have a sense of urgency over or an obsession for material possessions. They will attract money, recognition, and influential alliances when following their natural instincts to question everything. Sevens use the mind, cultivate the brain, and put their findings to a concentrated, practical purpose.

Maturity:

Adult number 7s want to be purists undisturbed by practical realities or earthy people. They need to be surrounded by timeless treasures and may seem to be out of this world most of the time. They desire to be perceptive, contemplative, and erudite. These desires and accomplishments put them in a class by themselves.

Sevens want to use their minds and are constantly developing their inner resources. They are visionaries comfortable with the mystical side of life. After slowly and surely assessing all they want to know about a subject, they may become authorities. It is rare for number 7 self-motivations to scatter interests or make light conversation. They are the thinkers who become clairvoyant, clairaudient, or telepathic when freed from material concerns. Their ability to experience psychically has made religious, scientific, and technical history.

Number 7 people do not like to be surrounded by frenzied business people, jangling telephones, or clanging typewriters. Rarely gregarious or animated lovers, they just need to know that constant shows of affection are not expected and they will provide the perfect criteria for a patient soulmate. Sevens are not comfortable when expected to be obsessed with sensuality or pressed into a demanding social whirl. On the other hand, any theoretical discussion, enlightening television program, or gourmet recipe will intrigue them.

When unbalanced, these individuals may be despairing escapists, obsessed fanatics, or commercially aggressive dreamers. When balanced, they are rational, discriminating, conscientious originals. When under number 7s' care, youngsters are taught to be investigative, meticulous, and resourceful. Able to follow their natural instincts, number 7 adults are astute, broad-minded, poised parents.

Commercial ambitions do not rule number 7s. Money is usually spent only on quality acquisitions. However, these individuals will not sacrifice necessary thinking time to take action if cash is not readily available. Unconcerned about fads and trifles, 7s have their own philosophy and faith about material freedom. However, number 7s are students of life and can push buttons, if necessary, to put themselves and others on a rigorous schedule. Once they get going, they only aim for perfection.

One may expect the balanced, ingenious, attentive, and patient number 7 to figure out how to attract the things or lovers that fit his expectations. It is highly improbable that one will ever meet a balanced number 7 self-motivation who is self-satisfied, overtly affectionate, or dramatically excitable.

Problems for those with a number 7 self-motivation are feelings of moodiness, melancholy, and emotional poverty. They often fear their own desire for separatism; 7s dislike living hand-to-mouth, but cannot be true to themselves in routinely competitive business environments. If they follow natural instincts to become academics, professionals, and specialists, prospects for financial happiness are good. In spiritual or metaphysical pursuits, 7s tune in to a realm of deeper truths, and their findings may be extraordinary.

Number 7s may worry, dislike sudden changes, and lack the urge to sympathize or display understanding. If they allow themselves to stand out in a group and build a reputation, it is more likely for intelligence, detachment, or elegance. Vague, bawdy, or amateurish people make them shudder and retreat. Sevens enjoy skillful conversationalists and are not particularly domestic, hospitable, tied to home, family, or children. They will do the "right thing" when they are not inclined to be antisocial. One may expect a leather-bound book, an antique chess set, or a piece of pre–Columbian pottery as concrete testimony that number 7s have fallen in love.

You may find the introspective 7 self-motivation living in an attic, a seaside cottage, or a penthouse. Just as long as there is privacy, calm, and quiet, he will mind his own business and do his own thing. The sound of waves rising and retreating from the shore may be the only background noise he will tolerate or want to hear. Living near the water and observing its fluctuations calms the mind and soothes the tensions of this contemplative individualist.

Marriage for cerebral 7s is never totally comfortable; however, with practical planning they can live with cooperative, elegant, detail-conscious, intuitive mates. Separate baths and bedrooms are usually ideal, but a home office, den, or private space of relaxation for 7s can easily serve as a retreat from too much closeness or constant observance of another presence in the house.

It takes a mentally stimulating, sensual, well-built person who shares similar ideals to attract a 7 for a long-term relationship, as he needs emotional support all the time yet only occasional companionship. A relationship will not last between a 7 and a partner who is paranoid or becomes distressed by the number 7's moods and meticulousness. Before contracting for life, one should note and compare his own numbers and the basic numbers within a 7 lover's chart.

The marriage of two number 7 motivations will begin and end in silent contemplation. Two people who may keep thoughts to themselves, seek physical privacy, and choose not to aggressively seek the other out to reconcile differences are destined for the marriage counselor's couch. One often cannot convince the analytical 7 to accept love without intellectual discourse, and he may examine wounds too impersonally. When feeling rejected, the aloof 7 may not bother to put Band-Aids on little bruises.

It is a sure bet that two uncommunicative number 7s will not make small talk about their own or another's feelings. If one tries to compromise, everyday accommodations, conflicting emotions, and the resulting inner turmoil will make a drunk or a sleepaholic out of one or the other. An intimate relationship between two number 7s is definitely not going to make it without financial security, sophisticated mores, and separate living arrangements.

SELF-IMAGE

Youth:

When lying on the bed, listening to music, and imagining "What am I going to be like when I grow up? How will I walk, dress, and talk?" number 7 youths visualize an aristocrat. They dream of living a serene life of quality, free to investigate, select, and analyze. Little boys see themselves authoritatively lecturing on a beloved specialty to intellectual equals; little girls see themselves as the reincarnation of Margaret Mead or Madame Curie, surrounded by quiet, earnest students in a room walled with leather-bound books or an extensive, perfected laboratory. Children with the number 7 self-image may picture themselves as proud, dignified, confident royalty—above the mundane and earthy obligations of youth—and are often referred to as little princes or princesses.

Sevens may appear to be self-assured, thoughtful, quiet children who have the intellectual capacity to mix with elders. When number 7s say they want to be scientists, photographers, or clergymen, they see themselves in the appropriate positions to use their scholarly, technical, or mystical ideas. When living up to their self-image, these individuals will be first to read a gourmet recipe, follow each ingredient and instruction to a tee, and critique the menu after tasting the fruits of the labor they assign to others. These tots, teens, or young adults dislike getting their hands dirty or working themselves into a sweat. They try to avoid mundane work and often assume a position of expertise or authority.

Youngsters with dreams based upon the meaning of the number 7 may have discriminating tastes. They are hard to please, and will assert themselves in order to maintain physical, mental, and spiritual privacy. Their overall appearance is carefully coordinated, with muted tones and soft materials. They are not inclined to attract attention, so they may wear classic styles rather than making a fashion statement. When in tune

with their self-image, their style sense is impressively harmonious, and their tailoring and grooming is impeccable.

Sevens rarely appear emotionally expressive or mercenary.
Youthful number 7 expectations are not sensual or materially
ambitious; instead, for this aloof self-image, the heart's desire
is centered on private investigation, analysis, and deductions,
based upon the world above, beneath, and around them.

Maturity:

When walking out of an elevator or into a room—before
personality or intellect come into play—the adult with a 7
self-image sends out a dignified and refined vibration. His
attitude indicates a reserved personality and aloofness. The
first impression he gives is unruffled, sometimes curious, and
always well bred. If self-motivation and self-expression numbers are extroverted or unconventional, the number 7 will wear
unique combinations of colors and look decidedly chic. Clothing styles, posture, and attitude will not indicate his intellectual
or mystical self-image.

When these individuals are wearing the colors purple and
violet, the self-image is emphasized. Violet implies mystery,
and purple implies aristocracy. When their self-image is reinforced in this way, number 7s are inclined to make intuitional
decisions, think carefully before speaking, and speak with dignity or authority. Generally 7s will not try to stand out in a
crowd; in essence, they present a deliberate, contemplative,
unaggressive facade when observed by the public. It is the
number 7 heart's desire to give an authoritative, imperturbable,
unobtrusive impression. At first blush, number 7s never look
incompetent, uncertain or simple; however, they may appear
to exist in a world all their own.

Number 7 adults perceive themselves as experts or critics
and may be highly opinionated. When living up to their self-
image, their first impression may be intimidating, and they
may not get along with everyone.

The self-expression number may govern the first impression
if utilitarian or attention-getting clothing styles are indicated

by the career descriptions outlined in the number meaning.

The self-motivation number may influence the apparel of the bearers, if they are relaxing and doing what they want to do. However, when these individuals are living up to their self-image, they will not feature correspondent colors or styles indicated by numbers in another part of their numerology chart.

SELF-EXPRESSION

Youth:

It is obvious to adults when children have a number 7 self-expression, for in youth 7s' talents are based in questioning everything: asking why the sky is blue or how can birds fly. Because they do not accept superficial explanations and will investigate all responses, 7s keep parents mentally alert and send teachers to the reference library. As they get older they will delve into hobbies, read for hours, and enjoy playing or listening to stringed instruments. They will mind-boggle authorities and alienate less introspective peers. As accurate, perceptive, truth-seeking little helpers, they add refinement to a family project. It is difficult to stifle one's surprise at their intelligence and meticulousness.

Without intending to be fussy logical number 7s may assume a detailed and penetrating attitude toward rules and regulations. Each original, well-reasoned critique may be persistently and ingeniously argued. To flexible, excitable, active parents, they may appear to be too exacting, pretentious, or apprehensive. To cultivated, calm, cerebral adults, the 7s' instinctive nobility of purpose, intellectual curiosity, and sincerity is expected and welcomed. The children's need to probe to get to the root of everything will be respected.

Number 7 talents may lead these children to avoid risks, physically demanding sports, and manual labor. They have the analytical ability to plan football plays, enjoy bridge or chess, and manage finances for school outings. Sevens will be more sociable, flexible, understanding adults if encouraged to participate in extracurricular activities. Too often 7s become loners who do not enjoy or develop the art of casual conversation; for example, when attempting to get involved, mental 7s may appear humorless or self-conscious until their different wavelength is acknowledged and they are given respect for their expertise.

As teenagers, these bookish perfectionists may lock themselves in concentration and be impervious to noise, hunger, or entertainment. In spite of their general disregard for light hearted banter or conventional social interactions, when the mood strikes them 7s are capable of eloquent speech and pixilated humor. New puns, mathematical games of logic, cameras, and computers may fascinate them. They are intellectuals and should seize every chance to use their keen brains. Museums, ancient ruins, and excuses to take pictures will give them an opportunity to develop artistic interests. They are not slipshod, uninterested, or amateurish and will take a scientific or technical approach when left alone to do research.

Observant, discriminating number 7s will be hesitant and will not speak or take a leadership role until they are sure of their facts. They may choose to be sideline resources, but once they find a career interest offering mental challenges, a refined environment, and an opportunity to work independently, 7s prove themselves to be quality-conscious experts.

In youth, 7s prefer soft fabrics, tasteful clothes, and delicate, well-prepared foods. Once they discover the things that work for them, they do not make changes. Generally 7s disregard fads, foolishness, and dramatic displays of emotion. They are comfortable in noncompetitive businesses that do not require them to follow the crowd or dress uniformly. Sevens are uncomfortable when singled out, preferring a low profile and ignoring less evolved opinions. They appear to take everything in stride, aiming to control their emotions and act cool during crises.

Tots, teens, and youths should be given privacy and en-

couraged to see all sides of everything. They may learn from books and acknowledged authorities how to become outstanding scientists, technicians, and spiritual leaders. Their studiousness, intuition, and attention to quality is always impressive.
Maturity:

Suggested Occupations: Psychiatrist, psychologist, psychotherapist, scientist, technical expert, engineer, computer programmer-systems analyst–designer, mathematician, editor, judge, photographer, underwater explorer, scuba diver, oceanographer, geologist, historian, librarian, writer, preacher, metaphysician, holistic medical expert, dietitian, appraiser, antiques dealer, banker, certified public accountant, comptroller, investment counselor, watchmaker, gemstone cutter, jewelry designer, architect, astronomer, doctor, dentist, lawyer, prep school or college dean, anthropologist, gourmet cook, radio announcer, archivist, museum curator, magician, tea leaf reader, Turkish coffee grinds reader, investigative debunker, psychic, numerologist, astrologer, tarot reader, medium, parapsychologist. Expert: wine, aerospace, biomedicine, metallurgy, petroleum, agriculture, or hubcaps . . . any subject that captures their mind.
Options:

Careers indicated by the meaning of the self-motivation number may not make use of readily available talents but will allow the individual to feel comfortable.

Careers indicated by the self-image number meanings will encourage the individual to live up to youthful dreams.

Careers indicated by the meaning of the destiny number, if it is not the same as the self-expression number, will require that the individual learn from incoming personalities and experiences.

If self-expression and destiny numbers are the same, the individual's talents will be recognized and utilized early in life.
Maturity: Self-Expression Analysis

The number 7 self-expression has the potential for financial compensation for the ability to investigate all aspects of a subject, perfect techniques, and reveal findings with confidence. Recognition is possible for number 7s' superior intuition and talent for appreciating or producing quality work. Sevens attract positions for which expert information is required and keen perceptions are appreciated. Their communications are deliberate, accurate, and logical. These researchers are sincere, patient, and imperturbable. Sevens earn the limelight when probing an idea and proving its worth.

Sevens rarely consider money or material power the goal of their efforts. They do not accept people or experiences on the spot. These discriminating individuals are not frugal when they want something for themselves yet may be penurious when carrying out their responsibilities to others. Talented scholars, they know that it takes accuracy to get accuracy.

Usually at their best when left to work alone, 7s may prefer independent careers to the fast pace and competitiveness of the business world. Forever questioning, they take nothing for granted and are uncomfortable with people who do. Sevens maintain efficient routines and revise when necessary. Refined, dignified, and influential job situations appeal to them. In a business environment these responsible aristocrats will be unwilling adversaries; however, they are cunning, humorless, and skillful purists who will dogmatically argue to maintain authority.

Balanced number 7s automatically follow their first thought, and this trait gives them the gift of ESP. Sevens are visionaries and may be inspired teachers, counselors, or spiritual leaders. Their minds and spirits never take a vacation; they are always thinking and learning. Number 7 talents are centered in the mind, and because their energy goes into reflection and cerebral pursuits, they require more rest than most people. If 7s are physically and mentally active, the strain will make them lose their serenity. When challenged by the number 7 or being reclusive, 7s speculate unwisely, try to outsmart everyone, and may become out of touch with reality.

Innate mystical talents often make investigative 7s appear

eccentric. They should try to grow wise without forgetting about mundane necessities, financial stability, and domestic responsibilities. Explorations into channeling and a fascination with séances and the parasciences often deter the innately psychic 7 from focusing on accumulating practical assets.

If self-motivation and/or destiny number meanings indicate materialistic or emotional inclinations, those with the number 7 self-expression will use their extraordinary intuition in these areas. Number 7 achievers, supported by the numbers 2 and 5 in business and the number 4 in casual life, will benefit from the personality traits of the other numbers. Unaccustomed to responding to everyday intimacies and traditional thinking, number 7 talents are often otherworldly. Sevens need to learn how less detached types of people operate.

Generally 7s will not be escapists; however, the negative aspects of this number indicate moodiness, melancholy, and a lack of faith when finances are low and relationships tax their emotions. Unfortunately these introspective talents are not inclined to discuss their emotional problems. They may seem to be uncaring or aloof but really feel everything deeply. Sevens find it difficult to confide in others, so they reach inside themselves for information. When balanced, those with the number 7 self-expression know when to take actions based upon careful consideration. They withhold an opinion until a progressive plan is formulated and then reveal feelings in a dignified manner.

DESTINY

WE ARE NOT BORN KNOWING WHAT LIFE HAS TO OFFER. INDIVIDUALS WITH THE NUMBER 7 DESTINY LEARN TO DEVELOP WISDOM, REFINEMENT, AND IN- DIVIDUALIZED CONCENTRATIONS THAT ATTRACT AUTHORITY. THEY ENCOUNTER PEOPLE AND EXPE- RIENCES THAT TEACH THEM TO VALUE SOLITUDE,

INTELLECTUAL FREEDOM, QUALITY, AND THE MYS-
TERIES OF LIFE.

This destiny implies a lifetime of introspection, quiet accumulation of knowledge, and the perfection of the inner being.
The result is a mature thinker who is able to apply intuition
or spiritual beliefs to a practical lifestyle. To make the most
of numerology's ability to forecast, the number 7 must find
contentment when being alone, investigative, and analytical.

Number 7 destiny holders may choose not to marry or
form distracting partnerships. They may be born to older,
dignified parents who are inclined to be logical rather than
emotional and learn from books or theoretical discussions. The
number 7 lifestyle in youth may be either too formal and
unemotional or materially inadequate. In either situation these
children learn to depend upon inner resources for comfort.
The number 7 destiny will not be realized—the destiny holders
will be disillusioned by legal involvements and be malcontents—if commercial ambitions are the focus or too much
importance is placed on material acquisitions.

People with the number 7 destiny may not hold on to
success or feel content in mundane occupations. The aggressive, competitive business world upsets their perfections and
jangles their sensitivities. Sevens will find they will make sufficient money and material assets to satisfy their desires if they
maintain faith in themselves. In time, they build a reputation
for expertise or authority that may be based on a technical,
scientific, or spiritual concentration. In general, 7s are gifted;
as youths, they may choose to be social butterflies, yet find
in maturity that they are really more comfortable in a cocoon.

Prime examples of people given the opportunities offered
to this truth-seeking destiny are picky-picky drama critic Brooks
Atkinson (11/28/1894), analytical TV producer-questioner David
Susskind (12/19/1920), and unsophisticated, one-track-minded
U.S. President Harry S Truman (5/8/1884).

President Truman, a Missouri farmer's son, was an unsuc-
cessful, small-town retail haberdasher and a local politician

known for hard work. Truman used common sense and preserved his personal honesty in the midst of corrupt political machinery. He was destined to become a surprised and surprisingly effective president. The people and experiences President Truman encountered as he expanded politically taught him to question authorities. He listened to his conscience and took action based on his personal doubts. He faced the reconstruction of World War II–ravaged nations with the aplomb of a competent leader and mystically stretched his intellectual capacities to fight the Cold War with Russia.

Harry Truman marched to a different drummer as a young man. He proved to be an authoritative president in mid-life and sought privacy and serenity writing his memoirs in later years. History records that President Truman refused to be swayed by public opinion when he recalled demagogue General Douglas MacArthur from Korea. He stood alone to exert his influence, as all number 7 destiny holders must.

Sevens discover that personal concentrations are steady companions that invite them to contemplate in the morning and remain absorbing through the night. Any interest may earn them a unique, respected, and responsible place in history if authority is diligently, accurately, and honorably upheld.

If fertile-minded 7s remain uninformed, untrained, and vague, their presence will not be acknowledged and prospects will be limited. Only immature, foolish, or antisocial behavior will delay their progress. Number 7 destiny holders are best suited to becoming specialists and letting the universe benefit from their capabilities. Devout believers, learned seekers, and analytical thinkers open doors for these rational mystics and encourage them to continue to probe for perfect solutions, while dignified, well-bred, tasteful people add quality and respectability to their lives.

Throughout life, the 7's experiences and decisions may be highlighted by extrasensory perceptions, precognitive dreaming, and religious or metaphysical investigations of the people they encounter. The number 7 does not live in the fast lane:

he deliberates. After comparing his perfectionist theories and fundamentals with the way things are, he makes observations that may cause him to become uncompromising, cynical, and critical of mediocrity. When the peaceful number 7 realizes that his tastes are extraordinary and exacting, he will pace himself socially and guard his tongue appropriately.

Every stone will be overturned to find a solution to a problem when number 7s are interested. They are capable of digging in and unsettling boulders to get to the bottom of anything. However, simultaneous love affairs, adventurous careers, and physically demanding jobs are too taxing for these erudite students of the unknown. These individuals should avoid clinging to intimate relationships, living in cluttered, noisy, or ungracious urban communities, or becoming ineffectually thick-skinned. They are intended to be at peace with themselves, to live in a natural environment, and to remain open-minded.

Number 7 destiny holders discover that they do not like to do anything if they cannot do it well. As they become more and more selective, their probings for perfection will delay conclusions to slipshod group projects or compromising commercial competitions. Time will teach them that they are meant to learn, work alone contentedly, and speak up when the things they have to say will enable others to see all sides of an issue.

With this destiny's legal complexities the 7s may wonder why others are content with things as they find them. Actually people who accept dogma, follow traditions, and do not expect the perfection of their ideals respect the questioning number 7. Number 7 wisdom and quality-consciousness grows with each new experience. As time goes by the number 7 realizes that there is nothing to fear but his own demons. He may be a saint, a sorcerer, or a sinner and refuse to conform in an emotionally triggered society. For him, having greater wisdom than the average person is a blessing; knowing how to adapt to mundane realities without compromise is the problem.

BIRTHDAY INFLUENCES
WITHIN THE DESTINY

July

Individuals born in July learn in youth that they cannot be superficial, untrained, or scattered. They are exposed to serious situations, dignified attitudes, and spiritual or intellectual authorities prior to their twenty-eighth birthday. Situations arise that cause them to question and analyze. They may find a lack of financial freedom or companionship, and on account of the people and experiences surrounding them, they may develop an introspective nature, a private world, and a detached attitude. In youth, July–born may be misunderstood and secretive.

Childhood relationships may lack understanding, expressive communications, or the patient guidance that provides a social training ground. The resulting difficulties are not forgotten. Early years may be remembered as a time to dream, investigate, and escape from pedantic authorities. The youngster wants to question in a world where adults may have forgotten how it was to be a child. If there are no responses, the child retreats into private thoughts or is quiet and uncomfortable when pressed to be socially active or materially ambitious. July–born may be considered unconventional, eccentric, or out of touch with reality.

It is better for all concerned if these children's observations are acknowledged and valued. To learn to provide for themselves, these youngsters need an academic, technical, scientific, or spiritual education. As a rule, they are not businesslike go-getters during the formative years. People born in July rarely commit themselves to commercial ambitions or a career until they have established some authority and speak from knowledge. They do meticulous work, becoming resourceful researchers and discriminating originals when they decide to delve into a specialty.

Birthday: 7, 16, 25

THE BIRTHDAY NUMBER HAS AN INFLUENCE ON PERSONALITY AND DESTINY. IT ATTRACTS PEOPLE AND EXPERIENCES DURING MID-LIFE THAT EXEMPLIFY THE NUMBER MEANING. The mid-life productivity cycle begins with maturity. It lasts from approximately twenty-eight to fifty-five years of age and coordinates with the destiny during that time span. The birthday-number meaning adds its character traits and experiences to an individual's numerology analysis.

People born on the seventh, sixteenth, and twenty-fifth of the month, in addition to the character traits outlined by the number meanings for the name, are introspective, discriminating, and analytical truth-seekers. They may not be happy when undeveloped or comfortable with shallow or unrefined loudmouths. Individuals born on these dates want accuracy, logic, and peaceful surroundings in order to perfect their thoughts and dream their dreams. They are cerebral and controlled.

Between approximately twenty-eight and fifty-five years of age—the twenty-seven-year productivity cycle within the destiny—life will offer additional opportunities to develop intellectually and delve independently into specialized interests. Marriage may be uncomfortable because of a need for privacy. Mystical, religious, and philosophical experiences will add to the individual's perceptions and spheres of influence. He should not disregard his intuition and attraction to psychic phenomenon; he should strive for professionalism, enlightenment, and ongoing self-examination. People born on the seventh, sixteenth, and twenty-fifth need quality, not quantity.

PERSONAL YEAR

The number 7 is the seventh year in the cycle of nine years of experiences that results in a polish and skill of performance based upon the goals set in the first year. It is a time to rest, reflect, and analyze. Let go of the preceding year's domestic and emotional drains. March begins a time for personal values, noncommercial focuses, and self-analysis, as the spring and summer months are not conducive to commercial ambitions or physical strains.

For most, this is a slow year, filled with communication delays, legal questions, and unexpected feelings of loneliness. For others, the year focuses on a specialized course of study that was decided upon in October of the preceding year. It is an introspective year to look over the past and plan for the future. Money and practical attainments come in if one is not too changeable or aggressive. This is a nonmaterial year whose purpose is developmental and preparatory.

Many marriages flounder or stretch to reach a higher plateau in the 7 personal year. Some fail sadly or deepen extraordinarily, after one partner goes through the soul-searching inspired by the slow pace. One should keep spiritual, intellectual, and practical values in mind and wait until the year concludes before drawing conclusions or taking actions. Social activities should be kept to a minimum, and speculations should be put on the shelf entirely. This is not the year to marry, divorce, make major purchases, initiate a physically active sports program, or focus on commercial or financial ambitions. To get the best out of this year, one must relax, spend time alone, reflect upon the past, and plan for the future. A good look into the perfection of one's desires may make them realistic.

Do not be afraid to let business or material interests take a backseat. Recognize this once-in-nine-year chance to look over life, sort priorities, and learn from the past. Be still. Keep calm. Do not rush the seasons or manipulate each day. The most promising plans will work out whether you take control or allow things that are meant to be of benefit come in. If aggressive actions are taken, incoming financial and material activities are delayed. Problems arise that force you to wonder why you are feeling powerless or repressed. A serene attitude is beneficial. Whether or not you understand how things will happen for the best is not important: it is important to expect the best, to have faith, and to take a break from outside responsibilities and ambitions. This year is intended to remind you that there is more to life than meets the eye.

The number 7 personal year encourages one to develop new interests and deeper understandings. Ideas generate investigations that materialize into the next year's business achievements. In order to have mobility and freedom to pursue commercial or material ambitions next year, health is a factor to be considered now. Medical and dental checkups should be planned as preventive measures before July. Any physical discomforts should be acknowledged and promptly brought to the attention of a professional. If one ignores intellectual, spiritual, or physical preparations, one is not using this year wisely. The intuitive decisions made and filed for future use will determine the scope of maturity harvested during the past six years.

PERSONAL MONTH

The number 7 personal month within any personal year gives an opportunity to question plans, enlist the aid of professionals, and learn from the past. Actions should not be taken until next month. Wait to see how the incoming responses fit in with current legal dealings, questionable alliances, and progressive ideas. A broad-minded, probing, exacting point of view should take top priority. Aggressiveness, commercial ambitions, and unnecessary social interactions should be put on the shelf. Remember how to say "I'll think about it." Examine the opinions of others carefully, and think before speaking. Do not reveal thoughts; be a little secretive. This is not a good time to get telephonitis. Wait for the phone to ring to receive input. Take time to read, be self-examining, and enjoy philosophical discussions. Be patient, tolerant, and willing to spend time quietly. This may be an exceptionally enlightening month.

PERSONAL DAY

Wake up with a leisurely attitude, do not overextend physically, and avoid confusion or conflicts. Approach each experience calmly, quietly, and with poise. No matter the task, focus on preparation and exactitude. Analyze to get the most out of a situation. Be receptive and listen to another's ideas. This is a day to take a long look at personal plans, character traits, and the nonmaterial side of expectations. Commercial delays or technical questions will crop up, solutions will not be readily available, and actions should not be taken to solve problems until tomorrow.

On this day, other people are likely to postpone making commitments or living up to their promises. An expected phone call or letter may not arrive. But the moon will still rise and the sun will set as usual in spite of the day's slowdowns. It is best to remain passive and take in stride whatever happens. If possible, catch up on reading informative books, go to a movie, or let your imagination roam free while listening to music. Practical problems will solve themselves or wait until the time is right.

Make a personal commitment to self-improvement. Be honest and reflect upon past behavior to picture how unproductive habits may be altered or eliminated. Allow time to visualize a happier and healthier you. Your abstract thoughts may turn to practical accomplishments when you are inspired and have faith. Take care of medical or dental obligations. Talk to a psychologist, lawyer, or accountant if you require professional knowledge. Accumulate wisdom and counsel others—without thought of payment—if called upon to speak from an expert perspective. Tomorrow's focus on efficiency, stamina, and material objectives will give you the opportunity to achieve tangible results.

CHAPTER TWELVE

NUMBER 8

Material Power

Material Power

ATTRIBUTES:
POSITIVE—Efficient, Strong, Self-Reliant, Ambitious, Discriminating, Shrewd, Businesslike, Assertive, Intelligent
NEGATIVE—Materialistic, Intolerant, Straining, Dishonest, Spiritless, Undisciplined, Power-hungry, Militant, Gaudy, Crude

CORRESPONDENTS:
LETTERS: H, Q, Z
EVEN NUMBER: Receptive; Materially Aggressive
DISPOSITION: Clearheaded, Serious; Confident
NUMBERS: 17, 26, 35, 44, 53, 62, 71, 80, 89, 98, 107
COLORS: Rose, Red-Pink, Mauve
GEM: Diamond
CRYSTALS: Pyrite, Rose Morganite, Pink Beryl
VEGETATION: Begonia, Dahlia, Jasmine, Hickory, Pine, Rhododendron
FOODS: Cereal, Bacon, Rice, Cauliflower, Chicken, Tea, Apple Pie

MUSICAL INSTRUMENT/APPEAL: Ukulele; Choir, Soprano, Revue
MUSICAL NOTE: High C
LOCATIONS: State: Georgia, Nebraska, Pennsylvania, Vermont, Virginia, Wisconsin
City: Allentown, Cedar Rapids, Columbia, Fort Collins, Lima, Little Rock, Pueblo, San Bernardino, Santa Barbara, Savannah, Toledo, Tyler
PLANET: The Sun
MONTH: August
BIRTHDAYS: 8, 17, 26
DAY OF THE WEEK: Thursday
GENERAL COMPATIBILITY NUMBERS: 2, 4, 6
INCOMPATIBILITY NUMBERS: 7, 8, 9

Note: If an individual has the challenge to the number 8, these descriptions will swing from positive to negative until the challenge is balanced. Please be sure to read the challenge number meaning.

CHALLENGE OF THE NUMBER 8

This is the challenge to individuals' understanding of the values and purposes of money and power. As children, these challenge holders may have observed authorities with hard-driving ambitions who focused on the financial picture. High-level power and competitive spirit were the only available means to gain freedom—or the opposite extreme may have been experienced, in which case authorities may have had no interest in the accumulation of assets, community influence, or competitiveness. Either extreme gave the 8 youngsters a false sense of material values, and fostered a plus or minus obsession about material possessions and financial security. As a result, these individual challenge holders usually become self-made workaholics or self-destructive, nonachieving squanderers.

There are many reasons for number 8 challenge holders'

preoccupation with ownership. In youth, either too much or too little attention was paid to material judgments, organizational efficiency, and physical abilities. During the number 8s' youths, parents may have provided them with gifts instead of playtime and affection. As adults, challenged children do not have points of reference that are based on sentimental responses; instead, they show emotional concern by giving expensive or practical gifts, and, all too often, adults challenged by the number 8 judge others' love by the material tokens of esteem they receive.

To a child deprived of esoteric values, mothers may have appeared to live for shopping and fathers may have seemed to live for work. Parents may have been employed by extremely wealthy or influential employers, so when the child hears about or sees how the rich live, he may either say "That's for me" or feel too intimidated or overwhelmed to become a contender in the business world. The challenge may become an obsession compelling the holder to strain, lose sight of the joys of companionship, and become mercenary. He may use his accomplishments selfishly, unconsciously allying emotional, physical, and spiritual satisfaction with a drive to control everything and everyone.

As teenagers, challenge-holding individuals may excel at sports, schoolwork, and a part-time after-school job. They may be considered to be "super kids," or in the opposite extreme, these teenagers may be purposeless, inconsistent, and uninvolved. They may not be able to exercise good judgment, keep their affairs in order, or assume responsibility for managing time, money, and practical obligations. For these challenge holders, there is either too much or too little concern for self-control. They are usually either tornadoes or puffs of wind, with temperaments that match either extreme.

Adult challenge holders have little or no patience for less efficient or less ambitious people and are constantly concerned about appearances. After amassing money these individuals will use it for display. To make a good impression, they will furnish a library with obviously expensive leather-bound books, yet never have the time or inclination to open the covers. In the other extreme of the challenge, status symbols, fancy job titles, and the reflection they see in the eyes of affluent or influential people matter little—often *too* little to protect their own material security.

Number 8 challenge holders may ostentatiously tip a headwaiter lavishly for the most sought-after table in a restaurant and privately purchase mediocre, inexpensive products to compensate. Or they may tell the world about their charity donations and forget that charity begins at home. These challenge holders become easily caught up in the pursuit of money and image, devoting full efforts to overcoming any obstacles they encounter. In their rise to the top, they may forget tenderness, be consistently inconsiderate to loved ones, and assume that their mates will understand their behavior.

This challenge indicates a physical and material singlemindedness. Generally the teenager who is not an achiever but has a materialistic background will recognize that money slips through his fingers. The result is that he may never have enough to satisfy his wants later in life. The go-getting tiger in high school rarely relinquishes his expansive ambitions. Once his habits are established, it is too difficult for the aggressive, grand-scale achiever to slow down until physical pressures do it for him.

Professional athletes and coaches with this challenge are often unable to quit. Business executives refuse to let go of the reins and pass them to qualified associates, even when they have passed peak performance. When nonworking females marry, they may exert their materialistic pressures on husbands and offspring. Number 8 challenge holders often have lofty expectations and may imagine that no person or circumstance can force them to give up their right to push buttons or have the final say.

It is almost impossible to recognize when number 8 challenge holders are feeling stress, for they seem to thrive on it.

Initially these movers and shakers will exhibit integrity and use their clout to fight for the rights of associates. However, strain will turn their worship of materialism to unscrupulous, greedy, or cold-blooded business practices. Stomach muscle tension, outbreaks of nervous activity, or high blood pressure may be early indicators that it is time to take a vacation. But because number 8 challenge holders rarely have time to feel pain or notice labored breathing, physical-fitness regimens are a must. The challenge holders' caution is to maintain a regular schedule of physical checkups.

Gourmet foods, lavish, professionally decorated homes, custom-made clothing—and anything else that indicates to themselves and the world that the number 8 challenge holders are on the upward climb—is coveted and purchased. They may be downright cheap or extraordinarily generous, but they almost always overreact to money.

Number 8 challenge holders have physical stamina and the ability to coordinate body, mind, and spirit to fulfill their ambitions. They may put their businesslike talents to work at sports or any goal—if they channel their ambitions efficiently. The challenge-holding company president will focus on the bottom line—cutting budgets, maintaining a skeleton staff—using all problem-solving talents to surpass the previous year's figures. The challenge-holding competitive runner trains, meditates, and counts calories in order to sprint for a trophy. Tokens of success are very meaningful to the number 8 challenge holders: they are symbolic of love and approval based upon childhood standards.

These individuals may think Who would reject me if I have money, power, and prestige?; however, feedback indicates to them that people cannot be treated like corporate structures. Some 8s must learn that there is a higher power than the board of directors. To master the challenge of the 8, one must first master the number 7 challenge, that which places faith in nonmaterial values and recognizes the wisdom in Everyman.

Challenge bearers always have choice—with the same self-

awareness, self-discipline, and ability to solve problems employed for material ambitions, they may use their efficiency
to balance domestic, social, spiritual, and commercial interests.

The number 8 challenge may swing from one of the following extremes to another until it is recognized and new habits
are initiated that stabilize the material ambitions of the challenge holder.

Too combative or too apathetic.
Too unprincipled or too ethical.
Too aggressive or too slow.
Too ambitious or too undirected.
Too efficient or too incompetent.
Too defensive or too defenseless.
Too controlling or too unreliable.
Too limited or too expansive.
Too slipshod or too thorough.
Too oblivious or too conscious.
Too industrious or too lazy.
Too dynamic or too feeble.
Too wasteful or too thrifty.
Too showy or too uncaring.

PHYSICAL CHALLENGES OF
THE NUMBER 8

Challenges affect physical as well as mental health. Body chemistry changes when individuals are stressed, and when we do
not know what is good for us, our minds trigger anxious, angry,
or frustrated habits. When we are mean to ourselves, we get
sick. One's attitude sends the brain a message, and the brain
tells the body to scream for help.

To get attention for their dis-ease, often people get sick
or form negative habits. Numerologists believe that illness and
wellness depend upon attitude, and challenges indicate the
attitudes that result from needy feelings. When we do not feel
needy, we feel well and balanced and do not crave attention

from others. Essentially, if the personality challenges are balanced, the body chemistry is in balance, too, and therefore there is little chance of mental or physical dis-ease.

Challenge numbers indicate the ways people subconsciously punish themselves for not being consciously good to themselves.

The following list of dis-eases and negative habits relate to the challenge of the number 8.

Addictions	Herpes
Alcoholism	Indigestion
Allergy	Knuckle cracking
Appendicitis	Laryngitis
Asthma	Nervousness
Cancer	Numbness
Colds	Skin Problem
Eczema	Slipped disk
Epilepsy	Smoking Problems
Eye Problem	Strokes
Fainting	Varicose Veins
Heart Problems	Warts
Hepatitis	

TO BALANCE THE CHALLENGE OF THE 8 AND BRING IT OUT AS A TALENT . . .

The first step to balancing the challenge is to feel comfortable about saying "I need material freedom." Take a look at personal relationships. Take time to thank a secretary for consideration beyond the job specifications. Call a friend for a social lunch. Aim to organize your time to include a hobby, a brisk walk, or a quiet evening with your loved ones. Make yourself read books that describe the lives of multimillionaires, and find out if money really bought them *everything*.

Avoid overindulgence and lapses of sentiment. You will develop gout if you eat your way through both volumes of *The Gourmet Cookbook*. Lean on somebody once in a while, keeping in mind that you are entitled to some small weakness. Try turning down a business dinner to dine with your loved ones. You will be surprised at the dividends you will accrue from time spent with the people who love you. Be true to your mate, and remember that you really cannot buy eternal loyalty or good health. Material things and materialistic people have a predictable life span, so if you take care of your assets and are considerate of loved ones, they will be there when you need them.

Watch your temperamental outbursts. Do not show your charm and understanding at the office only to take your frustrations out on the people at home. Try not to be critical of or compete with your spouse or lover: you will wear out your welcome and his or her emotional stability. Habits are hard to break; however, you should try to save your intolerance for impersonal competition.

Remember that you meet the same people on the way down that you met on the way up. Be kind and considerate, and respect each person for the job he or she does. It is not possible to accomplish anything in a world filled with chiefs. Every chief needs loyal Indians to do the detail work, so protect your tribe and keep them happy.

Recognize yourself as an administrative, shrewd, business-like, industrious achiever who deserves peaceful security within and a piece of security without.

SELF-MOTIVATION

Youth:

As a tot, the number 8 child feels a great urge to be alert, self-reliant, and active. When reprimanded, this child may hold a treasured possession, stare confidently, and trade angers in order to soothe his wounded ego. This child needs exercise, practical chores, and peer interactions, as the number 8 youngster is, in general, courageous, managerial, and decisive. If surrounded by weak or unreasonable authorities, he will crack the whip. He wants discipline and will find a way to get it.

Parents may describe their number 8 child as capable, confident, and enterprising; however, these words describe the individual only when he is surrounded by efficient, positive, and responsible authorities. If the child's high-powered energy is misunderstood and parents are bullying or apathetic, the child may become too demanding or spiritless. The number 8 youngster wants to be given tasks, prove himself, and progress to greater responsibilities or challenges. If this child—who has a serious, sensible, industrious character—is disorganized for long periods of time, he will feel unprepared. The result will be a first-grader who is neither self-confident nor venturesome.

Number 8 children need to plan, build, and work consistently. Their cleverness, ability to concentrate, and intellectual curiosity should be coordinated with physical activities. A lack of interest in artistic self-expression or difficulty accepting others' vulnerability may be a problem in maturity. Eights are born organizers with a knack for talking anyone into assisting them. Since they have a talent for seeing through unrealistic people and are frank critics, to avoid disrespectful confrontations, parents need to practice what they preach or find that their children are leading *them*.

The strong-willed number 8 will be stubborn, impatient with restrictions, and possessive. The 8 individual is attracted to ambitious projects and shies away from petty details. He will attempt to avoid routine jobs or wasting time. If asked to help, he may quickly take charge, delegate responsibilities, and go on to a more personally productive interest. If he is disobedient and punished justly, he will deal with his penalty efficiently. On the other hand, if he knows that he is right and feels mistreated, he may become hotheaded and rebellious.

Tangible accomplishments and assets are foremost in the minds of number 8 teenagers. They have an urge to get what they want, so it is best to begin teaching money management when they are preteens to avoid grand-scale spending when they become wage-earning teens. Eights want to make a good impression, feel competitive, and enjoy status symbols. They will carry after-school jobs yet manage to have time for sports and social activity. If the number 8 is also a challenge number, they may be one-track-minded and should be encouraged to relax.

If these individuals have creative or artistic number meanings in other aspects of their charts, they will capitalize on them. Eights may be superb salespeople who discover door-to-door businesses while still in high school. Astute judges of human nature, they understand the value of impulse buying. In order to successfully fill orders quickly, they cram the family storeroom with their inventory of Avon, Fuller Brush, or Tupperware products and comb the neighborhood for prospective buyers. Eights are the third-graders who sold lemonade to passersby on hot summer days, saved the profits, and bankrolled themselves as high school juniors. They are eager to gain power and affluence independently as self-made young adults or—when prepared academically—as executives in the business or sports community.

Maturity:

Number 8 adults want to own and enjoy all the things money can buy. They strive to be influential and to maintain a well-organized, constuctive lifestyle, preferring to marry traditionally and raise a family that shares their ambitions. However, these 8s are the workaholics who have no respect for weakness, procrastination, or failure. They may therefore be oblivious of a lover's emotional anxieties or the concepts of carefree vacationing and nonbusiness social activities. They are also often capable of overestimating the capacities of employees and relatives: without realizing that only one out of nine people has their stamina or material ambitions, they assume that everyone wants to work an eight-day week.

Number 8 people do not like to be disobeyed, disorganized, or distracted by petty details. Rarely comfortable just paying the bills, they opt to wheel and deal with big shots. Eights *must* have the latest Gucci wallet, Mercedes-Benz model, or other status accessory. Unmistakable symbols of success and prosperity bolster their egos, and they dislike being outclassed. These individuals may swim thirty laps, lift weights, or run twelve miles before or after the workday is over. They have tremendous vitality and physical endurance, so outlets that relieve stress—on which they seem to thrive—are necessities. Resting or relaxing, on the other hand, only bore them.

The head rules the number 8 heart, yet 8s are sensual and search for a mate who will be an asset. Although generally loyal lovers, if home life is not supportive and their physical appetites are not met, they will find companionship elsewhere. Since the 8s take pride in home and community, family circumstances and behavior are expected to be exemplary. When disillusioned by marriage, they will try to avoid divorce in order to maintain a dignified outer image. It is difficult for number 8s to take a backseat at home, as they are unconsciously bossy. Pillars of the community when time and money permit, they add enthusiasm and sound leadership if they work for charities or other improvements.

A problem for self-established number 8s may be finding time to add polish and diplomacy to their accomplishments. In other words, they may have the appearance of a prince or princess and the social graces of a pauper. When sensitive and cooperative or born to wealth and power, 8s are self-possessed, honorable, and discriminating. But when overambitious, inflexible, or crude, they may be clumsy, opinionated boors. It is in their best interest not to be indifferent to less influential associates or unprepared to assume all the responsibilities of success.

A desire to look prosperous and to wield clout may cause number 8s to make major purchases and to display them all. These individuals have the desire to own things, but when bejeweled to go out on a golf course or a sailboat, they are really indicating a lack of inner security. When comfortable with themselves—prudent and conservative—they will cleverly research a new experience and groom themselves to communicate reputability and self-confidence.

Number 8 self-motivations have the souls of opportunists and minds like steel traps. Those with sound material judgment should quickly spot bargains and receive value for their money. And although 8s may be penurious and supermarket shoppers, they can also be lavish spenders when they want to make a splash. If number 8s decide to impress a client or superior at dinner, the guest may expect to dine on caviar, asparagus, and filet mignon. And depending on whether the evening is profitable or eventless, leftovers may be either tomorrow's lunch and supper or food for the cat. Number 8 individuals may not appear to be consistent or practical until they are established and secure; however, they are skillful manipulators and shrewd planners on their way up.

Eights may be self-indulgent, opinionated, sneaky show-offs or dynamic, persevering, principled authorities. In either case, they are not going to be ignored. It may be their physical strengths or their practical accomplishments that enable them to take the lead. With compatible numbers in their own charts or a destiny that brings in affluent and influential people who need their businesslike talents, they attract high-powered experiences and a variety of opportunities to become major problem-solvers.

The balanced number 8 will be serious about success. Fly-by-night scheming and careless work habits indicate a fear of failure and an underlying inability to be self-governing. The balanced 8 believes that it takes money to make money, and his approach to finances is realistic and conscientious; however, this insight does not compensate for the fact that he may be blind to intimates who offer love and comfort.

A lasting partnership and marriage will require 8s to make an effort to be appreciative, trusting, and totally committed. They may repeatedly delegate family obligations to a spouse and miss going to Little League play-offs or graduations. Eights do not believe in fairy tales and will persevere to find a solution to any problem they want to solve; however, if their personal ambitions and decisions are ignored, even the most honorable number 8s may take a walk around the block, find another shelter, and never return.

The marriage of two positive number 8 motivations may not include spontaneous, whimsical gift giving or amorous after-dinner walks in the moonlight. Two people who are industrious, pragmatic, and constantly on the go may systematize a lifestyle that is creatively limiting and emotionally detached. If these individuals are on the negative side of the 8, they may be unrealistic, devoid of a sense of material values, and unable to solve their individual practical problems. Positive or negative, two 8s add up to 16. In the numerology system, 16 is a testing number that rises to fall when allied with commercial ambitions. 16/7 is a number that indicates loneliness, emotional poverty, and erroneous ideas. Since the motivation-number meaning describes what one needs to feel comfortable, a long-term, intimate relationship between two 8s will be a ticklish affair for both.

SELF-IMAGE

Youth:

When lying on the bed, listening to music, and imagining "What am I going to be like when I grow up? How will I walk, dress, and talk?" number 8 preteens visualize a giant of industry, the hostess with the mostest, or a sports immortal. They dream of presiding as chairman of the board and leaving after lunch to talk business on the company yacht or receiving the Player of the Year award and managing a pennant-winning team until they die. Children with the number 8 self-image picture themselves as wealthy, chiefly winners—company presidents, professional athletes, and financial advisers.

Number 8 children may be eager to accept the challenge of a two-wheel bike, get a paper route, or open a savings account. They cannot pass up a chance to work, excel, or accumulate possessions. They are always ready to earn or spend money for assets. It is their greatest joy to get the best of a trade or a bargain. When they are encouraged to be self-reliant, assertive, and consistent achievers, they are happy.

The number 8 self-image coordinates ambitions and social interactions. These 8s appear to be sturdy, neat, and vigorous. It is their youthful wish to gain power and amass their own belongings. They are impatient to grow up and seem mature beyond their years. At times they may be bossy or self-important, but when feeling in tune with their self-image, they will alter their personalities and become persuasive, enthusiastic, and supportive.

As youths, number 8s will dress efficiently. They are not faddists or fashion plates unless dressing a part will make them appear older, more dignified, or important. Enterprising, opportunistic 8s are ready to do anything to command respect and to serve their purposes. When living up to their self-image, number 8s look dynamic and enjoy ambitious projects. When out of balance, they may be slovenly and unreliable. If the number 8 is supported by the same self-motivation or a self-expression number 8, these individuals may be hyperactive, hotheaded, inflexible workaholics.

Maturity:

When walking out of an elevator or into a room—before personality or intellect come into play—number 8 adults send out an impressive, genial, and fastidious vibration. Their attitude indicates a strong personality, and they seem to brim with energy. The first impression they give is prosperous, dominant, and dignified. If self-motivation and self-expression number meanings are artistic or modest, they will display status symbols and their clothing styles, posture, and attitude will indicate to the world that they are not cheap to keep.

When these individuals are wearing the colors mauve or rose, the self-image is emphasized. Those with the 8 self-image do not have to brag or take over. Their leadership qualities are obvious, and they have a businesslike charisma that inspires confidence. In essence, balanced 8s are perceived as go-getters who aim high and expect to be powerhouses. It is their heart's desire to gain control, make prestigious alliances, and earn financial independence. Their self-presentation is carefully calculated, for they consider the observations of others and strive to make the best possible impression.

Number 8 adults consider themselves to be rule-breakers and may rationalize anything that will get them ahead. When living up to their self-image, they have a sense of accomplishment and visualize unlimited possibilities.

The self-expression number may govern the first impression if inexpensive or unconventional dress codes or fads are indicated by the career descriptions outlined in the number meaning.

The self-motivation number may influence the apparel of the bearers if they are relaxing and doing what they want to do. However, when these individuals are living up to their self-image, they will not feature correspondent colors or styles indicated by numbers in another part of their numerology chart.

SELF-EXPRESSION

Youth:

It is obvious to adults when children have a number 8 self-expression number. In youth, number 8 talents are based in activity, stamina, and self-confidence. As they get older they discover that they have good coordination, attract positions of responsibility, and achieve goals more easily or quickly than their peers. When frustrated, they may act intolerant, dictatorial, or sneaky. As assertive, appreciative, conscientious little go-getters, it is difficult to stifle their problem-solving ideas or entice them to take a nap.

Without intending to be inconsiderate, high-powered number 8s may be blunt, ignore displays of affection, or show impatience with less efficient friends or authorities. Slow-moving or less strong people may get in the way of their objectives. To undisciplined, impractical, unmaterialistic parents, they may appear to be too definite, managerial, or possessive. To ambitious, businesslike, systematized adults, number 8 children are accepted as contributing family members who are given praise and material rewards for jobs that are well done.

Number 8 talents put the child to work early. They will be more competent, consistent, and industrious adults if encouraged to manage finances, time, and energy appropriately. To reach the ambitious goals they set for themselves, they require assertiveness, industriousness, and stamina. Even as tots they effectively manipulate others to do mundane tasks or thankless jobs; however, once given the chance to solve practical problems on their own, number 8 children prove their self-reliance.

As teenagers and young adults, 8s are always busy and should be taught how to relax. They have the ability to get good grades, play varsity ball, serve as class president, and make money after school. They are natural efficiency experts and have a talent for big business. These young people are serious students of finance and have a gift for making their physical efforts and commercial ideas pay off.

Capable number 8 children may be straight arrows, not flexible enough to know when they have outgrown their focus on sports. They become dedicated to disciplines and may feel lost without steady practice. These children should be encouraged to diversify. The world of business may be their oyster, but they should venture out to absorb the world of social graces. A university business degree is a worthwhile objective, even if these youngsters have to work days and go to night school to get it. Tots, teens, and youths do well to set their sights on executive positions or their own organizations. Material ambition is their key to success.

Maturity:

Suggested Occupations: Manufacturer, banker, stockbroker, stock market trader, commodities broker, financial adviser, sports professional, military officer, statistician, accountant, office manager, engineer, bandleader, drummer, school ad-

ministrator, purchasing agent, tax consultant, corporation lawyer, judge, building contractor, construction foreman, payroll
administrator, investor, cashier, comptroller, bank loan officer,
store owner, franchise operator, collection manager, public
official, union leader, sales manager, gentleman farmer, purchasing agent, importer/exporter, weight lifter, physical fitness
adviser, movie producer, stage manager.
Options:

Careers indicated by the meaning of the self-motivation
number may not make use of readily available talents but will
allow the individual to feel comfortable.

Careers indicated by the self-image number meanings will
encourage the individual to live up to youthful dreams.

Careers indicated by the meaning of the destiny number,
if it is not the same as the self-expression number, will require
that the individual learn from incoming personalities and experiences.

If self-expression and destiny numbers are the same, the
individual's talents will be recognized and utilized early in
life.

Maturity: Self-expression Analysis

Number 8 individuals have a potential for financial rewards
for their executive ability, efficiency, and commercial judgment. Recognition is possible for their physical stamina and
coordination. Eights are dominant personalities who plan, organize, and work to make their efforts pay off in a big way.
These individuals send out a vibration that puts them in the
driver's seat.

Number 8 talents must recognize their need to maintain a
positive approach. In a business or sports environment they
are powerhouse problem-solvers who radiate strength. If socializing and promoting are called for, 8s are well equipped
to charm and impress the most prestigious clients. They are
persuasive opportunists when they know what they want—
and they usually do. Balanced number 8s may be depended

upon to be conscientious employees and employers. They display a fastidious style and status in their dress, and enjoy creating an air of prosperity, power, and capability.

Number 8 individuals are progressive and must select a job or career that offers growth. If possibilities are limited, balanced 8s will find a more promising position in which to use their sound judgments and workaholic drives. All number 8 talents want creature comforts. They may be down-to-earth, common-sensical, and straight talking one minute and up in the air eating, drinking, and indulging sensually the next. Eights are not petty or small about anything. They are generally ambitious in their pursuit of unlimited money, influential alliances, and unconditional authority.

In selecting a career, businesslike 8s want security and far-reaching options for advancement. They are self-starters and are at their best in challenging competition. Consistent, strong, and dedicated, 8s have the talent to be professional athletes or corporate giants. Both careers require individuals to co-ordinate physical stamina, intellect, and intuition. The professional baseball player joins talents to bat a ball or field a grounder at the right time and in the right place, employing exact judgment to hit a home run or stop a runner from scoring. A company president brings his clearheaded decisions, disciplined energy, and courageous spirit together to increase the preceding year's income or take over a competitor. Both are playing for high stakes, and both are intent upon winning.

Those with the number 8 self-expression should not have trouble in any wheeler-dealer occupation offering a chance to manage, organize, and have the final say. Eights set the pace and ride in the financial fast lane. Their career problems may stem from their impatience, demanding leadership, and one-track mind, but mixing business and pleasure does work for balanced number 8s who know when to take family and personal obligations to heart. Negative aspects lie in the 8s' self-indulgence, intolerance, and hot temperament. They are easily bored by routine matters, mundane responsibilities, and limited potentials. They are, however, attracted to businesses that enable them to choose when and how they will get recognition or money for the tangible results they produce.

With an 8 self-expression, an academic education is a booster but not a prerequisite for success. This is the number of self-made, unpolished, get-an-idea-and-build-it-in-the-garage multimillionaires. Eights can be low-key listeners or bigmouthed tell-it-alls. They are generally pragmatic, self-confident, enterprising money-makers who want to see and taste the fruits of their labors. Number 8 go-getters do not let up on themselves and they thrive on stress. They may be loyal, dignified, honest commercial bankers or sleazy, bigoted, scheming moneylenders. With the power of the number 8 for material mastery, these individuals must select how to use it to gain financial freedom.

DESTINY

WE ARE NOT BORN KNOWING WHAT LIFE HAS TO OFFER. INDIVIDUALS WITH THE NUMBER 8 DESTINY ARE SURROUNDED BY WEALTH AND LEARN TO DEVELOP BUSINESS SENSE, EXECUTIVE SKILLS, AND MASTERY. THEY ENCOUNTER PEOPLE AND EXPERIENCES THAT TEACH THEM EFFICIENCY AND MATERIAL JUDGMENT AND HOW TO GET WHAT THEY WANT.

This destiny implies a lifetime of seeking financial freedom and maintaining a positive attitude toward commercial possibilities. To make the most of numerology's ability to forecast, the number 8 must be ready to think big, plan, and work to carry out the plan to the best of his ability. He may be born with a silver spoon in his mouth yet not know how to get and keep another. It may take a lifetime, but once the 8 learns to assume control, delegate responsibilities, and leave the details to others, he is on the road to success. The number 8 destiny should seek out a lifestyle that opens doors to commerce, wealth, and authority.

People with a number 8 destiny must learn to thoroughly and carefully direct others. Influential, financially secure people are the companions who help further this destiny's purpose. Number 8 destiny holders should focus on cultivating an interest in community affairs and investment procedures and building for future material growth. Those who are straightforward and farsighted moneymakers should set the example for the individuals who may choose to be indifferent to materialistic goals, misdirecting their energies to purely artistic, academic, or humanitarian pursuits. Life experiences will likely change this latter perspective as time goes on.

There are no limits to the possibilities that an efficient, aggressive, and dependable personality will attract to a number 8 destiny. He may enhance opportunities by dressing expensively, styling conservatively, and tailoring expertly. If the 8 understands the high power that surrounds his destiny, that he should go where the wealthy go, conduct himself appropriately, dress acceptably, and rub elbows with only the most progressive and successful people, his destiny will take it from there.

Children within this destiny do not become one-track-minded achievers unless the self-motivation or self-expression numbers are the same. As time passes these destiny holders create or look for ways to increase income or expand business interests. Opportunities will arise for them to meet the holders of wealth or power, and in time they themselves will reach for the brass ring. On this lifepath they learn to supply those in need of executive abilities in large corporate structures with administration, practical judgment, and solid solutions to problems.

It is essential that 8s find a way to take command. To progress, they must be directive, delegate details, and maintain personal integrity. Individuals with the number 8 destiny should not wait to be told what to do or how to do it; instead they must listen and watch for their chances to fill demands for effective leadership. Cockiness, bad taste, or inconsistent work habits will push away prudent, respected members of the commercial community. Eights recognize phony facades and entrepreneurial flashes right away and need both stamina and courage to keep up with potential boosters and friends who open doors for raises and promotions.

Marriage to someone with a number 8 self-motivation or self-expression makes life easier for the 8 destiny, as they are efficient and know what the 8 destiny must learn. In this situation, if the 8 is a late bloomer or lacks perspective in material matters, the spouse will pressure the 8 destiny holder to be more ambitious and try to teach what he or she understands. Depending on the challenges and name-number compatibility, this may be a shot in the arm or a kick-in-the-gut experience for the 8 destiny. The marriage of two number 8 destinies will be fraught with financial insecurities and will be a trial for both; however, name-number meanings may help, and this could be a loving relationship based on partnership and material growth. In any marriage, if the 8s strive for dignity, efficiency, and pride in work, destiny will direct their energies to succeed in areas where business and commercial interests are focused.

BIRTHDAY INFLUENCES
WITHIN THE DESTINY

August

Individuals born in August learn to foster material ambitions in youth. Situations arise that direct them to be concerned with practical realities—too much or too little money, family influence, or business activity. They may not be geared toward recognizing the need to earn or learn and therefore make naive material judgments after age twenty-eight. As children, these individuals are surrounded by high-powered workaholics, financially desperate weaklings, or nonmaterialistic intellectuals.

Making serious decisions about money or material security becomes a problem or a focus in mid-life.

Prior to age twenty-eight, these youths are caught unprepared by economic experiences. Because they come from environments frequented by people with ambitious aspirations, people born in August may develop a controlling or selfish attitude toward money and assets. Fears of poverty or of not comprehending how wise investments are made breed in August–born a fear of spending or venturing income and capital. As youngsters, if these individuals do not learn thrift and are not taught to work or build patiently, they will direct others to get them the things they want. People born in August usually get involved in talking business in youth and learn how to do business in maturity.

Birthday: 8, 17, 26

THE BIRTHDAY NUMBER HAS AN INFLUENCE ON PERSONALITY AND DESTINY. IT ATTRACTS PEOPLE AND EXPERIENCES DURING MID-LIFE THAT EXEMPLIFY THE NUMBER MEANING.

The mid-life productivity cycle begins with maturity. It lasts from approximately twenty-eight to fifty-five years of age and coordinates with the destiny during that time span. The birthday-number meaning adds its character traits and experiences to an individual's numerology analysis.

People born on the eighth, seventeenth, and twenty-sixth of the month, in addition to the character traits outlined by the number meanings for the name, are efficient, industrious, and ambitious. They may be unhappy when they cannot make sound business judgments or gain status. Individuals born on these dates want financial freedom, influence in the power structure, and a dignified, traditional lifestyle.

Between approximately twenty-eight and fifty-five years of age—the twenty-seven-year productivity cycle within the destiny—life will offer additional opportunities to be successful in commercial interests, to accumulate possessions, and to efficiently follow short- and long-term plans. Attention to organizing a well-run domestic life, complete with a family that lives up to expectations and a responsible community commitment, will bring pleasures. One should try to realistically take on ambitious projects and develop social activities that enhance business opportunities. Above all, those with an 8, 17, or 26 birthday must be self-reliant.

PERSONAL YEAR

The number 8 is the eighth year in the cycle of nine years of experiences that results in a polish and skill of performance based on the goals set in the first year. In February one sows ideas, which come to light in April. Then a variety of nuts-and-bolts options materialize, which are examined for impracticalities and made utilitarian in May. During the first and last weeks of September, activity intensifies and money and influential alliances are reaped. For most, finances improve, and new opportunities are the result of projects delayed and analyzed one year before.

Work and responsibilities keep one active during July, August, and September. October brings in a chance to draw personal and financial conclusions. It is the time to let go of deadwood and expand this year's commercial efforts. New material prospects and major steps to branch out are conceived in November. December slows the pace and attracts recognition. Surprises and unconventional behavior make the last two weeks a strain. This productive year closes with a reminder to keep up with details and reaffirm emotional relationships.

This is a year when one sees tangible results of past efforts. If romance is the objective, wealthy, healthy, and ambitious prospects are easier to come by. Seeking singles may find that June sparks sensual activity. If marriage is the objective, this is the time to get up the nerve to go after a significant relationship. The same businesslike approach is as effective when courting as in taking over a corporation. One should ignore petty problems, and efficiently utilize planning and management skills to work to achieve objectives. Now is the time to go after whatever one wants and expect to get it.

During the number 8 year the amounts of money and power plays that come in or go out are greater than what one usually handles. Things will not necessarily be on the plus side, and anything is possible; however, all things are attainable, and it's important to maintain a healthy attitude. The purpose of this year is to give one the opportunity to wheel and deal effectively. Advantages are available demanding unsentimental or hardheaded decisions. If one gets down to brass tacks, aims high, and visualizes success, the 8 temperament and outlook lends talents to goals for the duration of the 8 personal year.

PERSONAL MONTH

The number 8 personal month within any personal year gives one the opportunity to take control of business and financial matters. One must always be self-reliant, forceful, and resourceful. High-powered, enterprising, pragmatic associates are important now. This is not the time for vacations, sensualizing, or undisciplined behavior. After last month's delays, legalities, and unanswered questions, one must develop an efficient attitude and unclog the wheels of progress. The projects begun seven months before require one's best effort: to advertise, promote, and be shrewd. One should dress with dignity, be diplomatic, and pull out all the status symbols available. If one is organized and persuasive, exceptional results will be achieved.

PERSONAL DAY

Wake up with goals in mind, and set out to accomplish them. Streamline plans and expect to accomplish them. Check expenses and be prudent and farsighted, making this day profitable and orderly. Money comes in or goes out for bargains. Shopping, commercializing on ideas, and socializing for business are favored activities. Appear successful: remember, money attracts money and commanding impressions attract command.

If the time is right, ask for a raise, an office with a panoramic view, or first-class travel arrangements. Be straightforward, expect to get results, and things will go smoothly. Do not be ungracious, one-track-minded, or self-indulgent. Make your appearance dignified and assured, and boost self-confidence. Feeble attempts, fear of failure, or abusive language send out cowardly vibrations. Be courageous and expect to be respected; otherwise the high energy of this day will internalize into restrictions and frustration.

"Cash in" on markers if considerations are due. One is more likely to see debts paid or favors returned today. Do not take chances, get hot-tempered, or be inconsiderate. If situations are awkward, be the one to maintain refinement, trust, and conscientious leadership. Remember that people in power are watching. Today's energetic, enthusiastic, and upright executive efforts may bring in material rewards tomorrow. Success depends on common sense, logic, and constructive problem-solving. If you keep objectives in mind, this will be a memorable day.

CHAPTER THIRTEEN

NUMBER 9
(O)

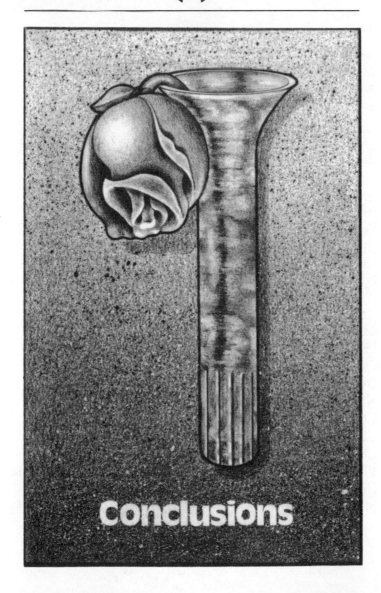

Conclusions

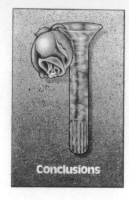

Conclusions

ATTRIBUTES:
POSITIVE—Compassion, Empathy, Artistry, Faith, Generosity, Compatibility, Bravery, Tenderness, Willingness, Tolerance
NEGATIVE—Bitterness, Bigotry, Selfishness, Jealousy, Indiscretion, Fickleness, Coldness, Deception, Cowardice

CORRESPONDENTS:
LETTERS: I, R
ODD NUMBER: Receptive, Aggressive
DISPOSITION: Cordial, Affectionate; Philosophical
NUMBERS: 18, 27, 36, 45, 54, 63, 72, 81, 90, 99, 108
COLOR: Saffron, Orange-Yellow-Gold
GEM: Opal
CRYSTAL: Alum
VEGETATION: Holly, Magnolia, Buttercup, Oak, Sycamore
FOODS: Milk, Cheese, Beef, Jello
MUSICAL INSTRUMENT/APPEAL: Violin; Tenor, Symphony

MUSICAL NOTE: High D
LOCATIONS: State: Alaska, Illinois, South Dakota
   City: Amarillo, Anchorage, Augusta, Buffalo, Daytona
   Beach, Hartford, Miami, New Orleans, Paterson, Rock-
   ford, South Bend, Spokane, Utica
PLANET: Aura and Influence of All or None.
MONTH: September
BIRTHDAYS: 9, 18, 27
DAYS OF THE WEEK: Monday (Alone), Friday (with Com-
   panions)
GENERAL COMPATIBILITY NUMBERS: 5, 6, 9, 1 (Artis-
   tic); 3, 8 (Business)
INCOMPATIBILITY NUMBERS: 4, 7

Note: If an individual has the challenge to the number 9, these descriptions will swing from positive to negative until the challenge is balanced. Please be sure to read the challenge number meaning.

CHALLENGE OF THE NUMBER 9
AND THE 0

Note: NUMBER 9, THE HIGHEST NUMBER, CANNOT BE SUBTRACTED FROM ANOTHER NUMBER AND REMAIN A NUMBER 9. NUMBER 9 IS NEVER FOUND AS A CHALLENGE NUMBER. ZERO IS SYNONYMOUS WITH THE 9.

Zero is actually the challenge to the meaning of the number 9. The numerological interpretation of the number 9 is that it contains all character ingredients of the numbers 1 through 8. Zero added to a number (20, 30, 40, etc.) raises the interpretation of the single number to a perfection of its meaning. Zero demands that the numbers 1 through 9 add practical conventions and humanitarian and universal responsibilities to its meaning. The challenge of the zero may be likened to a challenge to the number 90.

CHALLENGE OF THE 0

This is the challenge to the individual's understanding of human emotions and human frailty. The challenge holder is born with an "old soul's" maturity, is philosophical, and has more options than the average person. Therefore, the 0 challenge holder has immediate personal choice. He has the capacity to know what is wrong and how to fix it as well as a great potential for compassion, empathy, and charitable problem-solving.

This is not a challenge that is identified quickly; the *sub*-challenge number may be easier to spot. The 0 challenge holder should read all the preceding challenge number meanings, as the 0 challenge encompasses them all at once when out of balance. Or, when balanced by the intellect, the 0 challenge comprises none of the others at all. *Nine is the challenge to one's responsibility to oneself and the world around one . . . it contains the extremes of selfishness or selflessness.*

In youth, adults may have expected more from these youngsters than they could comprehend or attain. Usually these children are born to parents past the average childbearing years. In some cases they are middle children from large families, who walk a tightrope between answering to domineering older siblings and playing parent to younger siblings. A serious illness may have kept them in the hospital or attended by adults at home. These children were required to understand the serious personal problems or emotional highs and lows of the younger or older relatives surrounding them.

Parents may have relinquished their responsibility to these children and reverted to childishness or, because of the death of the parents, the children were left alone to fend for themselves. As a result, these children became older than their years, precocious little old ladies or gentlemen who spewed forth wisdom and listened with deep concern.

As preteens and teenagers, they are loners. They may become groupies searching for role models and looking to people who are the exemplars of a skill or craft. They fall in love from afar and have difficulty with intimate relationships, and, too often, they are in love with love. Nines either have so much to give that they cannot relate it to one person, or they become immersed in a lover's needs.

Number 9 youths may take on responsibilities, become group leaders, and deny themselves for the welfare of their peers. As adults, they may continue to give more than they get *or* meet the world selfishly. Subconsciously 9s feel deprived of the imagined joys of youth and may try to stay young forever. They often marry older, more cultured individuals or young, and needier individuals. They either serve the community or go on welfare, are novices or "old souls." The older these challenge holders grow, the more comfortable they become with their capabilities and capacities.

The zero challenge holder feels a deep satisfaction in sacrificing ambitions for others or giving up relating to others entirely. When beset by emotional disillusionments and disappointments, the number 9's broad-scoped point of view diminishes to that of an unevolved 0. The philosophy of the zero challenge holder is rooted in the observation "I felt sorry for myself because I had no shoes, until I saw a man who had no feet." At the most negative extreme, the challenged 0 has no feelings at all; a dispassionate 0 challenge holder is a cold associate and a formidable enemy.

Because the 0–9 understands the deepest emotions of others, when hurt, he uses all his depth to push an adversary's buttons. He can even be sadistic. It is difficult to comprehend the 9's changes when they occur, as he is a seasoned thespian and can appear caring when actually being self-serving.

When balanced, a 9 has the ability to look beyond immediate needs to understand another's problems. The 9–0 challenge holder unconsciously knows that "there but for the grace of God go I." This individual is born with the awareness that only something superior to humankind has the right to judge another being . . . unless the individual feels cheated.

The challenge bearers' balanced philosophy is based in a welfare worker's impersonal love and feeling for human suffering. These individuals must learn to understand the difference between being charitable and acting out of pity. In other words, 0 challenge holders must learn not to perceive *everyone* as being needy. When acting from the standpoint of pity, their good works usually result in an emotional boomerang.

Zero challenge holders may submerge their personalities in order to fulfill desires or compensate for weaknesses they observe in others. Intuition gives these challenge holders a superior talent for knowing what other people often do not know about themselves. Because of childhood experiences, these challenge holders sense that material matters are dealt with on a different level than are emotional upsets; they feel another's pain and forget their own material needs.

When watching a film, these challenge holders are emotionally involved in it. When someone is hurt, they feel the pain and they identify with the images. Nines cry or laugh and their bodies react accordingly. They may be exhausted upon leaving a theater, unable to shake off the experience as mere entertainment. Books, movies, and all other media of self-expression reach into the hearts of 9–0 challenge holders. They are born with culture and extreme responsiveness to all forms of artistry, or develop this strong tendency later in life.

After realizing that not everyone views humanity with their romantic style or emotional capacities, 0 challenge holders may train themselves to detach. As a result of rejection, heartache, or experiences with shallow companions, they guard against emotional responsiveness, often producing the extreme opposite reaction. "Charity begins at home" may become their credo.

When balanced, these challenged individuals know that

the everyday problems of living may strain their energy but will not kill them. They have the strength and knowledge to handle anything life can throw at them. They understand that people and life evolve at an irregular pace and that they cannot save all of humanity. Instead, they focus on strengthening their skills to do the best they can.

Yet an accumulation of survival problems or attempts to balance all challenges at once may swing these challenge holders to the opposite extreme. Zero–nine challenge holders solve problems while sleeping, so sound physical fitness routines are key to maintaining good health and balancing this challenge. Stressful times may be indicated by insomnia, high blood pressure, heart problems, or emotional apathy. The overly compassionate nature of these challenge holders may bring them to an energy level at which material problem-solving is impossible. In time, they realize that they take more to heart than the average challenge holder. These individuals may use their superb intuition and discernment to ease away stress when on overload.

Zero challenge holders may also be masochistic. If as children they were exposed to pain, loneliness, or sadistic authorities, they may find the habit of suffering hard to break. When awakened, however, zero challenge holders have the superior ability to know when and how to break away from unacceptable behavior. They reach a point in evolution that equips them to accept their own problems and modify behavior. These individuals may intuitively sense the foolishness of greedy, selfish, and inhumane individuals and take appropriate actions to remove themselves from such company.

The zero challenge may swing from one of the following extremes to another until it is recognized and new habits are initiated that impersonalize the emotions of the challenge holder and spur the individual on to make selections and changes.

Too selfless or too selfish.

Too broad-minded or too bigoted.

Too melodramatic or too unexpressive.
Too pleased or too discontent.
Too possessive or too liberal.
Too passionless or too romantic.
Too understanding or too narrow.
Too charitable or too greedy.
Too brave or too cowardly.
Too fickle or too loyal.
Too provincial or too cultured.
Too obstinate or too amenable.
Too devoted or too uncaring.
Too vindictive or too forgiving.

PHYSICAL CHALLENGES OF THE NUMBER 0–9

Challenges affect physical as well as mental health. Body chemistry changes when individuals are stressed, and when we do not know what is good for us, our minds trigger anxious, angry, or frustrated habits. When we are mean to ourselves, we get sick. One's attitude sends the brain a message, and the brain tells the body to scream for help.

To get attention for their dis-ease, often people get sick or form negative habits. Numerologists believe that illness and wellness depend upon attitude, and challenges indicate the attitudes that result from needy feelings. When we do not feel needy, we feel well and balanced and do not crave attention from others. Essentially, if the personality challenges are balanced, the body chemistry is in balance, too, and therefore there is little chance of mental or physical dis-ease.

Challenge numbers indicate the ways people subconsciously punish themselves for not being consciously good to themselves.

The following list of dis-eases and negative habits relate to the challenge of the Number 9 and 0.

Back Problems	Influenza
Bone Problem	Jealousy
Bronchitis	Knee Problems
Cellulite Problems	Lung Problem
Eye Problems	Pneumonia
Glandular Problems	Seasickness
Gout	Sinus Problems
Hay Fever	Stuttering
Headaches	Venereal Disease
Heart Failure	Warts
Hives	

TO BALANCE THE CHALLENGE OF THE 9–0 AND BRING IT OUT AS A TALENT . . .

The first step to balancing the challenge is to feel comfortable about saying "I need to be needed." Sort out priorities and remind yourself that you have every reason to follow your feelings. Take stock of your ambitions now; reflecting on deterrents from youth will not put you on the road to broadening your scope.

Be decisive and you will receive positive feedback. You have the capacity to see all the options. Analyze your priorities: find a comfortable vantage point from which you can cultivate your compassion, sympathy, and desire to elevate yourself.

It will be difficult for you to expand and grow if you are enmeshed in either purely commercial goals or personal love affairs. Your drives must bring you out into an environment filled with people who share your desires to serve humanity and who can help you polish your talents. Reach out to the people who exemplify skillfulness, quality, and purpose—you belong with them.

Open your heart to fight the urge to become possessive. You cannot be bound to purely domestic or community needs. You have the abilities to set an example others will follow; do not feel needy if your students eventually become your teachers, however. That is a great honor, and no one will deserve the credit more than you do.

Make your love of culture a highlight in your weekly plans. Go to the theater or an art gallery or read a classic novel. You are a born do-gooder and caretaker, and you deserve curtain calls for your expertise; however, suffering for your art or the world's needy may cause you to become the star tragedian. That type of action is a reflection of youthful misconceptions. Remind yourself that you can play Shakespeare without making the plight of Romeo and Juliet part of everyday life.

Let go of past relationships and ambitions when they have lost their usefulness. Growth requires changes; give yourself the same advice you would give to another in need of expansion. Do not trust everyone else yet ignore your own inner promptings. Philosophical discussions are profitable up to a point, but there comes a time when you must analyze the input and personally take action.

Yesterday is gone. You are the sum of your life experiences and intuitive self *today*. If you do not reach out, you may feel smothered in commitments. You have within your birthright independence, sensitivity to others, optimism, traditions, sensuality, responsibility, intelligence, problem-solving stamina, and compassion. Recognize the positive qualities of the numbers 1 to 8 within yourself.

Opt for the additional space you need. Focus on your personal ideals while keeping your eye on long-term domestic and business commitments . . . no need to become impulsive. Do whatever you need to do. Make your selections, pay your dues, and live life true to your desires and purposes.

Recognize yourself as an understanding, wise, philosophical humanitarian who deserves to control emotional responses, choose his own lifestyle, and grow far from his birthright.

SELF-MOTIVATION

Youth:

As a tot, the number 9 urge that the child feels is to be affectionate, empathetic, and aware of his surroundings. When reprimanded, this child will understand the feelings of the authority, become emotional, and apologize profusely or heatedly blame the accuser. This child needs love, sensitive social interactions, and a sense of being needed. The number 9 youngster is kind, responsive, and well intentioned. If surrounded by aloof authorities, he will become impassive or willful; he wants warmth and will go to extremes to get it.

Parents may describe their number 9 child as precocious, reasonable, and older than his years. Those words describe the child when he is surrounded by broad-minded, unselfish, and indulgent authorities. If the child's depth of feeling is considered to be ultradramatic and the parents are humorless and shallow, the youngster may become nervous, moody, and depressed. He wants to understand his own feelings and becomes very uncertain or submissive when misunderstood. The 9 finds it difficult to relate to peers, but once this child, who has his self-esteem rooted in pleasing others, is appreciated for his demonstrations of selflessness, he will be free to apply his energies artistically.

Nines want to be multitalented communicators. They should explore interests in music, art, sports, theater, and writing. If the environment is conducive to spiritual or religious observances, 9 children will be responsive; however, they may go from one belief system to another accumulating knowledge. Nines tend to spread their interests, charitable efforts, and romantic ideas. One week they may daydream that they are destined to be saints. When they learn that saints may live a hell on earth to be considered worthy, they may decide instead to play Helen Hayes or Richard Burton, becoming enshrined stage greats.

NUMEROLOGY HAS YOUR NUMBER

Nines have a broad scope of desires. The strong-willed want to get out of the domestic or neighborhood philosophy and meet the world with open arms. They will attempt to make everyone they meet one of the family. All are welcomed into their heart and hearth.

Possessions may not be important to 9 youths. Things are for sharing, feelings are for caring, and intuition is to be used to spare another suffering. These children are born wise and strive to give and gain knowledge. It is surprising how they comprehend the ways of grown-ups. As children, wherever and whenever it seems important, 9s know other people's thoughts.

Even as a youth, the 9 is attractive to notable and noble people and is drawn to learn from them. He spots people who are exceptionally talented or have polished a craft, and will follow their example. Without trying to upstage, the 9 novice soon sets an example others follow. If hurt by his own trusting nature, the 9 will not give up his romantic notions. He is filled with "brotherly love"—will give his last dime to a beggar and expect to be able to recoup the loss or meet a better person next time around. The 9 knows, without experiencing disaster, that things could always be worse.

If the 9 has more materialistic number meanings in other aspects of his chart, it will affect his desire to experience financial freedom. However, he will likely still find a means of being charitable and will not be unemotional in his attitudes toward money. Humanitarian causes, the Girl or Boy Scouts, and invitations to foreign students to learn about his lifestyle may occupy his after-school time. As a passionate missionary, a hospitable adviser, and an enthusiastic do-gooder, the number 9 youth is the knight on the white charger or an awesome inspiration to everyone in need of comfort, protection, or service.

Maturity:

Adult number 9s want to live a worthwhile life. They will find it difficult to narrow down interests and focus on mundane practicalities or immediate needs. Nines are drawn to helping others and creating—or being involved with—something of universal artistic merit. These are the altruistic inspirational healers and reformers who want to benefit the world. They are capable of self-sacrifice when they have little themselves, and they do big things when others are petty. Nines want security, but do very little to stabilize their economy, emotions, or movements.

Number 9 people do not like to be tied down domestically or squelched emotionally. Rarely able to confine themselves to one intimate relationship, they have many groups of friends. Nines must go where they are needed. Any less fortunate stranger, luckless charity, or repertory company in search of actors or audiences will touch their hearts, or pocketbooks. These individuals make generous, sentimental, impulsive gestures. They may donate the family rent money or leave a spouse with dinner on the table to answer a neighbor's call for help. They feel another's pain with a sense of immediacy that is difficult for intimates to tolerate on a day-to-day basis.

If they are to last, domestic relationships with 9s require a special kind of lover and an extraordinary friend. Nines are attractive to all and attract love. When relaxed, they have charisma. It is possible for 9s to make someone feel that meeting them was kismet. They are universal kindred spirits and without setting out to romance the world, 9s' thoughtfulness, empathy, and compassion find grateful soulmates.

The heart and soul rule over the 9 head. They are affectionate associates, devoted friends, and great lovers. Nines generally blame themselves if there are problems in an intimate relationship, making allowances for transgressions and letting bygones be bygones. Nines will judge each situation by the standards they set for themselves, but they realize that human beings are not perfect, and recall the times when they themselves have been jealous, possessive, and ready to place blame on others for their mistakes. Nines are "in love with love" and may submerge their practical or emotional needs to please a lover.

A 9 will forgive the person who repents but will not understand deceit or disloyalty. He may be a formidable enemy who suffers extreme emotional and physical stress when his love grows cold. Too often, prior to maturity, an isolated 9 does not find suitable emotional outlets and showers all his love on one person. In time, even the most appreciative mate may feel that reciprocating is a burden. If the 9 does not become exhausted by continual self-sacrifice, the mate may retreat. When a 9 senses a lover's detachment, he will become depressed, ambitionless, and aloof. The result is usually a bitter memory for both.

The 9 temperament and perceptions may run the gamut from Albert Schweitzer to Attila the Hun. When comfortable with themselves, those with 9 self-motivation enjoy the beauty of nature, never want a good thing to end, and are nonmaterialistic. They do not depend upon wealth or the use of money as a tool that enables them to bring happiness or comfort to others. Nines treasure personal memories; they realize that remembrances are the precious legacy one leaves behind. Balanced 9s expect nothing and give everything.

The heroic, caring battleground medic and the next-door neighbor who drops in daily to cheer a lonely old spinster both have the 9 self-motivation. These individuals are not afraid to get involved.

The 9 natural instinct is to be uninhibited and enthusiastic about love. Shy recipients of their romantic zeal may be wooed with charming conversations and bowled over by their charisma. Since helpful 9s must be free to leave the nest to reach out for new ideas, their intimate relationships usually suffer. Marriage may be hellish for those who simultaneously are singled out to be romanced by the 9 who wants to possess a lover, and also desires to share experiences with outsiders.

The best-remembered relationships involving the dramatic, romantic, bighearted 9 begin and end with courtship. After saying he wants security and a nest, he has second thoughts. The cloistering effects of a rooted day-to-day existence and a life of practicalities will not coincide with his personal ideals. To make a marriage work, the intuitive 9 will marry a much older or emotionally secure individual.

Nines set the stage by giving more than they get at the onset. When the honeymoon is over, they set out to serve, entertain, or beautify the world again. In a long-running relationship, 9s become the major contributor. If their mate remains unthreatened by the 9 need for loose ties, respects the 9s' purpose, and possesses a philosophical sense of humor, the necessary open communication is possible. However, when personal interactions are stifled, bigoted, or narrow, 9s will call it quits and never look back.

The marriage of two number 9 self-motivations will need some narrowing down to focus on domestic issues. Both partners will tend to drift from one interest to another without thought of expenses or future ambitions. As two romantic dreamers with vivid imaginations who avoid discussing or touching unpleasantness, they will find traditional marriage difficult. If 9s devote themselves to a purpose and have a professional manage their money—*and* one or both travel for business—they may succeed in the real world. But the ideal solution is for both to join the Peace Corps and forget about paying rent, budgeting, or maintaining conventional routines.

Deep in the soul, 9s want to be healers, counselors, and philosophers. They must shout out their creative message to touch others' emotions. Uplifting and magnetic when comfortable, 9s have a way with individuals and audiences. Fulfilled thespians, doctors, politicians, or charity organizers will want to make the world a better place to live. However, they must develop an incentive. Nines would like to believe in art for art's sake. Starving painters, writers, and musicians throughout history have had patrons motivated by the number 9 wish to keep them alive. Such number 9s may give money, time, affection, love, empathy, friendship, and unlimited understanding, because for 9 self-motivations, deep satisfaction is the only reward.

SELF-IMAGE

Youth:

When lying on the bed, listening to music, and imagining "What am I going to be like when I grow up? How will I walk, dress, and talk?" the number 9 preteen visualizes a wise counselor, dedicated artist, or selfless humanitarian. He dreams of receiving the Nobel Peace Prize and donating the cash to a needy charity. A child with the number 9 self-image pictures himself as a humane universalist: a physician-missionary, a polished performer, or a skilled artist.

Nines may be first to hear the bell and rush to drop their donation into the Salvation Army kettle. These individuals cannot pass up a chance to show their love of humanity and eagerness to be of service. They are always ready to offer a listening ear, share experiences, and expound that "there but for the grace of God go I." It is their greatest joy to live up to their heroic ideas and altruistic personal ideals. When they are well groomed, dressed to fit unobtrusively in any part of the world, yet making their presence felt, they are happy.

Number 9 self-images relate to pleasing others. They make promises and try to keep them. Nines' first impression is romantic, artistic, and strong. It is their youthful wish to possess the emotional and physical capacity to take on everyone's burdens and relieve universal signs of suffering. At times they may seem overly dramatic. When feeling in tune with their self-image, they will subjugate their personalities and material ambitions to uplift a lover or cooperate with a cause they respect.

In their early years, number 9s dress neatly and youthfully. They have an eye for beautiful lines and subtle accessories. Each outfit is complete and matches the personality focus for the moment. It is difficult to accurately judge number 9s' age.

Even as tots they are at ease with adults conversationally and have an assured manner. When living up to their self-image, number 9s are graceful, magnetic, and impressive. When out of balance, they may be listless, detached, or sullen. If the self-image number is supported by a self-motivation or self-expression number 9, these individuals may be indiscreet and foster lofty, impractical ideas as well as implement a sublime, self-sacrificing follow-through. Too many 9s in a numerology chart may put welfare-working 9s on welfare themselves.

Maturity:

When walking out of an elevator or into a room—before personality or intellect come into play—number 9 adults send out a cultured and amiable vibration. Often prematurely gray, 9s appear wise and dignified—never old or brittle. Their attitude indicates a gracious personality, and they appear brimming with well-intentioned interest. The first impression they give is magnetic. If self-motivation and self-expression numbers are introverted or businesslike, these number 9s will still attract the attention of exceptional humanitarians or celebrities. Their polish, versatility, and skillful conversation fit in anywhere.

When the color saffron is worn—a yellow-orange blend that highlights fall foliage—the self-image is emphasized. The individual with the number 9 self-image does not have to speak or move to make everyone like him. In essence, 9 includes the communication talents of the number 3, the acting and communication talents and community service of the number 6, and the teaching and communication talents of the high-minded thespian number 9. It is the individual's heart's desire to love everyone and be loved by all. The first impression of an emotionally stimulated number 9 may be intense and passionately animated. He is expert at sensing the needs of others and playing out the expected role. This impressionable idealist has the temperament of a great diva or an eccentric artiste.

Nines are born leaders. Without experience or preparation they join groups and set the example that others choose to follow. When living up to their self-image, 9s are affectionate, hospitable, and tolerant. They want to give and get knowledge and experience.

The self-expression number may govern the first impression if uniforms, current fashions, or unconventional garb are indicated by the career descriptions included in the number meaning.

The self-motivation number may influence the apparel of the bearers if they are relaxing and doing what they want to do. However, when these individuals are living up to their self-image, they will not feature correspondent colors indicated by numbers in another part of their numerology chart.

SELF-EXPRESSION

Youth:

It is obvious to adults when children have a number 9 self-expression. In youth, number 9 talents are based in mature, philosophical, and helpful observations and comments. As they get older they discover they can advise, question, and placate others with their self-deprecating brand of humor. When frustrated, they may appear too dramatic, passionate, and egocentric. As ultratalented, empathetic, self-motivated "old souls," it is difficult for them to behave like self-absorbed children or carefree teens.

Without intending to overact, compassionate number 9s may heroically run back into a burning building to save a pet or relative. Nines think of others' welfare, examine the big picture, and carry out unselfish actions. They will mimic grown-ups and parrot playmates. Nines are funny, free-form, and fanciful. They inspire confidence and are extremely intuitive. To materialistic, possessive, or narrow-minded parents, they may seem too emotional, generous, or expansive. To cultured, artistic, broad-scoped adults, number 9 children are students and teachers who should be enlightened at every opportunity.

Number 9 talents put these children at the top without the need for apprenticeship. Born with the ability to sense others' thoughts and ask the right questions, number 9 youths appeal to notables and highly skilled talents. Arts and crafts schools and a liberal university education will not be wasted on 9s with a thirst for knowledge. They will be more inspirational, contributing, and professional in positions of responsibility that allow for mental and physical freedom. Their flashes of unselfishness and compassion will be noticed by authorities, and once they receive appreciation, they let the world know they enjoy a pat on the back.

Number 9 teens and young adults are frank, thoughtful, and attractive. They have a world of friends and various interests that take them away from home. These teens have faraway pen pals, contribute time to the sick or elderly, and play Hamlet or Ophelia in the senior class Shakespearean festival. They have a way with words, and writing, acting, and conversing come easily. These children of universal love shy away from commercial ambitions, exclusivity, and pessimism. They are ready to save or serve the world and need to work at a job that has far-reaching benefits.

The "big brother—big sister" attitude expressed by 9s leaves little time or room for private relationships. Nines want intimate lovers but find one person too limiting and opportunities elusive. These children should be encouraged to exchange places with students from foreign countries or to travel during vacations; they need this type of exposure and will effortlessly absorb culture.

Number 9 tots, teens, and youths should bring their emotional responsiveness to their chosen careers. Since they respond sympathetically when others feel pain or joy, as babes they are precocious. As the years go by 9s grow far from their birthright to expand interests and means of self-expression. However, they remain precocious adults! Young job-seekers should find a noncompetitive, natural environment where human understanding, empathy, intuition, and dedication are admired. The responsiveness, magnetism, and high-minded contributions of 9s will attract awards or recognition.

Maturity:

Suggested Occupations: Publisher, writer, reporter, foreign correspondent, editor, circulation manager, teacher, teacher's aide, doctor, lecturer, artist, illustrator, social worker, welfare administrator, college administrator, preacher, healer, counselor, broker, entertainer, forest ranger, ecologist, environmentalist, conductor, composer, beautician, decorator, postal clerk, navigator, space scientist, astronomer, aviator, dental receptionist, nurse's aide, practical nurse, health spa owner, chemist, judge, lawyer, paralegal, singles club organizer, philosophical humorist, rabbi, priest, minister, nun, health services administrator, life scientist, urban planner, public relations specialist, publicity writer, financial adviser, charity organizer, art patron, hospital orderly, metaphysician.

Options:

Careers indicated by the meaning of the self-motivation number may not make use of readily available talents but will allow the individual to feel comfortable.

Careers indicated by the self-image number meanings will encourage the individual to live up to youthful dreams.

Careers indicated by the meaning of the destiny number, if it is not the same as the self-expression number, will require that the individual learn from incoming personalities and experiences.

If self-expression and destiny numbers are the same, the individual's talents will be recognized and utilized early in life.

Maturity: Self-expression Analysis

Number 9 individuals have a potential for financial rewards for their ability to communicate their understanding of human nature. They are artists—uniquely talented, polished performers who hone their skills and set a noteworthy example. Recognition is possible for their ability to empathize with people, to respond to others' needs, and to charm or capture large audiences. Basic attributes of the number 9 are universal appeal, nobility of purpose, and selflessness. These individuals send out a vibration that puts them on the receiving end of everyone's problems.

Number 9 talents must recognize their need to inspire, teach, and upgrade others. They have a great capacity for impersonal love and charity. In a business environment competitive associates or commercial aggressiveness makes them nervous and restricts their creativity. Nines excel in developmental or counseling areas. Sales and marketing may or may not be attractive to them. If a career requires a diversification of attitudes, they will skillfully fit a soft sell or a dignified promotion into a casual meeting. As lecturers, they excel with a wide variety of audiences. Balanced 9s may be depended upon to be frank, broad-minded, and trustworthy. They are generally artistic, charming, and neatly groomed—assets to any service or communication organization.

Nines must invest their passion, high-mindedness, and missionary enthusiasms in a position—not just a job. These individuals do not know how to do things halfway and are sensitive to environments, individuals, and groups. Imperfections bother them. A job, for them, must have a purpose—it must reach out to serve, beautify, inspire, or entertain. In order for 9s to survive commercialism, the job must mean more to them than just a paycheck: it must have the capacities to spread their ideals to a universal marketplace. They are impressionable, quality-conscious, indulgent teachers, students, and confidants. Nines have a talent for getting involved, and people who give recognition need a pat on the back. Nines can be humble, but they can also toot their own horns. These ardent do-gooders want their insights, talents, and ideas for reforms trumpeted to the world.

In selecting a career, the wise 9 allows the imagination to roam free. There are multiple choices, but the most inviting will not offer security or stability. Emotional, artistic, intuitive people surround the 9, who is happy at work. Because the 9 is an unselfish giver, there is an element of protection offered to him. A benefactor, teacher, or kindred spirit will guide or guard the number 9's survival when he is true to his desire for quality, craftsmanship, and artistry. The 9 will attract what he needs.

Those with a number 9 self-expression should not have difficulty working with people. However, in a coolly efficient, polarized, narrow-minded career environment, 9s will become unfriendly, aloof, or depressed. They may lack the practical judgment needed to fulfill their obligations and build instead a reputation for being all talk and no productivity. They absorb their environment whether it is beneficial or unhealthy. There must be emotional rapport if 9s are to use their talent for swaying opinion and attracting true believers. They must relate to coworkers as well as clients.

Too often, they are artsy-craftsy late bloomers who teach, dabble, or wander—unaware of their true feelings—and discover their exceptional talents in mid-life. From childhood to old age 9s are born philosophers with eccentric standards that relate to the healing professions, politics, art, religion, and philanthropy. If 9s are pressured and stressed, mental or physical health problems will arise. This appears to be bad news initially, but it is actually the tool that slows them down and forces a sorting of priorities. When they are reminded that good health and contentment are more important than status or wealth, 9s find a humanitarian cause or an artistic purpose worthy of their talents.

DESTINY

WE ARE NOT BORN KNOWING WHAT LIFE HAS TO OFFER. INDIVIDUALS WITH THE NUMBER 9 DESTINY LEARN TO DEVELOP CULTURALLY, ARTISTICALLY, AND UNSELFISHLY. THEY ENCOUNTER PEOPLE AND EXPERIENCES THAT TEACH THEM TO ABANDON PREJUDICES, SERVE JUST CAUSES, AND IMPROVE CONDITIONS FOR HUMANITY.

This destiny implies a deeply rewarding, self-expressive life that unfolds as one learns the meaning of "brotherly love." On this path one has the affinity for encountering notables from all walks of life. The universal obligations of this destiny may seem unattractive on paper, but the 9 attracts beauty, recognition, and awards for his charisma. If the 9 destiny holder's self-esteem is based on material possessions or commercial ambitions, accomplishments will be short-lived and financial stability will teeter. When staunch and self-sacrificing, he is given whatever is needed to support his devotion. Artistic or philanthropic contributions may be so extraordinary that the 9 destiny leads to a Pulitzer prize—or sainthood.

The 9 may be consumed with self-interest or competition in youth. He will grow wise, set an example of excellence, and live true to his altruistic nature as time passes. When the individual expects nothing in return for offerings of love, compassion, and tolerance, the end results are beneficial. The emotional highs and lows of the number 9's dramatic and philosophical lifestyle rival anything written by Eugene O'Neill and Neil Simon. With a discriminating eye and a generous heart his potential is unlimited.

People with a number 9 destiny may appear cosmopolitan or mature. They feel youthful. Premature gray hair is not an unusual common denominator among 9 destiny holders. Coincidence? Probably. However, 9 is a test until one learns to pay attention to the Golden Rule. Nines must be willing to strive for the best and let things happen without feeling remorse. These individuals clear the decks for expansion by accepting the freedom that is offered when relationships end. Friends are helpful, but the 9s often outgrow people and possessions. They must achieve a degree of unselfishness that will determine whether life on the next plane will be lived as teacher or student.

Exposed to unfamiliar races, creeds, and cultures, 9s learn how others live and love. They may be critical at first but in time become more liberal. Hospitable, forgiving, and unprejudiced 9s cross these individuals' path, and these exposures build character. A variety of responsibilities—marriage to a person with children, dependent siblings, or the care of ailing parents—may contribute to early maturity. Very often 9s are attracted to much older, very needy, or extremely sophisticated lovers or associates. They may seem masochistic, but they are not. They simply cannot avoid giving more emotional and material comfort than they get.

Nines cannot settle at one hearth or in just one person's life. If they favor artistic endeavors, 9s may have to respond to public demands. If they follow humanitarian professions, they will interrupt domestic intimacies. The divorce rate is high in the medical fields, which often attract 9s. When responding to a call for help, physicians may leave spouses with dinner on the table or disappoint children eager to share a day of fishing. The opportunities of 9s are more highly evolved than those of any other destiny. However, personal desires come second; the romantic drive to create a perfect world or heal its ills comes first.

On the 9 lifepath, one meets notables: people who are the cream of the crop in the arts, sciences, professions, and religions. Regardless of background, the 9 expands culturally in an unconscious effort to learn about life. To make the most of numerology's ability to forecast, the number 9 must expect to give whatever is needed—unstintingly, and without thought of payment. Some say "What goes around comes around." If that is true, the enlightened 9 destiny holder will always reap the greater rewards. The 9 will attract recognition, deep satisfaction, and peace of mind by understanding what makes people tick and treating them kindly.

The individual may be domestic, a nester by nature, and find that life does not offer permanent residences or relationships. He may desire status, money, and power and discover that material possessions are transitory—acquired and lost easily. From birth through the fifties, the individual's lifestyle may be restricted by his self-absorption. After mid-life the 9 may reverse the focus and squelch the ego. It is essential that careers or alliances are not chosen for personal acclaim and affluence, for if greed or avarice motivate the 9, he will never reach his greatest ambitions.

Career opportunities arise in widespread service or communication industries. When the 9 cherishes the beauty of friendship and virtue, people, places, and things take on new values. There may be childhood recollections of bigotry or narrow-mindedness that are swept away by encounters with warmhearted, tolerant, and patient people. In mid-life a crisis may develop that changes the number 9 focus from that of unconcerned lone wolf to that of compassionate welfare worker. Emotional growth is at the core of the lessons to be learned. The 9 realizes that nothing lasts forever and learns to gracefully bend to the inevitable.

As life draws to a close the balanced, numerologically unchallenged 9 may find himself beloved by many and an example who inspires others. Nines are recognized for their insistence upon excellence and the craftsmanship they bring to their work. Unlike the actor (3) who entertains for a moment, or the teacher (6), who bears the burden for education, the 9 is on the highest level of communication. He epitomizes the inspired thespian. In accordance with the depth of his caring and service, the 9 individual is elevated. He may bring Shakespeare's *Hamlet* to Kadoka, South Dakota, or slave in an infirmary or starve in a garret to become a novice on a higher plane. The most revered is remembered as "the teacher's teacher" and lives forever in the hearts and minds of appreciative students or audiences.

Individuals with the number 9 destiny should form partnerships or marry people with the number 9 as a self-expression or self-motivation number, as the latter two know what the number 9 destiny is intended to learn. The marriage or partnership of two number 9 destinies will result in a lasting friendship, but money and life purposes may be difficult to stabilize. Two 9s may meet at airports, at political activist rallies, or on line to donate blood for disaster victims. Life will often offer difficult domestic adjustments and too many personal restrictions; two people intent upon saving the world may not be able to give their all to an intimate relationship. Therefore marriage and partnerships are generally short-lived, although the love or friendship between two 9 destinies may continue on.

BIRTHDAY INFLUENCES WITHIN THE DESTINY

September

Individuals born in September learn to understand the feelings of others in youth. They are expected to put their personal desires, possessions, and worries aside when others need their time, energy, and sympathy. They grow up fast—situations arise demanding that they handle themselves and others without preparation. As youngsters, they are afraid and confused by adult problems. Frustrated because they cannot be like other kids, they are unwilling loners and precocious babes strained by their unique ability to comprehend the trials and tribulations of the grown-up world. Unable to cope with their own deep capacity for empathy and love, they become surrogate parents, teachers, or counselors. September–born grow far from their birthright culturally, spiritually, and practically.

Childhood's emotional upheavals and responsibilities are not conducive to playfulness, freedom, or self-development. September–born are highly emotional, artistic, and melodramatic. They meet notable people while in their teens and are brought out of the family culture or neighborhood mentality. A broad scope of talented, philosophical, intuitive people open doors for their expansion. Unfortunately there are upsets that are out of their control; people pass out of their lives and situations that they wish to maintain or change. Youngsters born in September offer understanding without getting anything in return.

Partnerships or marriage for number 9s are not recommended before twenty-eight years of age. The reasons for marriage before this time will not be based on these individuals' practical needs or the right reasons for gaining personal satisfaction, and therefore it is unlikely that commitments will last. Youngsters born in September make personal sacrifices above and beyond the call of duty, causing the years before thirty-six to be the most difficult time in these people's destiny.

Birthday: 9, 18, 27

THE BIRTHDAY NUMBER HAS AN INFLUENCE ON PERSONALITY AND DESTINY. IT ATTRACTS PEOPLE AND EXPERIENCES DURING MID-LIFE THAT EXEMPLIFY THE NUMBER MEANING.

The mid-life productivity cycle begins with maturity. It lasts from approximately twenty-eight to fifty-five years of age and coordinates with the destiny during that time span. The birthday-number meaning adds its character traits and experiences to an individual's numerology analysis.

People born on the ninth, eighteenth, and twenty-seventh of the month, in addition to the character traits outlined by the number meanings for the name, are loving, empathetic, and generous. They may not find happiness in long-term relationships or find success in the competitive business community; instead, they might enjoy spiritual investigations, artistic pursuits, and major service or communication projects.

Between approximately twenty-eight and fifty-five years of age—the twenty-seven-year productivity cycle within the destiny—life will offer these individuals additional opportunities for cultural expansion, a polish of skills, and service to worthy causes. Attention directed at boosting creative talents and broadening their potential will open doors for recognition and awards. The individual should expect to let go of outgrown people and accomplishments. People born on the ninth, eighteenth, and twenty-seventh cannot center on themselves; they must insist upon the mental, emotional, and practical freedom to view everyone as a sibling. In other words, they cannot afford to love too personally.

The individual learns to philosophically accept the inevitability of winter's demises before spring's reseedings. He must learn when to move on before intimacies grow and partings become too painful. Love affairs rarely last, so the individual learns not to put all his eggs in one basket. Similarly, he must learn to move on when he is no longer needed. During this time span he should also examine mass needs and tastes in the arts and humanities. Public recognition is possible, and loving friendships will blossom and grow. It is essential to the productivity cycle that the person refuse to be narrowed down by anyone else's expectations or acquiesce to another's possessiveness.

PERSONAL YEAR

The number 9 is the ninth year in the cycle of nine years of experiences that results in the polish and skill of performance based on the goals set in the first year. In the spring one receives recognition for creative efforts, takes inventory of past accomplishments, and prepares to begin new long-term goals. For most, old beaux, school chums, and personal ideals crop up for a final assessment. This is the year to discard unfashionable clothes, reread beloved books, and let go of lost loves. It is time for reflection and reevaluation. This year requires one to give unqualified love and accept another's burdens. Nothing new begins, so anything that will hinder a fresh start next year should be excised.

Love is offered but is of short duration or stems from impersonal admirers. The focus is on being patient; this is not the time to instigate or legalize innovative ideas or affiliations. Emotions swell and shrink when a panorama of past performances rekindle old flames. There is some disillusionment and disappointment in September as a result of romanticism and erroneous ideas run amok during the summer. This is the year to be a rolling stone that gathers no moss. It is difficult to let go of comfortable habits, whether they are pleasant or unpleasant. Endings take place, but only as the foundation for next year's rebirth and better future prospects.

Changes are necessary, so some things must be terminated. New goals instigated in October will melt when the year ends and should be kept on ice until April of the following year. Transitions come to light that seed in October. One should sort out priorities and may plan in the fall, but it is best not to instigate innovative changes until all the facts are in. Time should be spent working to improve relationships, entertain, counsel, or inspire others.

Travel is enlightening and should be enjoyed. Get out to smell freshly cut grass, feel the ocean breeze, or listen to the reminiscences of old friends. Imagine that this is Chinese New Year's Eve when, as is the custom, all debts must be paid in full before the old year concludes. If one does not start fresh, he will be hampered by old business, relationships, and obligations during the next year.

If a marriage went on the rocks two years before, during the number 9 year the divorce will become final. The cycle brings back things that have occurred during the past eight years—petty illnesses, lost articles, and discarded ideas reappear. A return trip to "the old neighborhood" is inevitable. Wives try on their carefully packed bridal gown, and husbands begin asking for dinners "like Mama used to make." There is a lot of living and a need for giving as the realization sinks in that we are all vulnerable.

November attracts petty annoyances and emotional irritants as a result of the delays from October's actions. Intimate relationships flourish if one is open to follow the other's lead. Be quiet, play Mona Lisa, and smile. Things are working underneath the surface that will come to light in December. Until the clock strikes midnight on New Year's Eve, expect December to be all talk and nothing concrete. On December thirty-first, before midnight, the most important finalization of the year will be decided. It will be the result of an unconventional and surprising observation. Someone or something will alter the course of next year's independent goals.

PERSONAL MONTH

The number 9 personal month within any personal year provides the opportunity to complete projects, be charitable, and increase cultural activities. Personal ambitions are not favored; nor is commercial aggressiveness. Instead, this is the time to inspire, counsel, and support others. The projects that began eight months ago crop up to either conclude or be abandoned. Situations arise requiring an altruistic, broad-minded attitude. Call on the sick, elderly, or needy and take a book, a tasty treat, or a listening ear. This is not the time to begin anything! Group interactions, auditions, and public appearances enhance your reputation and attract rewards. Use this month to meet with notable or helpful people who have the contacts or abilities to further ambitions.

PERSONAL DAY

Wake up with a pleasant word and the determination to settle all problems before sunset. Stop at a needy friend's home to do something thoughtful for him. Plan to share blessings, talents, and understanding. Make this the day to tell the bigot down the block to grow up and be sure that personal prejudices are not showing. Detail work may require a supreme effort. It is best to put off sewing, ironing, and talking to the bookkeeper for a few days. This is a day to think of major issues and be generous with lovers, friends, and business associates.

You will note that there are odds and ends that must be cleared away. There is a strong urge to take stock and get everything that is lagging out of the way. Make a personal commitment to be patient, indulgent, and well intentioned. Do not stir things up. Share knowledge and allow people who have lived and absorbed more than you have to be enlightening.

You will focus on culturally expansive people and merciful experiences. Go listen to music, see a play, or volunteer to donate blood. The only thing you can give that saves lives and replaces itself in six hours is blood. Remember that to be creative you must first appreciate another's artistry. This is a time to get deep satisfaction from relating yourself to your fellow humans and the universe.

Take whatever comes today and be agreeable. Realize that there comes a time when demonstrations of compassion, consideration, and tolerance are due. Some sacrifices may be necessary. This may be a day you take the blame for another's mistake or forgive and forget a slight. This day should be used to reflect, expand, or conclude, and plan for tomorrow's changes. Above all, use this time to tie up loose ends; expect nothing new to begin.

CHAPTER FOURTEEN

BEYOND 9

H ow to Use 9: Using ordinary arithmetic, 9 added to any number or subtracted from a larger number leaves the original number unchanged when it is reduced to a single digit.

When adding in haste, ignore 9. The result will be the same. Example: $1991 = 1 + 9 + 9 + 1 = 20$ and $2 + 0 = 2$. Ignore the 9s and $1 + 1 = 2$.

Subtract: $13 - 9 = 4$ ($13 = 1 + 3 = 4$)

When 9 is multiplied, it produces itself when numerologically reduced to a single digit.

Multiply: $9 \times 4 = 36$ and $3 + 6 = 9$

MASTER NUMBERS

There are masterly implications that go beyond the single reduced number meanings in a few double numbers. Some have special qualities as double numbers that inspire leadership and long-lasting benefits to others. Others are tests relating to the ancients' belief in laws of karma: a spiritual payment plan for past-life transgressions. Whether one agrees with the ancients is not the question; knowledge of the requirements made by these numbers does make life easier.

All numbers over and including 10 have the responsibility to unselfishly relate to their fellows. The meaning of the numbers 11, 22, 33, and 44 should be kept in mind when analyzing a chart. They offer the option to raise the reductions from 2, 4, 6, and 8 to universal proportions. For purposes of addition, the reduced number may be used. When numbers are reduced to a single number, the result will be the same.

11 + 7 = 18 and 1 + 8 = 9
 2 + 7 = 9
22 + 7 = 29 and 2 + 9 = 11 and 1 + 1 = 2
 4 + 7 = 11 and 1 + 1 = 2

These numbers indicate extraordinary nervous energy that must be used for selfish or unselfish purposes. Some people may not be able to live up to the demands of the higher number and will follow the lower number meaning. Beyond 9, people channel into the extraordinary perceptions of the mind and the spirit. As with all things in numerology, number meanings indicate options, but the choice remains ours.

DOUBLE NUMBERS BEHIND THE PRACTICAL NUMBERS 1 THROUGH 9

Note: When a group of numbers is added, the result is usually a double number. All double numbers *behind* the 1 through 9 numbers have meanings, too.

Numbers larger than 9 are understood when read as two individual numbers with an overall result. Example: number 23 = 2 + 3 = 23/5. Read 2 and 3 to add background for the 5. The 3 works through the 2; in other words, the 2 sets the stage for the 3's meaning. Example for 23/5 self-motivation: The person wants cooperation and intimacy (2) and needs beautiful, youthful, imaginative partners (3). Overall, he is comfortable learning from experience, enjoying sensual pleasures, and traveling mentally and physically (5). Example for 23/5 destiny: The person is to learn cooperation and how to enjoy intimacy (2) and will meet beautiful, youthful, imaginative partners (3). Overall, the destiny will offer opportunities to learn from experience, sensual pleasures, and mental and physical travels (5).

WARNING NUMBERS

Doubles may also be warning numbers. The number 13 is filled with superstitions that are explained productively by numerology. The numbers 14, 16, and 19 have testing meanings that describe lessons passed down from the ancients. In addition to the mystical meaning of the double number—and a simple meaning for the single reduced number—awakenings, tests, or challenges apply to the double number. When one pays attention to the warning and does not repeat patterns, the tests are passed and rewards are possible.

LEADERSHIP AND INSPIRATION NUMBERS

Beyond 9, there are special numbers of leadership and inspiration—11, 22, 33, and 44. Do not read the meanings of the 2 (11), 4 (22), 6 (33), and 8 (44) unless it is obvious that the higher double numbers are being ignored.

The double numbers 11, 22, 33, and 44 are not given to anyone who is not capable of inspiring others and serving humanity. They are called *masters*, or *visionaries*. Master numbers have both positive and negative potentials. Those who have master numbers behind the single numbers in their chart have the power of the basic reduced number accentuated and have an opportunity to leave a lasting impression.

All things are relative—if an ordinary, hardworking 22 self-expression owns a neighborhood grocery store, he will possess the drive and foresight to build a business that may be passed on to his children. An extraordinary multimillionaire named Rockefeller had a 22 self-expression, and when the nation's economy caved in in the 1930s, he passed on his assets to fund Rockefeller Center. Rockefeller Center was built to help New York City during the Depression by providing work for the unemployed. The individuals in both these examples could have or did perform a public service, which stemmed from their own scope of experience.

The numbers 11, 22, 33, and 44 are inspirational and creative, and leave a mark on humanity. The power of 11/2, 22/4, and 33/6 cannot be maintained: the higher, metaphysical meanings of the 11, 22, and 33 fluctuate with the meaning of the lower, practical meanings of the 2, 4, and 6. They are reflecting, perfecting, quiet, even, and receptive numbers to plan and take actions that build for the future.

The 44/8 is thoughtful and receptive, but also an efficient, humane problem-solver who works to leave a materially therapeutic lasting mark. The talents of a physical therapist exemplify the self-expression of the 44/8.

The 55/10/1, 66/12/3, and 77/14/5 are public-spirited and sociable, and intensify the attitude of the double numbers. Individually, if reduced to 1, 3, and 5, they are active, ambitious, and expressive. They make ripples in the mainstream, and the basic reduced number meanings are accentuated.

The 55/1, 66/3, and 77/5 provide the chance to be discriminating, develop reputations, and change for the better. They demand the mental and physical dedication that generally leads to distinctive careers or lifestyles. The 77/14/5, however, is not without personality flaws. The base number 77 is a double of the introspective 7. The 14 reduction, then, is a testing number having lessons and debts that require payment. The final 5 reduction of the 77 presents a conflict between its clever spontaneity and the number 7's brilliant deliberations. This is a number that has to abstain from melancholy, addictions, and escapist diversions to benefit anyone—even himself. The 77 will leave a noncommercial transition in his wake—and the way the 5 sails around, it will be unconventional.

The 88/16/7 has great conflict when he tries to use material power and/or commercial ideas to build spiritual, scientific, or technical perfections. This number experiences legal and romantic testings. The tests of the 16 indicate that he will rise to fall. However, 88/16/7 begins at a greater height and has a longer way to tumble. When he is dedicated to perfecting an expertise—using his efficiency and courage to further investigations—88/7 may be an electrical, material force that awakens the spiritual roots of humanity.

The 99/18/9 is receptive and aggressive for humanity. He gets results from his independent, executive leadership and his unselfish, charitable actions. This is the courageous, compassionate person who, when a ship is sinking, gives his lifeboat seat to someone who—it seems to him—needs it more than he does. The 99/9 indicates great public services in artistic, healing, and counseling fields. These abilities are brought to practical use after many extreme self-sacrifices. The progressive, innovative therapist who uses classic fine art forms to spark a patient's creative self-expression may exemplify the 99/18/9.

All double (12), triple (123), and quadruple (1234) numbers may be understood by interpreting each number behind the reduction. Prime importance is placed on the final number, with insights garnered from the background numbers. (Number 26 = 8 . . . 2 + 6 = 8. Background number is 26. Prime number is 8. Number 1234 = 1 + 2 + 3 + 4 = 10 . . . 1 + 0 − 1. Number 1234 = 1. Background number is 10. Prime number is 1.)

EXTRAORDINARY NUMBER MEANINGS BEYOND 9

Number 10/1:

A number 1 who is not self-serving. One (versus 1) who is conscious of public service. The number 10 stands for perfection of the higher self on an inner conscious plane where there is no time or space. In metaphysics, personality challenges do not exist. In the mundane, single-digit expression of a number, personality challenges account for extremes and stresses. Unless the 10 is selfishly reduced to a mundane 1, he will not be selfish or impatient. Every "one" is willing to stand up and be counted, and exhibits a unity of mind and spirit resulting in unique ideas that are universally progressive. The 10/1 takes the lead for innovative change in his community. With other active numbers in a complete chart a 10/1 may pioneer methods, control national policy, or win the heart of royalty to affect world changes.

SELF-MOTIVATION: Intense, inventive, fortunate in family and business ambitions. Very reflective; wants to make changes based upon past emotional experiences.

SELF-IMAGE: An ambitious, compassionate, unemotional leader.

SELF-EXPRESSION: A brilliant self-starter. Progresses by changing goals and gains stature and money from past efforts. Inspires subordinates and peers to extend boundaries of aspirations.

DESTINY: To influence and lead. To meet opportunities in which innovations, uniqueness, and decisiveness bring about fortunate changes. Advances by bringing back an old idea that promotes a new public service. Learns how and when to control major issues.

Number 11/2:

Visionary with opportunities to serve humankind by attracting supporters and publicity for unique personal ideals. Mystical, avant-garde, and evangelistic, the 11/2 attracts fame when unselfish. Constantly making decisions that are sparked by extremely high-strung and nervous energy. The 11/2 will simmer down occasionally to rest as a receptive 2, but when out of balance or challenged by the number 2, he may suffer from fears of aging, constipation, chronic nervous disorders (allergies), diabetes, or throat problems.

SELF-MOTIVATION: Wants to do something—anything—special. Pretends responsiveness when actually absentminded or lost in dreams of detailed perfection. Desires associates with same psyche. Selects close friends true to his personal ideals. Needs to be an inspiration to others.

SELF-IMAGE: Aims to live, love, and work above the crowd. Appears modest, reserved, and smoothly tailored. Intuitive, individualistic, and inspirational. Either a dreamer or a human dynamo.

SELF-EXPRESSION: Attracts the "silver screen," publicity, and leadership in an elite field. Talents lead to teaching, inventing, philosophizing, performing, computer programming, writing, or metaphysical or spiritual interests. Must follow personal ideals, set an example, and be willing to be different in order to live up to the master possibilities of the 11. May revert to a 2 when too self-absorbed.

DESTINY: Must learn to specialize, be an elitist, and retain humility. Attracts publicity and the limelight. Intimate love and partnerships may be difficult to maintain when personal ideals are threatened. Will succeed on the path of the 2 effortlessly if no attempt is made to learn and share insights (11). Childhood religious or spiritual beliefs are continued when the intuition (11) is not followed. Should cultivate interest in invention, acting, metaphysical, or universal philosophies. This is a master destiny in which opportunities arise that enable the bearer to specialize in a unique inspirational talent for uplifting or supporting others. The 11 is expected to serve the public and publicly espouse personal beliefs that entertain, inspire, or elevate. The 11 leaves a lasting image and is a magnet for groupies who sense that he is a kindred spirit.

Some 11/2 destinies: ALVIN AILEY, EDDIE ARCARO, BURT BACHARACH, FRANCIS BACON, ROGER BANNISTER, CECIL BEATON, JACK BENNY, SHIRLEY TEMPLE BLACK, JULIAN BOND, LOUIS BRAILLE, RICHARD BURTON, MILT CANIFF, AL CAPP, COCO CHANEL, GENERAL GEORGE CUSTER, BOBBY DARIN, CHRISTIAN DIOR, W. C. FIELDS, KATHARINE HEPBURN, BARBARA HUTTON, ROBERT KENNEDY, ROSE FITZGERALD KENNEDY, JACQUELINE KENNEDY ONASSIS, FRAN-

CESCO SCAVULLO, GEORGE C. SCOTT, NEIL SE-
DAKA, GENE SISKEL, GLORIA VANDERBILT.
Products and real estate with 11 model or serial numbers
have chronic, annoying, petty problems. They appear unique
and attract a following of elitists, but they generally turn out
to be more trouble than they are worth. Number 11 in home
and business addresses attracts high-strung, creative, visionary
people. Collecting rent from these individuals may be a problem for a landlord.

Number 13/4:

The tarot card for 13 details a skeleton, and the title of
the card is Death. No wonder superstition places 13 in the
hands of "the grim reaper." It did not help the number's original
reputation for reconstruction to sit thirteen at Christ's dinner
table and to have death follow. And in the vivid imaginations
of power-hungry ancient priests who needed a story to put
fear into the minds of the masses and keep Pharaoh at a respectful distance, the number thirteen was sold down the river
of superstition with the babe Moses.

Numerologically 13's meaning precedes the Last Supper,
going back to 600 B.C. and the philosophy of Pythagoras. The
number 4, 13's root number, was the foundational number for
tests of proficiency, work, and material stability in the Pythagorean Greek mystery school. Thirteen does not mean a cutoff;
it indicates evolution and change, the ending of one belief and
the birth of a new consciousness. Thirteen does not relate its
warnings to the demise of people. It relates to the death of a
consciousness and the construction of another based upon the
profits of the last.

There *is* a caution and a mild test attached to 13. When
the number relates to a person's self motivation, image, expression or destiny, it warns of frivolity—laziness, disorganization,
and indifference. One may lack the honesty and common sense
to put an effort into gaining material stability. Before a consciousness transformation the person with the 13/4 may lie and
cheat to gain acceptance or security. When a transformation

occurs, a down-to-earth approach to life's conventions, self-disciplines, and practical realities shows that one is heeding the warning that nothing is gained without hard work. Intolerant, frivolous, selfish, and overindulgent wastes are over.

The bearer of the 13/4 becomes aware of ways and finds the means to accumulate material assets of benefit to himself and others. A 13 in any category in a chart indicates that one will face one's moment of truth. When a change in consciousness is effected, the rewards are great.

Some 13/4 destinies: FRED ALLEN, WOODY ALLEN, P. T. BARNUM, CLARA BARTON, DAVID BEN-GURION, GERTRUDE BERG, EDGAR BERGEN, CHARLES BERLITZ, SHELLEY BERMAN, DIAMOND JIM BRADY, FANNY BRICE, LENNY BRUCE, BUTCH CASSIDY, DICK CAVETT, HOWARD COSELL, SIGMUND FREUD, JEFF GOLD-BLUM, EUGENE McCARTHY, STEVE McQUEEN, BETTE MIDLER, MIKE NICHOLS, ARNOLD SCHWARZENEG-GER, FRANK SINATRA, DANNY THOMAS, JOHNNY WEISSMULLER.

Products having a 13/4 model or serial number will break and be used entirely, or in parts, to construct a better product. These products will be attractive and unique, but their end function will be entirely utilitarian. Homes or businesses with a 13/4 address are those of fighters who will rise again after failures.

Number 14/5:

Knowledge of its meaning makes the trials of a testing number easier to handle. With self-awareness and self-discipline discomfort may be avoided. According to the ancients, 14 is the karmic number of physical man. Its lessons and tests relate to sensual abuses and excesses. To learn the lesson, one must not repeat the same mistakes; in time, reconstruction takes place. The 14/5 cautions against lust, gambling, and insatiable curiosity. The test bearer may change commitments before he is satisfied and restlessly grab freedom at another's expense.

The number 14 begins by being self-destructive and does not profit from past experiences. The selfishness of the negative 1 and the lack of self-discipline of the negative 4 make a hodgepodge of the lifestyle of the erratic, restless, impatient 5. Sex, drugs, drink, and all passionate, physical sensations are tasted to excess. Impulsive, erratic, indiscriminate temptations rule the uninformed 14/5.

Absorptions and overindulgences bring on losses, delays, accidents, sickness, sudden death, or physical defects. Material development is delayed because of the negative traits of the 1, 4, and 5 until the 14/5 settles down, practices self-denial if necessary, and makes practical use of personal freedom.

SELF-MOTIVAIION: The person does not understand how to be comfortable and free at the same time. He has emotional setbacks and receives little satisfaction in sensual relationships. A 14/5 may be irresponsible, impatient, and absorbed in physical sensations until a lack of material accomplishment forces him to make a conscious effort to change.

SELF-IMAGE: The 14/5 does not know that he appears ready to try anything and sends out a vibration inviting new encounters. Frustrations and disappointments may occur until the 14/5 understands that he attracts attention and adventure.

SELF-EXPRESSION: People with the 14/5 hold on to lost causes and jobs that have passed their prime—or they quit before a job demands responsibility. Until 14/5s stop allowing a restless feeling to take them over, and stay long enough to gain expertise, they will not build material security in an exciting job. They will undergo many unfulfilling career changes until they exchange their impulsiveness for self-discipline.

DESTINY: The 14/5 may be an "accident" or have an unconventional incident or unusual circumstance related to him or his parents at his birth. To meet this test, he must learn not to be possessive or overindulgent and not expect to live a conventional lifestyle. To him the physical senses are too important. He does not understand his own feelings and is confused by trying to understand a lover's motives.

The 14/5 experiments to learn. Results may bring on losses, illness, and extremes. Surprising events and sensual temptations lead to delays in reaching goals. There are repeated incidents of bad timing and incautious speculations. It may take half a lifetime of disappointments before the individual realizes that some changes are out of his control and some uprootings are repetitions of past mistakes.

The holder of the 14/5 destiny may not get value for his money. He experiences instability or a lack of material accomplishments until he understands that he does not have to restlessly sever ties to feel free.

Some 14/5 destinies: ANTHONY ARMSTRONG-JONES, DESI ARNAZ, F. LEE BAILEY, YOGI BERRA, CHASTITY BONO, PAPPY BOYINGTON, MARLON BRANDO, SCOTT CARPENTER, JOHNNY CARSON, MOSHE DAYAN, JOHN DILLINGER, CLINT EASTWOOD, ZELDA FITZGERALD, ZSA ZSA GABOR, ALDO GUCCI, GARY HART, ADOLF HITLER, JUDY HOLLIDAY, BETTY HUTTON, LEE IACOCCA, STACY KEACH, BILLIE JEAN KING, CORETTA SCOTT KING, NASTASSJA KINSKI, MEYER LANSKY, JANET LEIGH, SHELDON LEONARD, ABRAHAM LINCOLN, RICHARD LOEB, HUEY LONG, LEE MAJORS, DUDLEY MOORE, WILLIE NELSON, ARISTOTLE ONASSIS, LEE HARVEY OSWALD, EVA PERÓN, JUAN PERÓN, DIONNE QUINTUPLETS, HELEN REDDY, JOAN RIVERS, KENNY ROGERS, LINDA RONSTADT, CAROLE BAYER SAGER, GENE SAKS, CARLY SIMON, JACQUELINE SUSANN.

Products with a 14/5 model or serial number are surprising and do not do what is expected of them. This number is only fortunate on unconventional items.

Number 16/7:

The karmic test of optimism, faith, and willpower. The ancients believed that 16, the number that indicates past illegitimate love, ungovernable pride, and vanity, foretells of upcoming disgrace, deception, and disillusionment. Erroneous ideas cause adversities—love won and lost, power gained and drained.

If this individual builds material worth on hedonism and corruption, he achieves his desires, thinking he has what he wants, but actually losing everything. A husband or wife may cheat, leave an aging spouse for someone younger, marry, shower the new lover with unaffordable luxuries, borrow on the house to pay bills, and then find that the younger person is keeping a lover. Hanky-panky will not go unnoticed. Disgrace, bankruptcy, or imprisonment may be the result of superficiality, ignorance, and wrongdoing in this number 16 fable.

The spiritual test of the person bearing the 16/7 is met if when a true love—or commercial ambition—is found, he takes no actions that hurt anyone or leave behind feelings of guilt. He should maintain faith and trust in love and money. Self-discipline is required for him to overcome his selfish fears of loneliness and poverty.

SELF-MOTIVATION: Desires, love relationships, and promises will not live up to expectations.

SELF-IMAGE: Repeated broken relationships and love affairs will continue until the 16/7 appreciates the momentary things he has and realizes that neither love, lust, nor promises last forever.

SELF-EXPRESSION: Career or business may flourish, and possessions may become too important. Finances, assets, lovers, domestic bliss, reputation, and community status—whatever is gained—may be forfeited. The 16/7 is intended to learn that true wealth is not added by a lawyer, subtracted by a lover, multiplied by an accountant, or divided by the IRS.

DESTINY: Lessons are likely to be learned and are more obvious when the 16/7 rises to fall in the destiny. Inner strength and peace of mind are tested, and the birthright is questioned. The child may be illegitimate, born with difficult-to-treat infirmities, or have legal problems surrounding his birth. Mental, physical, emotional, and financial problems may arise. The 16/7 cannot hold on to loves or possessions; he becomes affluent and influential only to lose everything because of a lack of caution or self-discipline—or through succumbing to sensual vices—and finally, through questionable actions, is possibly faced with disgrace, bankruptcy, or imprisonment.

The 16/7 meets the test when he is not resentful, foolish, bitter, overindulgent, or abusive. When he acknowledges the debt, he speeds payment by not repeating mistakes. He will require strength of character and faith in metaphysical guidance to accept an obligation he cannot remember incurring. If he recognizes the pitfalls, he can satisfy obligations before discomfort occurs.

Some 16/7 destinies: ALEXIS, CZAR OF RUSSIA, MUHAMMAD ALI, ARTHUR ASHE, DAN AYKROYD, CHARLES AZNAVOUR, HOWARD BAKER, CANDICE BERGEN, POLLY BERGEN, CARL BERNSTEIN, VALERIE BERTINELLI, NEVILLE BRAND, MEL BROOKS, ELLEN BURSTYN, GEORGE BUSH, JOHNNY CASH, RICHARD CHAMBERLAIN, JOE COCKER, GARY COLEMAN, WALLY COX, SANDRA DEE, DIANA, PRINCESS OF WALES, ELIZABETH II, QUEEN OF ENGLAND, FABIAN, GERALDINE FERRARO, DAVE GARROWAY, FARLEY GRANGER, BOB KEESHAN, JOHN FITZGERALD KENNEDY, JOHN FITZGERALD KENNEDY, JR., PEGGY LEE, BARRY MANILOW, MARILYN MONROE, JIM NABORS, SHEREE NORTH, TONY ORLANDO, DONNY OSMOND, MAUREEN O'SULLIVAN, AL PACINO, JEAN PETERS, CHARLIE PRIDE, DONALD K. REGAN, PEGGY RYAN, ARTHUR SCHLESINGER, JR., RICKY SCHRODER, LIZABETH SCOTT, JOE SPANO, BETTY WHITE, MICHAEL WILDING, JANE WITHERS, SUSANNAH YORK.

Products and properties with the 16/7 model or serial number will have difficult-to-diagnose motor and electrical problems. Any property or commercial business with this number will become successful, have legal problems after it is successful, and end up getting only a modicum of the anticipated results. Money or commercial ambitions and the 16/7 are not friendly partners. Correspondingly, the 16/7 is to be avoided in business ventures if possible.

Number 19/1:

When 1 and 9 are reduced to 1, there are karmic implications that selfishness and greedy power plays have been the motive for acts of universal or humanitarian service. The lesson and test imply that the 19/1 must either give selfless service and understanding during his lifetime or endure one sacrifice after another. Since the 9 demands tolerance and completion, the 19/1 will be pushed to his limits until the best interests of others take precedence over his ego's needs. If the 19/1 shows one lifestyle to the world and secretly enjoys another, he will deny his individuality. He must awaken his true spirit by being creative, self-assertive, and progressive while compassionately providing others with "brotherly love," time, and money. The 19/1 is the "collector" and gets from life whatever he gives.

SELF-MOTIVATION: Hidden matters will be revealed for all the world to see: the 19/1 will have to suffer the indignities of being unmasked. Since this is a rebirth number, the individual may have a crisis that mentally or physically brings about change through a near death. Once reality sets in, the individual sees his life realistically and as something to be lived. He will never be given more than he can handle.

SELF-IMAGE: Intimate relationships are uncomfortable, for the 19/1 is a testing number. This individual's desires are denied, and he is unlikely to hold on to personal dreams. If the 19/1 becomes a loner—acts antagonistic or is discontent—he will never feel satisfied or fulfill the obligations of the test. When he accepts the actuality and gives impersonal love through humanitarian interests, he is comfortable because the test is being met. Like the self-motivation, he is never given more than he can handle.

SELF-EXPRESSION: This individual will have ambitions, put great effort into them, and watch others take the credit. The 19/1 should not become inactive or give up goals. Like the other 19/1s, he is never given more than he can handle. It may take a very long time, but success is possible. It is also possible that results will be taken away after they have been achieved.

DESTINY: There are restraints and repression for past self-importance and self-indulgence. Present-day burdens, which are tied to past relationships, curtail freedom to make changes or to expand upon ambitions. Life will be spent trying new ideas and actions aimed at getting free. This destiny's debt must be paid in personal effort, money, and a loss of ego needs. None are ever given more than they can handle.

Some 19/1 destinies: ALAN ARKIN, DANIEL BOONE, FRANK BORMAN, TRUMAN CAPOTE, SEAN CONNERY, JIMMY CONNORS, SAMMY DAVIS, JR., STEPHEN FOS-TER, H. R. HALDEMAN, STERLING HAYDEN, ERNEST HEMINGWAY, O. HENRY, JACOB JAVITS, PAUL LYNDE, RALPH NADER, JAY NORTH, NANCY REAGAN, DELLA REESE, TOKYO ROSE, PIERRE SALINGER, NANCY SIN-ATRA, RINGO STARR, GLORIA STEINEM, SARAH VAUGHAN, BILLY DE WOLFE.

Number 22/4:

The master builders who get an idea, plan the details, and work to achieve trangible results. They take on, organize, manage and complete jobs others cannot complete and problems others find unsolvable. Their potential for gaining wealth and influence is extraordinary. Spurred on by nervous, mental, physical, and spiritual energy, individuals with the 22/4 are usually confident talkers and workaholics.

Number 22/4 marriages and relationships may be depended upon to go well when the individual is down-to-earth, practical, and tension-free. Inspirations stem from his highly developed intuition. Influential, tactful, and diplomatic, the 22/4 stretches to reach a worldwide marketplace. His personal ideals are humanitarian, visionary, and altruistic. The individual becomes very authoritative, creative, and intense when organizing uplifting reforms. When operating under the 4 energy, the pressures of the 22 are lessened, but the accomplishments are less likely to have a beneficial influence or a broad scope of operations. Still, the 22 belongs in industry, politics, or other professions in which 4 accomplishments can fluctuate with the 22 potential for outstanding improvements.

In the self-motivation, self-image, self-expression, and the destiny, it is impossible to maintain the 22 influence for a prolonged period of time. The individual will swing among the constructive stability, self-discipline, and orderliness of the 4 and the genius, recognition, status, and affluence attracted by the dynamic 22.

A perfect work project for the 22/4 self-expression is the reconstruction and restoration of a landmark home or building. In order to make a more beautiful world, government service and lawmaking are prime occupations for the idealistic and no-nonsense 22/4. As a teacher, writer, or efficiency expert, he influences others and opens them up to material progress. The 22/4 has influence that has no boundaries. He may choose to navigate with his 22 side to fulfill secret desires or reach goals under the slow but sure-moving 4 side.

Some 22/4 destinies: LUCIE ARNAZ, FRANKIE AVA-LON, ANNE BANCROFT, ORSON BEAN, SID CAESAR, KIRK DOUGLAS, ALLEN FUNT, HUGH HEFNER, ROSE MARIE, DON RICKLES, BOBBY SHORT, FRANK YERBY.

Products with 22/4 model and serial numbers are classic workhorses that endure. Homes or businesses leave their lasting mark and benefit materially from a 22 address.

Number 33/6:

The master number 33/6 will be found in the self-motivation, self-image, and self-expression. The 33 serves the community and powerfully inspires the birth of service organizations. The person with a 33/6 finds a special mission, sacrifices personal considerations, and strives to lead reform movements. Despite his courage, self-sacrifice, and humility, the 33/6 is rarely given—and rarely expects—praise. He dresses for comfort and takes actions that serve his purposes. If 33 convictions take the 33/6 out of the immediate neighborhood, the 6 aspect is disturbed, and the 33 aspect will take a backseat.

The 33/6 may use the lower 6 energy or apply it to the wisdom of the 33. Self-expression opportunities take the 33 into areas of expertise that entitle him to be known as "the teacher's teacher." Employees who realize the need for a company credit union and volunteer to start one are prime examples of the 33 community concern.

A child cannot handle master-number energy. In younger years, the energy of the 33 is internalized and the child may indicate frustration by throwing temper tantrums. Generally quiet and happy adult-pleasers, occasionally, the 33/6 youngster will display puzzling behavior. Just as the 11 and 22 add an inspirational and visionary master vibration to the 2 and 4 child's practical number meanings, the 33 also inclines a child toward getting lost in his thoughts.

The 6 is a protected number, so 33 comes under the 6 provisions. Number 33 individuals always get help when in trouble. The 33 and 6 work to maintain group harmony. The 33 shares knowledge, wants to be comforting, and attracts occupations that take the place of a spouse, although he attracts the love of many. The 6 is a domestic vibration that dotes on home improvements and love from the family few. The 33/6 provides for others and, in turn, ways will be provided to assure the continuation of his helpfulness.

Number 33 products and addresses are desirable and durable.

Number 44/8:

Master number 44 is found in the self-motivation, self-image, and self-expression. The prime personality factors in the 44/8 are his ability to accept an imperfect situation, to heal with his hands, or liberate others from various handicaps with his practical dreams. He uses discipline, repeated practice, and a steadiness of purpose to achieve his goals. The physical therapist, military disciplinarian, or "down-home" politician who serves an economically deprived community best exemplify the 44/8.

Children with the extreme energy of the 44/8 should be encouraged to go out for sports or be otherwise kept very active. Children with this high-energy level may act as if they were fighting for their own possessions or were at war with tradition. Adults with this number are rewarded with success, and often inspire reevaluation after garnering recognition. Individuals with the 44/8 may let go of financial objectives to serve a humane cause. The number 8 need for self-reliance and commercial ambitions may never change to the metaphysical 44, but the opportunity is there, should these individuals choose to be more courageous.

44 products and addresses give buyers material advantages.

DOUBLE REDUCTION, MASTER NUMBERS 55, 66, 77, 88, 99

Number 55/1:

The master number 55/10/1 is found in the self-motivation, self-image, and self-expression. Innovative ideas that pioneer progressive changes bring the 55/1 into public service. When vibrating to 55 individuals, the corresponding energy acts as a universal catalyst. Number 55 puts emphasis on cleverness and curiosity, while 1 deepens reasoning and independent leadership. This is an extremely active and unconventional number. Parents may wish their 55/10/1 children were not as demanding, bright, or unique as they are. Youth is the soil where 55/10/1 ideas are seeded yet cannot be sown or reaped. Number 1s want instant gratification: the impatience and self-centeredness of 55s, who learn only by experiencing, may be legendary. Childhood will set the pace for their confused or discriminating personalities. The results of tasks undertaken depend on the individuals' ability to be patient and exercise self-control.

Pioneering, eccentric, and enthusiastic spiritual leaders, writers, investigators, and aviators fall under the influence of this number.

Products with 55 model or serial numbers are originals. They are not proved, dependable, or conventional. They are, however, promoted in exciting ways; and they make a quick profit for the manufacturer, although they usually require refinements to become lasting purchases. Number 55 as a home address is not conducive to a nurturing, peaceful, or traditional lifestyle: too many surprising changes occur under the 55 roof. The styling of this home looks different or trendy. Unique, gambling, or sensual businesses profit from publicity at a 55 address, but conventional people are not attracted to the pioneering, offbeat vibes of the 55.

Number 66/3:

The master number 66/12/3 is found in the self-motivation, self-image, and self-expression and indicates a unique, non-aggressive, tolerant style of social consciousness. Concern for the comfort of others draws the 66/3 individual away from home or family responsibilities to serve the public in some way. He is a multitalented partner and spouse, and at his best when serious and self-reliant. Given and accepting of responsibilities, his characteristic elements are poise, self-expression, and presence of mind. His rewards come through carrying out current duties in working toward a bright tomorrow. This number must be discerning and not accept people or things at face value in order to enjoy a variety of life's pleasures. The individual changes points of view frequently and needs an opulent environment to maintain his reputation as a materially ambitious, practical, and enduring problem-solver.

Products with the 66 model or serial number will be enduring and attractive. Number 66 business addresses are conducive to service and communication industries. Home addresses invite family social and creative artistic activity, and 66 is an ideal long-term residence number.

Number 77/5:

The master number 77/14/5 is found in the self-motivation, self-image, and self-expression. Wealth, ease, and honor are bestowed on those with this number as long as they are independent, practical, and self-disciplined. The 77 reflects an active, elegant, and creative personality. This is *the* combination of unconventional aristocrat and serious swinger. The 77 has time and money to indulge himself. Challenges spur his ambitions, and he becomes skillful by learning from books and experiences. Negatives stem from the sensual tests of the 14, and carelessness with money may lead to loss of face, funds, and family. $77 = 7 + 7 = 14$ and $1 + 4 = 5$, the number of aristocracy, elegance, and extravagance, which should result in good fortune.

Products that have 77 as a serial or model number will provide more than is expected of them. Extravagant price tags on conventional items usually indicate "top of the line" models. Electrical 77 products are exceptionally well made. Number 77 home or business addresses attract publicity and surprising material rewards. However, 77 represents a transition vibration that does not indicate long-term commitments. The number 77, therefore, is a steppingstone address.

Number 88/7:

The master number 88/16/7 is found in self-motivation, self-image, and self-expression. Material satisfaction and perfection of desires are possible for individuals of this number. Independent ideas lead to public-service positions, and the efficiency, courage, and self-possession of the 8 makes the 7 shrewd as well as wise. Good taste, financial awareness, and an analytical mind govern 88 investigations.

To avoid the 16 test, "rising to fall," 88 must not be corrupt or greedy. He must be educated, experienced, and qualified for any commercial venture. To be a competitive 88 professionalism is a must. Although family burdens and community responsibilities interfere, he must keep the peace and be accountable. He should appreciate lovers and partners and make time for self-expression and the arts. The 88 selfish loner will fail miserably and face disgrace, while the logical, meticulous truth-seeker will rise to become affluent, influential, and sublimely happy.

Products with a serial or model number total of 88 should not be purchased impulsively. After giving excellent service, they have electrical or difficult-to-identify problems. As an address for homes or businesses, 88 will appear classy but will require major financial investments over time. Because communications are cloudy, it is best to verify and investigate every aspect of a lease or verbal agreement. Legal, electrical, or termite problems may be at the root of home-related delays or difficulties. If problems are solved, however, a profit will be made on a house or product turnover.

Number 99/9:

The master number 99/18/9 is found in the self-motivation, self-image, and self-expression. A 99/18/9 efficiently organizes the 9 healing and service vibration to produce far-reaching results. In the self-motivation, the individual desires to live simply in a natural environment, while in the self-image, he appears a dreamer. Finally, in the self-expression, he talks a good job. A 99 talent is best suited to artistic, counseling, or philanthropic professions. The 18/9 courage, as well as constant mental activity, helps the 9 detach himself from heartfelt empathy and intense emotions. This is a number of practical problem-solving, bravery, and wisdom, demanding self-sacrifice to live up to its potential.

Products that have 99 model or serial numbers are classics and may be purchased for investment. Homes or business addresses with 99 attract cultured people. These homes inspire high-level communications but are not geared to intimate relationships. Therefore, 99 is an excellent address for a charity, university administration building, or private medical facility.

Campbell, Florence. *Your Days Are Numbered.* Ferndale, Penn.: The Gateway, 1931.

———, and Edith L. Randall. *Sacred Symbols of the Ancients.* Hollywood, Calif.: Tora, Inc., 1947.

Crowley, Aleister. *The Qabalah of Aleister Crowley.* New York: Samuel Weiser, Inc., 1973.

Goodman, Morris C. *Modern Numerology.* No. Hollywood, Calif.: Wilshire Book Co., 1945.

Goodwin, Mathew Oliver. *Numerology: The Complete Guide.* Vols. 1 and 2. No. Hollywood, Calif.: Newcastle Publishing Co., Inc., 1981.

Gruner, Mark, and Christopher K. Brown. *Mark Gruner's Numbers of Life.* New York: Taplinger Publishing Company, 1977.

Haich, Elisabeth. *Wisdom of the Tarot.* trans. D. Q. Stephenson. New York: ASI Publishers, Inc., 1975.

Hall, Manley P. *The Secret Teachings of All Ages.* Los Angeles: The Philosophical Research Society, Inc., 1976.

Heline, Corinne. *Sacred Science of Numbers.* La Canada, Calif.: New Age Press, Inc., 1971.

Hitchcock, Helyn. *Helping Yourself with Numerology.* West Nyack, New York: Parker Publishing Company, Inc., 1972.

Javane, Faith, and Dusty Bunker. *Numerology and the Divine Triangle.* Rockport, Mass.: Para Research, 1979.

Johnson, Vera Scott, and Thomas Wommack. *The Secrets of Numbers.* New York: The Dial Press, 1973.

Jordan, Juno. *The Romance in Your Name.* Marina del Rey, Calif.: DeVorss & Co., Inc., 1965.

————. *Your Right Action Number.* Marina del Rey, Calif.: DeVorss & Co., Inc., 1979.

————, and Helen Houston. *Your Name—Your Number—Your Destiny.* No. Hollywood, Calif.: Newcastle Publishing Co., Inc., 1982.

Jung, Carl G. *Man and His Symbols.* London, England: Aldus Books Ltd, 1964.

Line, Julia. *The Numerology Workbook.* Wellingbourough, England: The Aquarian Press, 1985.

Moore, Gerun. *Numbers Will Tell.* New York: Grosset and Dunlap, 1973.

Ostrander, Sheila, and Lynn Schroeder. *Psychic Discoveries Behind the Iron Curtain.* New York: Bantam Books, 1970.

The Random House Dictionary of the English Language, Unabridged ed. New York: Random House, Inc., 1966.

Rogers, L. W. *Reincarnation and Other Lectures.* Wheaton, Ill.: The Theosophical Press, ca. 1930.

Roquemore, Kathleen. *It's All in Your Numbers.* New York: Harper and Row, 1975.

Schuler, Carol Ann, and S. Kovacs Stein. *Love Numbers.* New York: G. P. Putnam's Sons, 1980.

Seiss, Joseph A. *The Great Pyramid: A Miracle in Stone.* Blauvelt, New York: Multimedia Publishing Corp., 1973 (originally published in Philadelphia, 1877).

Sepharial. *The Kabala of Numbers, Part 1.* Van Nuys, Calif.: Newcastle Publishing Co., Inc., 1974.

Stanley, Thomas. *Pythagoras.* Los Angeles: The Philosophical Research Society, Inc., 1970.

Stebbing, Lionel. *The Secrets of Numbers.* Sussex, England: New Knowledge Books, 1963.

Taylor, Ariel Yvon. *Numerology Made Plain.* United States of America: Newcastle Publishing Co., Inc., 1973.

———, and H. Warren Hyer. *Numerology—Its Facts and Secrets.* No. Hollywood, Calif.: Wilshire Book Co., 1956.

Taylor, Thomas. *The Theoretic Arithmetic of the Pythagoreans.* New York: Samuel Weiser, Inc., 1972. (London: 1816.)

The World Book Encyclopedia. Chicago: Field Enterprises Educational Corp., 1960.